Literary Criticism and Cultural Theory

Edited by
William E. Cain
Professor of English
Wellesley College

A Routledge Series

LITERARY CRITICISM AND CULTURAL THEORY

WILLIAM E. CAIN, *General Editor*

UNSETTLED NARRATIVES
The Pacific Writings of Stevenson, Ellis, Melville and London
David Farrier

THE SUBJECT OF RACE IN AMERICAN SCIENCE FICTION
Sharon DeGraw

PARSING THE CITY
Jonson, Middleton, Dekker, and City Comedy's London as Language
Heather C. Easterling

THE ECONOMY OF THE SHORT STORY IN BRITISH PERIODICALS OF THE 1890s
Winnie Chan

NEGOTIATING THE MODERN
Orientalism and Indianness in the Anglophone World
Amit Ray

NOVELS, MAPS, MODERNITY
The Spatial Imagination, 1850–2000
Eric Bulson

NOVEL NOTIONS
Medical Discourse and the Mapping of the Imagination in Eighteenth-Century English Fiction
Katherine E. Kickel

MASCULINITY AND THE ENGLISH WORKING CLASS
Studies in Victorian Autobiography and Fiction
Ying S. Lee

AESTHETIC HYSTERIA
The Great Neurosis in Victorian Melodrama and Contemporary Fiction
Ankhi Mukherjee

THE RISE OF CORPORATE PUBLISHING AND ITS EFFECTS ON AUTHORSHIP IN EARLY TWENTIETH-CENTURY AMERICA
Kim Becnel

CONSPIRACY, REVOLUTION, AND TERRORISM FROM VICTORIAN FICTION TO THE MODERN NOVEL
Adrian S. Wisnicki

CITY/STAGE/GLOBE
Performance and Space in Shakespeare's London
D.J. Hopkins

TRANSATLANTIC ENGAGEMENTS WITH THE BRITISH EIGHTEENTH CENTURY
Pamela J. Albert

RACE, IMMIGRATION, AND AMERICAN IDENTITY IN THE FICTION OF SALMAN RUSHDIE, RALPH ELLISON, AND WILLIAM FAULKNER
Randy Boyagoda

COSMOPOLITAN CULTURE AND CONSUMERISM IN CHICK LIT
Caroline J. Smith

ASIAN DIASPORA POETRY IN NORTH AMERICA
Benzi Zhang

WILLIAM MORRIS AND THE SOCIETY FOR THE PROTECTION OF ANCIENT BUILDINGS
Andrea Elizabeth Donovan

ZIONISM AND REVOLUTION IN EUROPEAN-JEWISH LITERATURE
Laurel Plapp

SHAKESPEARE AND THE CULTURAL COLONIZATION OF IRELAND
Robin E. Bates

Shakespeare and the Cultural Colonization of Ireland

Robin E. Bates

Routledge
Taylor & Francis Group
New York   London

First published 2008
by Routledge
270 Madison Ave, New York NY 10016

Simultaneously published in the UK
by Routledge
2 Park Square, Milton Park, Abingdon, Oxon, OX14 4RN

Routledge is an imprint of the Taylor & Francis Group, an informa business

Transferred to Digital Printing 2009

© 2008 Taylor & Francis

Typeset in Adobe Garamond by IBT Global

All rights reserved. No part of this book may be reprinted or reproduced or utilised in any form or by any electronic, mechanical, or other means, now known or hereafter invented, including photocopying and recording, or in any information storage or retrieval system, without permission in writing from the publishers.

Trademark Notice: Product or corporate names may be trademarks or registered trademarks, and are used only for identification and explanation without intent to infringe.

Library of Congress Catalogin-in-Publication Data
Bates, Robin E., 1971–
  Shakespeare and the cultural colonization of Ireland / by Robin E. Bates.
    p. cm. — (Literary criticism and cultural theory)
  This study explores how Irish writers such as Sean O'Casey, Samuel Beckett, W. B. Yeats, George Bernard Shaw, James Joyce, and Seamus Heaney, resisted English cultural colonization through a combination of reappropriation and critique of Shakespeare's work.
  Includes bibliographical references and index.
  ISBN-13: 978-0-415-95816-5
  ISBN-10: 0-415-95816-4
  1. English literature—Irish authors—History and criticism. 2. English literature—20th century—History and criticism. 3. Nationalism and literature—Ireland—History—20th century. 4. Nationalism in literature. 5. National characteristics, Irish, in literature. 6. Ireland—In literature. 7. Shakespeare, William, 1564–1616—Influence. 8. Shakespeare, William, 1564–1616—Appreciation—Ireland. I. Title.

PR8722.N27B37 2008
820.9'9417—dc22
                                                                                    2007034641

ISBN10: 0-415-95816-4 (hbk)
ISBN10: 0-415-87576-5 (pbk)
ISBN10: 0-203-93080-0 (ebk)

ISBN13: 978-0-415-95816-5 (hbk)
ISBN13: 978-0-415-87576-9 (pbk)
ISBN13: 978-0-203-93080-9 (ebk)

Contents

Acknowledgments — vii

Introduction — 1

Chapter One
Cultural Impressment — 13

Chapter Two
Macmorris and the Impressment of the Irish Servant — 36

Chapter Three
Richard II, Irish Exiles, and the Breath of Kings — 60

Chapter Four
Hamlet and Other Kinds of In-between-ness — 81

Chapter Five
Question and Answer — 109

Notes — 135

Bibliography — 159

Index — 165

Acknowledgments

I have incurred debts of gratitude to several people for their assistance and support while I wrote, rewrote, revised, and re-revised this work. First and foremost, I must thank Constance C. Relihan, she of the most apt given name, for encouragement and guidance that can be described only as relentless; I also thank Jon Bolton and Patrick Morrow for insight and excellent counsel. My wonderful family has always offered unquestioning support, even overlooking the times I brought work along with me during Thanksgiving and on family vacations. I have been fortunate in my friends, and I would like to mention specifically Tracey, Elizabeth, Amanda, and Terri for assistance both emotional and logistical. I must thank Evan, who has reminded me how to celebrate accomplishments, for his unwavering assumption that I can do anything I set my mind to. My dear friend Kat, without whose generous friendship this whole thing would have been impossible, has my eternal gratitude for letting me talk through ideas during countless late night phone conversations.

Many thanks to the following for permission to reprint material:

David Bevington, for use of quotations from his edition of *The Complete Works of Shakespeare,* updated 4th edition. Copyright © 1997 by David Bevington.

Faber and Faber Ltd., for use of quotations from "Whatever you say say nothing" and "Bone Dreams," from *North* by Seamus Heaney. Copyright © 1975 by Seamus Heaney.

Farrar, Straus and Giroux, LLC for excerpts from *Opened Ground: Selected Poems 1966–1996* by Seamus Heaney. Copyright © by Seamus Heaney. Reprinted by permission of Farrar, Straus, and Giroux, LLC

The Society of Authors, on behalf of the Bernard Shaw Estate.

The Estate of James Joyce.

Introduction

Probably in private, perhaps even in their souls, those who colonized the world were certain that they had the best of intentions. Exploration, expansion, correction, salvation—these are the positive words used by an empire that finds itself in the right, and believes that any who are not of their mind have not yet been convinced. These words do not take into account the values to the invaded culture which are cleared in exploration, squeezed out in expansion, erased in correction, and demonized in salvation. In the encounter between empire and invaded culture, those values and the people who hold them become othered, subjected. When a culture which has been invaded and subjected to a dominant empire works culturally against the constructions it finds of itself in the dominant literature, it must reappropriate the image that has been constructed or write against that image.

Writing against something and reappropriating it should be mutually exclusive acts. Writing against a negative image deconstructs the logic and power of the image and dismisses it. Reappropriating a negative image rehabilitates the negativity of the image for one's own purposes of self-description. The two acts are separate—they require separate means and create separate results. They should not be possible together. To do both would require a combined colonial identity of something othered and something which belongs.

Doing both, however, is exactly what was taking place in Irish literature in the first part of the twentieth century. Irish writers simultaneously write against British constructions of themselves and reappropriate the characters and images used in those constructions while writing their way towards an independent experience for themselves. They are grappling with their relationship to the writers of literature which they inherited as a part of the empire but which oppressed them in its constructions of the relationship of the colony to the empire. Shakespeare was one of those inherited writers. W. B. Yeats, Sean O'Casey, George Bernard Shaw, James Joyce, Samuel Beckett, and Seamus Heaney are among the writers who struggled with Shakespeare as both their own cultural inheritance and yet a cultural representation of their colonial oppression. As writers seeking to engage with the traditions of English culture on their own terms, they found themselves contending with Shakespeare in complicated ways. They were writing from a nation that had been dominated by, or at least involved with, the English for eight centuries and the literature of that dominant culture included representations of the Irish for its own defining purposes. The Irish find themselves in Shakespeare's work, but in ways that they sometimes find troubling and sometimes find validating. What, then, was Shakespeare doing in his representations of the Irish that make their paradoxical relationship to him possible?

The vast work available in New Historicist/Cultural Materialist and Post-Colonial studies lays bare issues of cultural hegemony and how dominant and subversive elements contend with each other within texts. Within these discourses, the perceptions of the powerful and the marginalized necessarily become shaping issues, but the applications of these discourses have directed their uses towards either imperialist or post-colonial texts.

Presenting nation and community as constructs, Benedict Anderson's *Imagined Communities* reveals that all nations understand themselves to have defining origins, boundaries, and common purposes and that nations construct all three things as part of self-identification and can be distinguished "by the style in which they are imagined," or, by the structure and terms they set up for themselves as unique to themselves.[1] Concerned with the phenomenon through which a nation is created by a pluralist construction of people who will never meet each other, Anderson roots the emergence of this larger-than-life nationalism in the Enlightenment, when secularism began to bring into scrutiny the larger nation of faith and separate people into smaller, location-based groups. What Anderson does not take into account, when he presents the eighteenth century as the period in which this transformation became possible, is that the ideas emerging in the early modern period of the sixteenth and early seventeenth centuries were early versions of the changes so important to the Enlightenment. A serious focus of nation-building in the early modern period was this seeking of an "immemorial past" which the English employed through a number of investigations which historicized religion, custom, and identity to racial and social origins.[2] Anderson's application of this theory covers a broad, almost global, scope, and so its investigations, while many, are at times necessarily brief and shallow. But Anderson's crucial contribution, of the ideology of imagined commonalities which tie nations together, has been fundamental to subsequent studies of culture in Britain in the early modern period.

Two applications of Anderson's theory specifically to the idea of Britain are David J. Baker's *Between Nations* and Richard Helgerson's *Forms of Nationhood*. Both of these works apply the idea of an "imagined" Britain to specific texts from early modern England. Baker's *Between Nations* points out the shaky senses of belonging that held the empire together by a thread of imagined construction in the early modern period. His premise is that, while this sense of belonging was written ostensibly as stable, it should instead be viewed suspiciously because of the strenuousness with which it is written. Leaning on Anderson's ideas of the place of a constructed ontology in nation-building, Baker is interested in discovering what was "unwritten" while Britain was being written. Baker reads Shakespeare's *Henry V,* Spenser's *A View of the Present State of Ireland,* and Andrew Marvell's "An Horation Ode upon Cromwell's Return from Ireland" and "The Loyal Scot" with a view to the uncomfortable plurality of the nations being subsumed within the idea of Britain and the unstable definition of the empire that resulted from attempting to make these nations both different enough to require justification for inclusion and similar enough to be included.[3]

Helgerson's *Forms of Nationhood,* on the other hand, focuses less on the difficulty of consumption by empire and more on the means through which that empire was written. Helgerson, intrigued by Spenser's question of why the English should not have "a kingdom of our own language," investigates the texts through which one can trace an almost communal attempt to insert England and the English language into the world stage as a contending language and nation. Those texts include poetry, plays, law, and even maps in a self-conscious path set out upon by English artists at a time in which being a contender amongst dominant cultures seemed possible. Their project was the project of a nation-state.[4]

New Historicist pioneer Stephen Greenblatt examines the construction and deconstruction of dominant discourses. Investigating the social context of appearance and social standing in the construction of outward identity, Greenblatt focuses his attention in *Renaissance Self-Fashioning* on the means of appropriating social discourses (verbal and visual) used for the purpose of creating a temporary narrative reality.[5] Appropriation of these discourses both reinforces the writer's entry into them as outsider and constitutes a comment on them. Greenblatt's ten rules for self-fashioning, which are now widely known, all pivot on issues of order and disorder, belonging and othering. Because an "achieved identity always contains within itself the signs of its own subversion or loss," investigation of that identity can allow for a probe into the subversion at play.[6]

In *Shakespearean Negotiations,* Greenblatt argues for the appropriateness of an historicist approach to early modern texts, pointing out that the historicist reader's resistance to a "single, master discourse" allows recognition that even the desire for such discourse among early modern writers "was itself constructed out of conflicted and ill-sorted motives." He points out that "Even those texts that sought most ardently to speak for a monolithic power could be shown to be sites of institutional and ideological contestation."[7] He offers *Shakespearean Negotiations* as a study of how early modern experiences were "shaped" and "offered for consumption."[8] He questions whether bringing alien discourses "into the light for study, discipline, correction, transformation"[9] creates contained subversion or subversion of containment and he examines how dominant discourses become and remain dominant, and at what cost to the alien discourse.

Jonathan Dollimore and Alan Sinfield investigate the potential for dissident readings, describing the space for subversion as "creative vandalism" or "intellectual vandalism" and so while a New Historicist such as Greenblatt will focus on the strength of the dominant discourse as evidence of that which is being suppressed, Dollimore and Sinfield read the text's presentation of that suppression as a potentially, if inadvertently, subversive act in itself. "Creative vandalism" is Sinfield's term, and "intellectual vandalism" is Dollimore's. The difference is slight but interesting. Sinfield's use of the word "creative" indicates dissident usage of dominant discourses as an artistic endeavor, while Dollimore's use casts it as a critical endeavor.[10]

In *Radical Tragedy,* Dollimore contends that the mere representation of a dominant discourse as dominant brings into question its stability and creates an ambiguity in its superior power. Jacobean tragedy has endings which are too perfunctory to be real reassertions of the *status quo.* But it is the fragility of surrounding power structures of that *status quo* with which Dollimore is most concerned, when he asks: "did these plays reinforce the dominant order, or do they interrogate it to the point of subversion?" Dollimore characterizes his own difference from Greenblatt as being that, while Greenblatt reads for the process in which "subversive social elements are contained in the process of being rehearsed," *Radical Tragedy* looks for a "subversive knowledge of political domination, a knowledge which interrogated prevailing beliefs."[11] Dollimore goes on to apply this theory to several early modern tragedies, including Shakespeare's *King Lear, Antony and Cleopatra,* and *Coriolanus.* He finds in them closure of subversive elements which is in many cases superficial, but he finds that those elements are given room to

Introduction 5

speak and perform before being closed out. Perhaps most important for this study, Dollimore discovers that once subversive elements have been given voices, their voices are never entirely erased by the dominant forces at the end of the play, because in the act of speaking they have stated their case and created the potential for the audience to identify with them. Those perfunctory endings may close out or attempt to erase the subversive elements which were presented as threats to be eliminated. Once represented, however, they have been identified as a threat and one with which cultural subversive elements might identify. The play, as long as it is performed, will continue to re-introduce those voices, even if it continues to close them out.

Alan Sinfield, with whom Dollimore has often worked, focuses *Faultlines* around the gaps between dominant and subversive discourses which are not resolved through containment.[12] Sinfield characterizes his project as being "designed to epitomize a way of apprehending the strategic organizations of texts—both the modes by which they produce plausible stories and construct subjectivities, and the faultlines and breaking points through which they enable dissident readings."[13] Sinfield applies his theory to works by a range of writers including Shakespeare (also Sir Philip Sidney and Christopher Marlowe). In his focused chapters on *Othello, Arcadia, Macbeth, Henry V,* and *Hamlet,* Sinfield discovers that the dominant frequently appropriates what parts it can of the other which it works to contain, and that it is the parts which cannot be made useful that the text villainizes and erases. Using much the same terms as Dollimore, Sinfield examines attempts by a dominant discourse to represent and then apprehend threats, but Sinfield is more interested in remaining gaps through which subversive elements may self-identify. Throughout *Faultlines,* Sinfield works to reveal the split between legitimacy and actual power. He, too, investigates "contained subversion," examining maneuvers that seem designed to challenge the system but actually help to maintain it.

In *Political Shakespeare,* which Sinfield and Dollimore co-edited, Dollimore writes that not only can a dominant force appropriate elements of the subjected which it seeks to contain, but that "appropriation could also work the other way: subordinate, marginal or dissident elements could appropriate dominant discourses and likewise transform them in the process."[14] Building on the theoretical insights made possible by the New Historicist and Cultural Materialist investigations of dominant and subversive ideologies, post-colonial critics study the means through which the dominant force characterized the other and the means through which the other read itself and re-imagined its place in the empire.

Post-Colonial theorists focusing on Ireland, such as Declan Kiberd, Terry Eagleton, and Seamus Deane, examine Irish writers in the context of the imperial control from which they emerged or the residual structures in which they still operate. Declan Kiberd's massive works, *Inventing Ireland* and *Irish Classics,* study the narrative of Ireland as it emerges through Irish literature of the last two centuries.[15] *Inventing Ireland* is the more helpful to the argument of the following chapters, as it focuses more on the Irish writers under investigation here—O'Casey, Beckett, Yeats, Shaw, and Joyce—and their literary maneuvers in the context of empire.

Kiberd's work has a similar thrust to Helgerson's—a study of self-consciously Irish writing as a collaborative enterprise to re-imagine Irish culture as an authorizing structure in the emergence of nationalism. He states his purpose as "to trace the links between high art and popular expression in the decades before and after independence, and to situate revered masterpieces in the wider social context out of which they came."[16] Kiberd examines text, context, style, and choice of language in the explosive movement of Irish writing that articulated both the frustrations of imperial dependance and ambivalence towards political autonomy. Finding that "it was less easy to decolonize the mind than the territory," Kiberd traces the links between the inherited British imperial culture and the Irish response, including how Irish writers responded to Shakespeare.[17] Kiberd seeks to find patterns in this literature that try to "imagine Ireland," but despite the tenuous connections, he finds that the patterns are a challenge to articulate because the independence movement in Irish culture "produced a great experimental literature" from "a people of immense versatility, sophistication and multiplicity of viewpoint."[18] Covering the broad reach of those multiple viewpoints accounts for the immense scope of his study. *Inventing Ireland* examines not only a range of writers and the historical situations in which they wrote, but also the unique achievements of those writers through their own relationships to the fracturing country in the early twentieth century.

It is the multiplicity of viewpoint which focuses Terry Eagleton's study of Irish culture, *Heathcliff and the Great Hunger.*[19] Concerned with the processes through which the divided Irish culture responded to imperial oppression through literature, Eagleton digs through the ideologies of Irish and Anglo-Irish writing to investigate the sliding degrees of interaction with empire for a nation he describes as oppressed through literature and education as well as through more obviously violent imperial hegemonic practices. He sets up his argument through the image of Heathcliff in *Wuthering Heights* as Irish by pointing out that Emily Brontë's brother Patrick Branwell had traveled to Liverpool (Heathcliff's only known origin) just before she began writing the novel, and could certainly have returned home with tales of the destitute Irish immigrant children who thronged there even before the

Introduction

mass exodus from the Famine. Briefly mentioning the Brontës' own Irish origins, Eagleton speculates about the novel's preoccupation with development of an Irish Heathcliff and his inability to conform to English expectations.[20] Eagleton applies the idea of an Irish Heathcliff as the necessary dark side of the Heights as an analogy to the cultural relationship between the empire and its colony and to the cultural relationship between the factions within that colony. Figuring Ireland as Britain's subversive and unruly unconscious, just as Heathcliff is the disruptive unconscious of the Earnshaws, Eagleton reads an array of Irish works including those of Yeats, Joyce, Wilde and Shaw to find their replies to the British inability "to decide whether the Irish are their antithesis or mirror image, partner or parasite, abortive offspring or sympathetic sibling."[21]

Kiberd and Eagleton investigate the dissonant and dissident relationship between Ireland and England. Ireland, however, while having a unique relationship to the empire, was one of many colonies, and broader studies of the imperial relationship to its colonies have established and developed the arguments Kiberd and Eagleton are using. Edward Said and Salman Rushdie examine more generally the condition of post-coloniality in terms of the interior conflicts caused by discordant identities. Said's landmark *Culture and Imperialism* studies literature participating in overseas expansion, rather than as reacting to, commenting on, or exposing it.[22] Focused primarily on the novel as a "cultural artifact of bourgeois society," Said argues that it is impossible to separate the novel from imperialism.[23] But while the novel is central to Said's work, the key concepts of *Culture and Imperialism* apply heavily to an examination of Shakespeare and Ireland: Said's emphasis on structures of attitude and reference in post-colonial writing reveal that "There is no way in which the past can be quarantined from the present" because the structures that newly independent nations emerge from remain, at least in part, as both the means of their struggle and the culture that they work in and against.[24] He also argues that imperial literature accomplishes its goals through the "silence of the native," creating either acquiescence in the speech of representations of the colonized or by removing their speech entirely from the narrative. The post-colonial response is then both limited and prompted by their character as reactions to imperial literature.

While Said's collection, *Reflections on Exile,* involves a wide examination of issues in the writings of many post-colonial writers, the essays create a loosely arranged body of work on issues of identity.[25] The title essay most closely informs the following chapters and in particular centers on the divided nature of the post-colonial identity and the process through which exile, self-imposed or otherwise, both separates an artist from the context which created him or her and also creates a new context for self-identification. Attempting to separate the literary motif of exile from the reality of it which is experienced by millions, Said writes that "On the twentieth-century scale, exile is neither aesthetically nor humanistically comprehensible," but while a literary exile figure cannot be understood as the total representation of the condition of exile, a poet in exile contains "exile's antinomies embodied and endured with a unique intensity."[26] The writing produced by exiles is then unique in its goals with the audience, because for the exiled writer, "nothing is secure" and so "What you achieve is what you have no wish to share."[27] The exiled experience is unnatural and so resembles the fiction the artist creates. The work is then a sort of new home which the writer attempts to create in shared art, driven by a sense of "defiance and loss."[28]

Said's words on exile, as a experience in permanent displacement between the broadly national and the deeply personal, could just as easily be a description of Salman Rushdie's essay collection, *Imaginary Homelands*.[29] In seventy essays, Rushdie writes about separation, culture, popular culture, censorship, nationalism, fundamentalism, commonwealth, and immigration. The common thread between them all is encapsulated in the title essay which leans on the relationship of the artist to society, original or adopted, for good or ill. Arguing in that essay that all vision is fragmentary, Rushdie contends that the artist who is perhaps best equipped to capture this is the one who is separated from home and so required to admit to and grapple with incomplete memory. Rushdie characterizes the separation from origins as displacement, and as a writer who has left his home and is now "partly of the West," Rushdie asserts that the displaced writer has an identity "at once plural and partial." He qualifies the grimness of this statement, however, with the observation that "however ambiguous and shifting this ground may be, it is not an infertile territory to occupy."[30]

The fertile territory of Irish writing in the twentieth century is the shifting ground of writers displaced from, and seeking, starting places. Displaced from their own past by eight centuries of British colonialism, the Irish found that anything like a recognizable past was never an entirely Irish one—it was always a past including English administrators in The Pale, English texts in the classroom, English plays on the stage, English soldiers knocking on the door. Salman Rushdie, sensitive to the connections between military and cultural invasion, writes: "One of the key concepts of imperialism was that military superiority implied cultural superiority, and this enabled the British to condescend to and repress cultures far older than their own."[31] Revivalist Irish writing reacted by writing both in a recovered Gaelic and a triumphantly thorough English and took as its models both the

Introduction

stories of Irish folklore and the English stories of imperialism. Shakespeare's participation in the nationalist writing of early modern England was part of a larger attempt by many to define Englishness and the English language as both traditional and unique, as precedented in a glorious history and unprecedented in its superiority.

Shakespeare's use of Irish characters as belongings of the empire and his attribution of Irish characteristics to those who fall providentially for the benefit of the empire is part of a larger scheme to press the Irish culturally into the service of British imperial writing. Militaristic language has been used frequently to describe imperial cultural practices: Declan Kiberd writes that English educators never "expected Irish students of Shakespeare to treat his works like captured weapons which might one day be turned back upon the enemy."[32] But literature is not a weapon that can be captured, because it is still in the hands of the empire as well. No writing remains in the exclusive control of anyone from the moment it leaves the author's hands. The same work is read with different agendas. The empire triumphs in an ending's order, even if, as Dollimore and Sinfield contend, that ending is a superficial reinforcement of an ideological framework and the subversive elements which are consumed or erased at the end were identified. The colony identifies with the subversion that is represented to authorize the force of that reinforcement. The writing that responds to the subversion both inhabits it and rejects the means of its representation. We are able to read them together. With the luxury of retrospect, we can examine the relationships between texts that are separated by time and distance but which stand side by side on our shelves. That luxury affords us the ability to find the means through which a work creates for the empire a colonial subject which is plural in its identity—both separating it from its origins and yet insisting upon them. And we can read for the response of the subject who is displaced from an autonomous home and kept in the periphery of a new home.

To do this, we need a more apt metaphor and model for reading, one of both separation and inclusion, one that positions the writer as both a member and an other. The military practice of impressment into service is more apt for this: the forced service of those whom the state thought would be useful to fill the ranks of the military in time of need. Press gangs live in popular imagination as roaming the streets and rooting through taverns to violently trap unsuspecting men and force them to join the military. The community of the ship was one of hierarchies and demanded service, like the ship of state and its administrators, volunteers, and victims. Kiberd uses a number of military metaphors to describe imperialist discourse, and briefly stumbles upon the press gang, writing that the English helped invent

Ireland, creating the situation from which modern Ireland emerged. Imperially, "Ireland was pressed into service as a foil to set off English virtues."[33] While Kiberd is hinting at cultural practices, he is speaking more practically of Ireland as a physical place enlisted politically and economically. But the idea of Ireland as enlisted into Britain imaginatively and culturally needs expansion.

Rather than attempting to decide for myself which characters and structures represent "Irishness" in Shakespeare, I will defer to nationalist Irish writers of the twentieth century and allow them to decide for me. I will then limit the bulk of this study of cultural impressment of the Irish in Shakespeare to works which appear most prominently in the writing of the early twentieth-century Irish nationalist movement. These works are *Richard II*, *Henry V*, and *Hamlet*, in which Shakespeare demonstrates pragmatism winning over idealism, and characters from these plays are re-read and recycled in Irish writing in unexpected ways.

While Chapter One will seek to establish cultural impressment as a metaphor for the depiction of other societies in acts of service to imperial goals, subsequent chapters will investigate how this operates in the three major plays with which Irish responses to Shakespeare seems to be preoccupied.[34] Chapter Two will focus on the great English panegyric, *Henry V*, and investigate how it sets up a model of subservience to the English crown which includes all of the Celtic nations surrounding Britain. These holdings are arrayed in Henry's captains, listed in the *dramatis personae* as "officers in the King's army": Fluellen, Jamy, and Macmorris the Irishman. This arrangement of captains impresses the Irish by representing English-occupied territories, specifically for this study in the character of MacMorris, cheerfully serving the ambitions of a king who is the very symbol of all that is English. Leaning on Sinfield's questions about the invasion of France as a metaphor for Ireland, this chapter will also look into references to Henry as the pragmatic Englishman in Irish literature. Kiberd finds the "two major Irish stereotypes on the English national stage" to have been first "conflated by Shakespeare in the sketch of Captain Macmorris" from *Henry V*. Kiberd identifies them as "the threatening, vainglorious soldier" and the "feckless but cheerily reassuring servant," recycled by Sean O'Casey and Samuel Beckett, whose plays this chapter will explore for their versions of servitude.[35]

Service to national interests does not have to take place in the visible form of a servant character, but can instead be depicted through a character whose inability to rule originates in character flaws which are the same as those of an "othered" nation. *Richard II* has long been read as a play which moves from a medieval emphasis on spirituality to a Renaissance emphasis on pragmatism. Chapter Three will focus on Shakespeare's use of idealism as a weakness which makes one unable to rule and it will explore the dissident readings in Yeats's "At Stratford-on-Avon," in which he dismisses books he has read at the Stratford library which venerate the success of Henry and in George Bernard Shaw's reviews of an English actor whom he felt inadequate to the task of understanding Shakespeare's language and purpose. Shakespeare's impressment of the Irish in *Richard II* is achieved through demonstrating Richard's inability to rule and Henry's rescue of the "sceptered isle" from the corruption of Richard's court. While Richard's fall from power is necessarily tragic, he is made ridiculous in several scenes as being weak from mysticism and idealism. Their readings of Richard as being an unappreciated sympathetic character are telling: Richard, the poet king, would necessarily appeal to an Irish poet who devoted much of his own life to mysticism and to an Irish playwright who himself contended with English dominance of the stage.

Yeats writes in that same essay that "Fortinbras was, it is likely enough, a better king than Hamlet would have been."[36] Shakespeare's depiction of Hamlet as a prince kept from his throne and unable to avenge his father can be read as a critique of heightened idealism, but Hamlet would not be the complicated and nuanced character that he is were he not also a celebration of an idealist intellectual. These complications make him a character no one can truly unravel, despite the appeal of such a project to idealist intellectuals. Continuing the study of idealism as an Irish trait which was crucial to Chapter Three, Chapter Four will explore the impressment of Ireland through the construction of Hamlet as separated from his throne and at the mercy of the pragmatist king who took over Elsinore. The ghost of Hamlet's father serves as an identifier for Ireland, and the tragedy of Hamlet's demise comes at the ghost's prompting. While this chapter is perhaps inspired by Yeats's comments, it will focus on exploring the dissident reading in the Scylla and Charybdis chapter of *Ulysses*, in which Joyce places the Irish relationship to Shakespeare in conflict in a reading room of the Irish National Library.

Chapter Five will expand the scope of the Irish relationship to Shakespeare to include works which struggle against Shakespeare more generally as a writer. Focusing more on Northern Ireland as a place of continuing political involvement, Chapter Five will consider how Irish artists insert themselves into Shakespeare performatively, despite conditions which silence them in their self-expression. Including a range of shorter texts such as a puppet show by George Bernard Shaw, Chapter Five will investigate how the practice of Irish artists deliberately inhabiting the roles they feel

Shakespeare prescribed for them allows them a limited but crucial control over the fragmented identity of an impressed subject.

The effects of enlistment are those of a permanently fragmented identity—having belonged by force so long to a larger and distant authority, the Irish can imagine themselves only in or against those terms. Shakespeare's cultural impressment of the Irish made them part of his work, and so it belongs to them as much as it belongs to those who used it against them. As Shakespeare continued to investigate Irishness and the qualities it brought to the empire, qualities that may well need erasing for the benefit of Englishness, he created an ambivalent identity for this enlisted other. The Irish responded as one pressed into service may well respond to an oppressor and a leader, with a combination of respect and resentment that shaped their use of Shakespeare as a literary father.

Chapter One
Cultural Impressment

When Essex returned from his inept Irish exploits and paid the Lord Chamberlain's Men to stage *Richard II*, his disordered attempt at rebellion went along with a subversive reading of Shakespeare's play which cast the current hegemony of the state in the role of the fallen rather than as the victor. Essex then hoped that he could effect such a change in reality, as the staging of the play was meant to prepare the way for a march on the capital and a declaration of himself as the new authority.

His entire attempt was a disaster.

The irony of his position lies in its balance between his own desire for the crown and his failure to have quelled restive Irish rebels.[1] His would not be the last subversive reading to come out of Ireland. Plays like Shakespeare's which the British celebrated as their literary heritage and as evidence of their cultural superiority were taught in colonial classrooms and performed on colonial stages. And the colonized read the representation of themselves on those stages in ways which might have surprised the English. At the beginning of the twentieth century, when the Irish responded through their own nationalist writing movement to the cultural violence which had accompanied the physical signs of their oppression, Irish writers centered their engagement with English texts around questions rather than the intended acceptance.

What can make acts of cultural violence so easy to perpetrate, particularly when they are embedded in works of cultural production, is that they can appear to the oppressors and even to observers to be quite harmless. The psychological effects can seem trivial, even when they are conspicuous, when compared to the physical violence that is at the front of imperialism. The combat zone of culture is no less harmful because its battles are fought through works of artistic expression.

Shakespeare, as part of what Richard Helgerson describes as a national self-defining project in English writing,[2] represented the Irish as needing

English governance, even as happily accepting that governance, and he did so in a vein that was common to the time, but he also created complex protagonists in which the Irish read themselves. The well-rehearsed argument that Shakespeare was either promoting the status quo, or he was not, does not take into account the possibility that Shakespeare could be interested in investigating political assumptions rather than just promoting or overturning them.[3] While his plays had to get past the censors, and writing what would appear to be a full-scale promotion of the current monarch would earn approval of his works by the Master of the Revels, a play complex enough to be an object of fascination for centuries must be up to more than that. A play cannot offer answers without first spending time searching for them. Part of that searching is an investigation of national origins.

Benedict Anderson argues in *Imagined Communities* that the idea of nationhood is a development which began around the period of the Enlightenment and is related to, although not a direct cause of, the disintegration of religious communities and dynastic realms. While the community is of course seen by those in it and creating it as a continuation of "immemorial past" and something which will continue into the future, the imagined community is in fact created to serve the same function which religious communities and solid monarchial dynasties once served: to offer to human life a sense of something larger which turns a sense of "fatality into continuity."[4] With the Enlightenment period's disintegration of both reliable religious feeling and of reliable monarchial succession, the need to turn the "fatality into continuity" is transferred to the "nation." He states that "it is the magic of nationalism to turn chance into destiny."[5]

What Anderson does not take into account, when he centers his argument around the statement that this is a phenomenon of the Enlightenment, is that the very vulnerability of dynastic succession he uses as a related factor to the development of nationhood was, as Irving Ribner points out, prevalent towards the end of the Elizabethan period.[6] Ribner argues also that, when politics and religion became inextricably intertwined for Elizabethans, texts such as history plays presented moral choices as being determined by "national and political, rather than personal, concerns."[7] It is for this reason that Anderson's ideas apply to a study of Shakespeare. Yet it is the model of imagining the expansion of territory and the lifting of the nation into greater significance in the world which makes Anderson's idea most applicable to the period.

The Elizabethan period was a time of burgeoning national sentiment—there was already a long history of military conquest, although much of the historically claimed property, such as France, had been lost—

and a shift in nationalist and imperialist vehicles led to a newfound collective work towards improving the place of English vernacular on the world stage.[8] This had already been taking place in the pre-Elizabethan period, as King Edward VI and his councillors put in place the first *Book of Common Prayer*, which was intended to unite the country through a common means of worship in a common language.[9] It was not only the various religious factions in England which the *Book of Common Prayer* sought to unite, it was all of current and longed-for British holdings. With an eye for national expansion, mainly control of Ireland and union with Scotland, a provision was made for diversity in private worship which shut down the public Latin practice of Catholic recusants, but also relegated any differences from the provided English standard to the private sphere while requiring a public conformity. Diarmaid MacCulloch writes that by the time a union between England and Scotland would take place, it "seemed a natural outgrowth of the religious links set up in the Edwardian era, instead of the bizarre mismatch of ancient enemies which it would have been a century before." But the attempt during the regime of Edward's councillor Somerset was clear, as Somerset attempted to claim Scotland through invasion and through marriage of monarchs, and "sought to charm the people of Scotland into a union, using a newly coined rhetoric of British identity."[10] Somerset's use of a rhetoric of national identity to attempt to persuade the Scots into a feeling of union points to the absence of union. An imperial rhetoric is used to imaginatively combine disparate identities under pressure to unify, as David J. Baker points out in *Between Nations*.

Baker's thesis, that Britain is "not an achieved nation, nor even such a unified polity in potential, but an unresolved political and cultural problem," points out that his question, "What is Britain?," has been a question since the early modern period. He contends that "Nations that were not at all nations in the contemporary sense were asked to subsume themselves within a union that we might recognize as a nation, but that bore little resemblance to any polity that the diverse British peoples were prepared to think of as their own."[11] But what may be unrealized in actuality may be realized in imagination, particularly in writing which takes the state as its subject and the location of its argument.

Baker states that to be "English in the time of Shakespeare, Spenser, and Marvell meant taking part in nation-creating traditions of exclusion and denial,"[12] and it is important to note that he places exclusion and denial in "nation-creating traditions." In calling them "traditions," Baker acknowledges that the processes of nation-building, and the practices of doing so, in the sixteenth century were processes with much earlier origins. Nation building through language had a heady tradition—one that pervaded all areas of English life. Baker argues that any constructed hegemony must "subsume" pluralities as a part of its construction.[13] The insistence on a common English vernacular, implicit in the insistence that a certain vernacular is "English" and "common" and should be used by all, negates the variety of experiences and "Englishes"—other languages like Irish and Cornish—and considers all those who are subjects of the king as being English. He later states that "if we broaden our sense of what early modern England was as a nation, and nations, and that England *always* implies Wales and Ireland and Scotland, then, at the very least, we will be alert to the operations by which these other nations are being written out of the English national text, more or less conspicuously."[14] The very modes of writing which he points out for his evidence—primarily, ignoring the plurality of the diverse British peoples in favor of a common "English" identity which is synonymous with a "British" identity—had a precedent.[15] Those modes violently included other cultures in the imperial project.

Such a goal—to unite through language—experienced a shift predictable in the early modern period from religious to secular texts. The areas in the British Isles which came to be included in the imagined Britain were suppressed, not entirely as "others," but rather as lesser belongings of the British nation—prodigal children who must be forced back into the fold. Certainly these included others had their own discourses, but such materials, as Baker points out, are not extant. The methodology then becomes one which investigates a history by locating the responses of those who lost the contest to get to write that history.

Stephen Greenblatt addresses the depiction of other languages in his essay, "Invisible Bullets," in which he points out that the "recording" of other languages is an important method by which English speakers could seek to contain other languages, and a process by which the other culture could be constituted as a culture, and "thus brought into the light for study" as well as for "correction, and transformation."[16] It is the purpose of this chapter to argue that the act of recording and constituting as a culture could also claim that culture as a property of the imperial power.

The content of representation is important, but should be understood in the context of the action of representation. In other words, there is what an author writes ought to be done, and then there is what he is doing by writing it. The characterization of the represented "other" tells a great deal, but the first statement about the character is made by having represented him or her in the play at all. The behavior of Macmorris in *Henry V*, for example, reveals a textual vision of Irish complicity in the empire, but before that character speaks or acts, he walks on stage in an English play about England. His very presence creates a textual England in which Ireland is an issue. Constructing the character as inhabiting a particular textual world (in this case "Britain") with the concomitant textual agendas forces that character into complicity with the closing demands of the play. Regardless of the choices that character makes, the choices are made in the habitat of the author's own imagining, a habitat which casts light on the character's choices, simply by his or her being in it.

Such representation is an act of violent inclusion, a shift from "other" to "our other," and enlists the recorded culture in the self-defining project of the empire. By doing so, the writer culturally impresses this "our other" into service. The othered culture finds itself serving the empire by repeatedly being represented as succumbing to it. In the case of Ireland, the other was impressed into service by being repeatedly represented as a problem for the empire, and a problem which was a preoccupation for writers, many of whom served the state in a military as well as literary capacity.

VIOLENT IMAGININGS

It should not be assumed that proposals for drastic or violent military action in Ireland were necessarily written to flatter the wishes of the queen. Nicholas Canny makes clear in *Making Ireland British* that, while Spenser and others of the Munster Plantation favored an any-means-necessary to subdue the Irish and bring them under English control, the queen frequently leaned more to passive actions such as legislation and concessions. The queen's position on extreme military action wavered, in a fluctuation Canny characterizes as either a reluctance towards incurring financial cost, or scruples in incurring loss of life. Either way, the queen alternately gave and retracted permission for extreme measures, and the short tenures of governors and others given authority to make decisions regarding appropriate measures in Ireland demonstrate the frustration to be found in quelling subjects the queen believed to be her own. The problem lay in this claim of ownership: whereas England gave no quarter in wars with foreigners, the Irish were considered part of the empire, and the queen, despite the intractability of Ireland in submitting to English rule, was reluctant to brutalize "her subjects of Irish birth."[17] As to financial costs, the crown instituted the "innovative" practice of raising some of the necessary funds for military occupation and policing through forced local subscription, so that the Irish were in effect partially funding the measures that kept them subjugated. Despite uneven success controlling areas other than the Pale, the English rulers of Ireland uniformly write of Ireland as belonging to Britain and of the Irish as being the queen's subjects.[18] Canny reveals that officials in Ireland had to "take account of the natural reluctance of the queen to engage in undertakings which implied a failure on her part to retain the allegiance of her subjects" and that while Sir Henry Sidney's policies in his first tenure as Lord Deputy of Ireland were too harsh to be popular with the Irish or with the queen—Canny describes them as "expensive and divisive"—the queen favored his later return to his post in Ireland because his revised policies were popular with the Irish people.[19]

While proposals for control of Ireland may have demonstrated less reluctance to employ violence, the rhetoric of the period reflects the queen's views in its depiction of Ireland as a territory included in the empire of Britain. Shakespeare's depiction of the Irish may at times complicate understood portrayals of the people as entirely uncivilized, but his work nonetheless participates in a trend of writing about the Irish which seeks to contain them within an imagined Britain.[20] That tradition rarely works out the Ireland problem in isolation from the empire, instead constantly forcing a comparison between the Irish and their supposedly superior English brethren. The separate history of Ireland is alternately ignored or excused, and depictions of the Irish characterize them as problems according to their failure to be appropriately British.

When Sir Philip Sidney wrote the "Discourse on Irish Affairs," his defense of his father's stringent policies in Ireland, it was the persistent refusal of the Irish to conform to Englishness which drove Sir Philip's vision of his father's rightness. Initially prompted to write by a disagreement between his father and the queen and some of her favorites over the enforcement of the "cess" or taxes within the Pale, Sidney broadens his argument to include the general stubbornness of the Irish and the need to forcefully subdue them. A difference between Sidney's argument and those of his counterparts lies in his personal division of self in understanding the possible counter-arguments. In arguing that the poor Irish are having to pay the tax while the rich Irish are complaining of the expense, Sidney writes: "And this I speak as an Irish advocate." However, his next statement readjusts his loyalty: "But now like a true English subject . . ." The Irish advocate must give way to the "true English subject," and use of the word "true" immediately places advocating for the Irish in opposition to that. To demonstrate sympathy for any Irish plight might give one credence in argument, and credibility in knowledge of the problem, but maintaining that side meant, apparently, not being "truly" English. Perhaps it is just as well that he repositions himself, since he promptly questions the queen's typical stance of the Irish as her own subjects. Sidney argues that "there is no cause, neither in reason nor equity, why her most excellent Majesty should be at such excessive expenses to keep a realm, of which scarcely she hath the acknowledgment of sovereignty."[21]

Sidney, despite considering himself capable of being an "Irish advocate," has little compunction about what he feels must be done: "For until by time they find the sweetness of due subjection, it is impossible that any gentle means should put out the fresh remembrance of their lost liberty."[22] Perhaps the most interesting aspect of this statement is his acknowledgment of the "lost liberty." Unlike other writers who more simply characterized the Irish as needing the rule of the English, Sidney remarks on the freedoms the Irish must lose in order to get that rule.

The failure of the Irish to demonstrate sufficient Britishness also drives some of the writings of Barnaby Riche, but Riche has no such compunction over what the Irish must lose in order to receive the blessing of Britishness. While Riche is deeply concerned with the perceived rowdiness of the Irish, it is their disobedience to the crown which irks him most. That disobedience is, apparently, impelled by an adherence to Catholicism. But Riche as often as not swerves from discussion of the Irish and Ireland to use the failings of the Irish as a metaphor for the shortcomings of English society.

A Short Survey of Ireland, has the continuing title: *truely discovering who it is that hath to armed the hearts of that people with disobedience to their Prince. With a description of the Countrey and the condition of the people. No less necessarie and needfull to be respected by the English, then requisite and behouvefall to be reformed in the Irish.* Riche seeks to correct the English and uses the example of the Irish, and comparison with them, to demonstrate the direness of the misbehaviors. Much of *A Short Survey* is concerned with identifying the anti-Christ (whom he identifies as the Pope). But Riche's descriptions of the Irish are telling, and vacillate between condemnations of their barbarousness and something almost like pity for their mistreatment at the hands of the priests, "their ghostly fathers."[23] Riche's initial description of the beauty of the land stops short at the point that however lovely, fertile, and well-situated Ireland may be, it is a puzzle that the people should remain "more uncivill, more uncleanly, more barbarous, and more brutish in their customs and demeanures then in any other part of the world that is knowne."[24] Clearly for Riche, the blame lies primarily with the Catholic church, which he alleges is ridiculously cheating the Irish out of progress. But the intended use of the text, the correction of behavior, applies as much to the English—"no less necessarie and needfull"—as it does to correcting the Irish. Any English who might fail to meet Riche's standards of behavior are compared with these "uncleanly," "barbarous," and "brutish" people.

The theme is continued in *The Irish Hubbub, or the English Hue and Crie*, which claims to be "briefly pursuing the base conditions, and most notorious offences of this vile, vaine, and wicked age."Riche suggests that this work is "a merriment," written for amusement, and dedicates it to the Lord Deputy of Ireland. The *Irish Hubbub* is not specifically concerned with Ireland, however, and condemns the behavior of women, drunks, adulterers, "suttle Lawyers," "deceitfull Tradesmen,"[25] and stage players, to name a few. Those needing correction in this text are primarily English, but the barbarous Irish serve as the controlling metaphor for a work which Riche intended to "make the wise to laugh and fooles to be angry."[26]

The behavior under scrutiny here is a refusal to adhere to order and comely conduct. While the metaphor of misapplication of standards for orderly society is used to critique problems amongst the English, Riche inadvertently provides in that model a description of the Irish which is unlikely to provide the Irish who read it much besides a sense of their own difference and a description of their own refusal to adhere to the rules of customs belonging to another place. The "Irish Hubbub" described in the title had, apparently, a good original purpose. According to Riche, when robbers or thieves or other lawbreakers are about, locals are to raise the Hubbub as an alarm, that local inhabitants "might combine and gather themselves together in a maine strength," to repel the lawbreakers, recover stolen property, and at the very least to protect the area "from any further spoile." Unfortunately, the Irish have taken, Riche writes, to raising the Hubbub "upon other sleight occasions" not worthy of such an alarm:

> If a couple of drunkards doe chance to fall together by the eares. If a man being drunk, or howsoever otherwise distempered, doth fortune to strike his wife. If a Master or Mistresse do but beat a servant that hath well deserved it, they will raise the *Hubbub*.
>
> Of these Alarmes and outcries, we have sometimes three or foure in a weeke, and that in *Dublin* it selfe, among the base and rascall sort of people, and as these *Hubbubs* are thus raised in cases of anger and discontent, so they use to give the *Hubbubs* again in matters of sport and merriment. And there is not a people under the face of heaven, that will sooner deride and mocke at any thing that is not in use and custome among themselves, then the Irish will do.[27]

Clearly, breaking up drunken brawls, preventing domestic abuse, and saving the skins of lazy Irish servants do not qualify as sufficient reasons for the Hubbub. Each case Riche cites is a case of preventing harm to a person, but for

Riche, this application of the provision for public order is being misused and applied instead to purposes less worthy. Perhaps the most alarming part of this application of the Hubbub for Riche is that the Irish are banding together to protect individuals whom they themselves deem in need of protection.

Use of the Hubbub in "matters of sport and merriment" may be the most subversive Irish application of banding together "in a maine strength" and one which may well give the English pause. It is a complete reapplication and reappropriation of this provision to maintain order as it is prompted not by outside forces but by a communal inclination of the Irish themselves. What Riche did not take into account was the possibility that the same insulting description of Irish behavior could be construed by the Irish as a matter of pride. The statement that the Irish are more disposed than any other group of people "under the face of heaven" to look merrily askance at customs not their own is more likely to be a matter of amusement than of concern to them. For what group of people would such a description be an insult? An adherence to one's own customs and a resistance to an oppressor's attempts at control are unlikely to be restricted to the Irish, but Riche is appalled that anyone would protest English control and pervert English systems. An account of the Irish as stubbornly resisting the invasion of another culture may, for Riche, be an indictment, but his disclosure of their obstinance reveals an Irish sense of self that the English are having difficulty overcoming. Riche's description of the Irish refusal to adhere to his English standards creates an "other" in which the Irish can cheerfully read themselves.

Such is not the case in what now is perhaps the most notorious writing of the period about the Irish problem: Spenser's *A View of the Present State of Ireland*. Edmund Spenser, self-appointed leader in the English panegyric, sought to codify the Irish problem in minute detail in his argument for a whatever-means-necessary approach to quelling the rebellious Irish. In describing the abhorrent starvation and destruction of the Irish in the process of the English holding onto the Munster Plantation, he advocates a violence that has made his writing a persistent subject of morbid fascination for scholars and problemitizes his place in the pantheon of great English writers. While the measures he advocated may have been violent enough to turn the stomachs of many, including the queen who preferred legislative measures, Spenser presents his willingness to go to any lengths to subdue the Irish as evidence of his loyal service to the crown.

Baker points out the extent of Spenser's devotion to his queen when he writes that Spenser "rendered some eighteen years of loyal service in Ireland to Elizabeth I and her administration. He coveted and accepted the queen's rewards of land and position in the kingdom and was concerned to defend them," but Spenser had no intention of being a merely military or colonial participant in the empire project, since, "he thought of himself as a royal servant, not just by employment, but as a self-appointed apologist and theorist."[28]

Spenser's "theoretical" production included *The Faerie Queene* and *A View of the State of Ireland*. While *The Faerie Queene* is persistently located in what Richard Helgerson calls an "antiquarianism," it depicts Irish subjects, frequently as Catholic villains which the Protestant English heroes must overcome.[29] In *The View*, Spenser, like Riche, distinguishes the problem as being inherently one of the people themselves, and not at all tied to the fertile and lovely land. It is not the place, apparently, but the people and their barbarous resistance to civilization that must drive the English to drastic measures.

Spenser, too, attaches a certain amount of the problem of Irishness to religion, and like Riche centers much of his criticism in the perception that the Catholic church kept the Irish people in ignorance. In the *View*, Irenius argues that not only are the Irish all Catholics, but that they are nominally so, as "not one amongst a hundred knoweth any ground of religion, or any article of his faith, but can perhaps say his Pater noster, or his Ave Maria, without any knowledge or understanding of what one word thereof meaneth."[30] To be Catholic is bad enough in Spenser's view, but to be Catholic and ignorant, to be at the complete whim and mercy of the Catholic church, is far worse. Like Riche, Spenser depicts the Irish as a sort of herd being poorly shepherded by local priests who determine their destinies.

Spenser devotes some space in the dialogue to an explanation of how the English themselves were once as barbarous and ignorant as the Irish he wishes to reform. He sets up the origins of English superiority in a way which allows him to not only demonstrate the lengths to which the English have come to reach their present superiority, but also to provide a precedent for what intervention is necessary to bring a people into a trajectory towards progress. Eudoxus points out to Irenius that "the English were, at first, as stoute and warlike a barbarous people as ever the Irish, and yet you see are now brought unto that civillity, that no nation in the world excelleth them in all goodly conversation, and all the studies of knowledge and humanitie."[31] Irenius responds that through all the "civill broiles" and "tumultuous rebellions" England suffered, it was the constant presence of a king which kept them in check and allowed them to eventually overcome their warlike nature. The implicit suggestion here is that the Irish, too, could experience such progress were they to submit to an English monarch and follow that single lead. Irenius argues that it was the harsh implementation of Norman law in England which brought order to that land, but that the Normans failed to force the issue in Ireland. In England, the Norman conqueror "followed the execution of [the laws] with more severity, and was also present in person to overlook the Magistrates, and to overawe these subjects with the terrour of his sword, and countenance of his Majesty."[32] Had the Normans had the wherewithal to govern Ireland with like "severity," Spenser indicates, that people may have been civilized much earlier. It is also the very individual attention that comes with a direct presence in that land which makes effective governing possible and Irenius suggests that the implementation of law and order requires individualized execution, suited to the specific people those laws are meant to regulate, and that such a plan might be put in place for the "tempering, and managing, this stubborne nation of the Irish to bring them from their delight of licentious barbarisme unto the love of goodnes and civilite."[33] Unfortunately, the Irish "delight" in "licentious barbarisme," and they will not embrace given opportunities to be civilized, so they must instead be forced to espouse them. Irenius's rhetoric of bringing civilization to the Irish will quickly move from "tempering" to more drastic measures.

Later in the dialogue, Irenius states that the Irish are so corrupt and unsalvageable that reform as it is being practiced will not work because it seeks to adapt current behavior and wrest it into English models, and "ere a new be brought in, the old must be removed."[34] While that particular statement is made regarding religion, the removal of spiritual corruption is not the end of Irenius's design. Irenius presents to Eudoxus the direness of the Irish situation, claiming that the troubles have grown so grave that they are irreversible. Only once they have been reversed may laws be put in place to protect a new peace. When Eudoxus asks Irenius how such a change is to be brought about if not by the imposition of laws, Irenius replies:

> Even by the sword; for all these evills must first be cut away by a strong hand, before any good can bee planted, like as the corrupt braunches and unwholesome boughs are first to bee pruned, and the foule mosse cleansed and scraped away, before the tree can bring forth any good fruite.[35]

Spenser's trope here is clever; he uses the metaphor of natural growth and presents the Irish corruption as the sort of unpleasant natural chaff which any good gardener would remove in order to make the plant productive. The extended and strongly pastoral metaphor lessens the alarming effect the reality of cutting away the "unwholesome boughs" which impede the progress of natural growth—trimming and weeding are acts which must be done to ensure production and are protective acts for a plant. To protect the empire, the "foule mosse" must be removed. Since, as Irenius has already established, the problem lies in the people rather than in the land, it is people he speaks of removing. When Eudoxus reminds Irenius that "the sword" is "the most violent redresse that may bee used for any evill," Irenius agrees but adds that "where no other remedie may bee divised, nor hope of recovery had, there must needs this violent meanes bee used."[36]

Should the faint of heart be reluctant to perceive the Irish people as something which must be "cut away," Irenius also establishes what is at stake. The Irish are a danger to more than themselves, according to Irenius—they are a danger to any English people with whom they have close and friendly contact. The Old English, the early colonial settlers, have become more Irish than English, Irenius argues, and have taken on their language, their customs, and their unruly behavior. They have become "degenerated and growne almost mere Irish, yea, and more malitious to the English then the Irish themselves."[37] Eventually centered on readings of both the *View* and *The Faerie Queene,* Andrew Murphy's *But the Irish Sea Betwixt Us: Ireland, Colonialism, and Renaissance Literature* first traces how sixteenth-century efforts (all presented as partial and stop-gap measures) were frustrated by the confused results of the cultural merging of English in Ireland and the powerful Irish.[38] Murphy examines Spenser's indictments of both the Old English and the New English, and contends that Spenser, himself a part of the New English, presents the Old English as the greater obstacle to English imperialist agendas than the new settlers, or even the Irish themselves. It is Murphy's suggestion that Spenser's stronger indictment of the Old English can only be seen clearly in the *View* because the allegory of *The Faerie Queene* obscures the distinctions between the Old and New English—the primary indictment in the *Faerie Queene* is of Catholic and non-English elements. The didactic dialogue of the *View,* on the other hand, has plenty of room to clearly identify obstacles to English dominance in Ireland. The danger then extends to the heart of the empire, if the English whom the crown sends to settle unruly lands find that land seductive enough to turn good Englishmen against their own origins.

Spenser's devotion to the empire is unquestionable and his depiction of the Irish is unmerciful. In Spenser's *View,* subduing the Irish is not only the right act of a civilized nation, it is the pragmatic step necessary to secure order in a land just across a narrow sea. The Irish not only resist English authority, but also teach resistence to the English with whom they have unmonitored contact. They are a people who are inherently incapable of taking advantage of the civilizing opportunities offered them but who are taking up space on a rich and beautiful land they are too ignorant to steward properly. According to Spenser, these ungrateful subjects of the English queen should be brought to heel.

Spenser's sense of historical place for the British empire was strong and Richard Helgerson centers his introduction to *Forms of Nationhood* and the crux of the work on Spenser's question: Why "may not we, . . . have the kingdom of our own language?" Helgerson's list of works from the period which attempt to ask and answer this question covers a wide range of genres and, by looking at them together, Helgerson finds in them a determined national purpose. He states that, while early modern writers were not involved in any organized writing project, they found in the constraints of their time, place, and cultural situation "that England needed to be written in large, comprehensive, and foundational works and that they were the ones to do the writing."[39]

VIOLENT FASHIONING

In the context of these violent imaginings, Shakespeare, too, offered questioning depictions of the Irish place in the British empire. As questions vary from play to play, each depiction represents the Irish as characters whose function brings about a closure in which characteristics on which the English prided themselves are rewarded and valorized. Closure is perhaps less than stable, however, with play endings which are followed by epilogues based on questions and hints at sequels, or which politely eulogize the fallen. The complex systems of self-identification which go along with an understanding of selfhood are necessarily dependent on a depiction of other places and peoples, in order to differentiate the self from them and to privilege domestic national interests. For Shakespeare, the nation was a question, and so characters who participate in the plays which work out "nation" and "order" are defined by their own questions.

In *Renaissance Self-Fashioning*, Stephen Greenblatt identifies where Spenser and Marlowe place the essence of identity: Spenser locates identity in "loving service to legitimate authority," and Marlowe attributes it to "those moments in which order . . . is violated." For Greenblatt, a writer's notion of identity is yoked to questions of power. Locating a writer's notions of identity can be accomplished by examining the writer's heroes, fears, audience, and response to order.[40] By this model, Shakespeare would see identity as a question of one's own power. Shakespeare's heroes question their own places in power structures, their power over other people, their power over themselves, to what powers they are duty-bound, and what powers they have at their disposal. Henry V's captain MacMorris questions, "What ish my nation?" Henry V questions, "Have I the right?" Richard II questions, "How far off lies your power?" Hamlet questions nearly everything, and it is just that for which the character is perhaps most famous. We know more about Shakespeare's characters by their questions than we do by their answers—it is the inquiry which establishes the character.

Greenblatt argues in the same segment that in Spenser there is a "fear of the excess that threatens to engulf order" and in Marlowe there is a "fear of the order that threatens to extinguish excess." In Shakespeare, the fear is that order may be difficult to define. The Henriad, for example, is an exercise in questioning "what *is* order?" The succession of kings who rise and fall through varying degrees of legitimacy, strength, and charisma creates a study of what constitutes a good ruler, and asks: does an effective and admirable ruler qualify as a good ruler if he got the crown by questionable means? Other plays—*Hamlet, Julius Caesar,* and others—expand the range of questions about order. Should one subvert an order that has been established nefariously? Does order extend from legitimacy or from ability to rule? What if the price of order is counted in lives or in rights? We are given examples of what order is not: order is not Falstaff, or a clown of any kind. Shakespeare's lauded ability to put wisdom into the mouths of fools only further complicates the question.

If the character is defined by his own questioning, then a nation can be the same—a group of people defined by their questions about who they are and what that means. A nation in question is implicitly a nation which is not static or certain, not a given but a possibility. Like other English writers, Shakespeare employs Ireland in the process of his questioning. By considering Ireland's place in the empire, Shakespeare yokes that country into his questioning of English order. What place in that order does he give Ireland? By using Ireland in the process of questioning the nature of the empire, he includes that country in the equation. Shakespeare's own relationship to the center of the empire may offer a helpful perspective on why his vision of the empire leaves such ample room for dissident reading by outsiders that his works are able to play the role that they have in postcolonial re-imagining of selfhood.

Jonathan Bate's reading of Shakespeare's own positioning of himself in his writing offers one possible answer. In a panel titled "What DID Shakespeare Invent" at the 2004 annual meeting of the Shakespeare Association of America, Bate argued in his paper, "Deep England," that Shakespeare "invented" the common understanding of the "shires" of England—the non-London, non-urban part of England. Bate contends that Shakespeare, unlike his contemporaries, resisted setting his English plays in the city and his emphasis on the pastoral and his depiction of that "outer," non-urban England created a pervasive conception of the English countryside. Such a positioning of Shakespeare as an "outsider" in the empire's center may offer an insight into what affinity the Irish may have for Shakespeare's approach to the "English question." If Shakespeare perceived the center of the growing empire from the position of an outsider, his perspective may color his characterizations in a way that appealed to other "outsiders." It may be going too far to find an analogous relationship between the "shires" and Ireland, but the "upstart crow," as Bate points out, wrote no London comedies, and rarely missed an opportunity to make thorough use of the green space and other non-urban areas, even in his history plays.[41] Even in what might be called "London plays," Shakespeare makes full use of "outsider" areas like Eastcheap.[42]

VIOLENT INCLUSION

Whether outsider himself or no, by employing the Irish as "others" in his own questioning, Shakespeare employs them as participants, against their own will, in his own nation-defining project. They are put into service to the empire, dreamt up and represented according to the imagination of an Englishman. A writer creating such a representation is committing an act of cultural violence best described by the term "cultural impressment," which I define as an act, perpetrated through cultural production, of forcibly enlisting another in the service of the empire. I use this term because the cultural practice of representation in the service of an empire-building project bears a similarity to the act of impressment which the English military used for recruiting. It was used throughout the military, but is most frequently associated with the navy, when men with some sailing competency were forcibly included on ships' rosters after being handed the requisite payment of the "king's shilling," which was theoretically to be a fair exchange, but was sometimes paid to the man targeted for impressment by slipping it into his pocket or into his pint of ale. Once the man found himself to be in possession of the required payment for service, he was considered a member of the royal navy and subject to the same punishments inflicted upon any other sailor. But it also offered the same benefits. While naval impressment became most notorious during the period of Admiral Nelson in the late 18th and early 19th centuries, as a system it had existed in one form of regulation or another for centuries. Impressment has a long, if not glorious, history in England. While the term for forced enlistment according to royal prerogative later grew almost exclusively into "impress," the word was originally used interchangeably with "arrest."[43] "Arrest" is the term most commonly used by William Soper, whose papers are collected in *The Navy of the Lancastrian Kings: accounts and inventories of William Soper, Keeper of the King's Ships, 1422–1427*.[44] According to the introduction, the crown arrested shipping vessels into defensive service since "time immemorial," and began investing in direct ownership of exclusively royal vessels (called "galleys") as early as

Henry II, but the size and royal ownership of fleets grew and waned alongside need and available funds.

By the administration of Edward III, arrest had become a fully organized and institutional part of royal fleets. The position of the Clerk of the King's Ships was established in 1344, and by 1405 the duties of this position were clearly stated: the administration of "ships of the crown," their repair, and "safekeeping and victualling and payment of their crews." He would also occasionally "be responsible for the payment of the monies due to the masters and crews of arrested ships."[45] The duties grew to include renting out galleys for merchant operators in order to defray the costs of maintaining an "action-ready" fleet of ships.[46] Initially, arrest centered around English merchant ships, but during Henry V's war in France, several of the galleys were "prizes," seized from Spanish "pirates" by English captains who were virtually pirates themselves but were acting on behalf of the crown, and included the *Christopher of Spain* and the *Marie Spaniard*. The cost of maintenance of these arrested ships grew wasteful for the government, which realized that the ability to require enlistment from anyone meant that it did not need to pay for its own fleet. When Henry V died, the terms of his will required that much of the royal fleet be sold so that the money from the sale could pay off any remaining financial obligations, but the income from the sale was considerably in excess of the payment of his few debts. Henry VI's administration deposited the income in the exchequer, and realized that maintenance of a royal fleet was unnecessary when the crown could arrest back any of the very same ships they had sold, allowing the new owners to pay to provision the ships until the state again required a fleet. William Soper kept the accounts for the few ships that were remained in royal ownership, but was directly affected by the crown use of individually owned ships, as his own barge, the *Julian of Hampton*, had been "arrested for the expedition led by the Earl of Arundel in 1418."[47]

What the history of impressment in England demonstrates above anything else is the power of national prerogative. Individual ownership crumbles in the face of state need; individual will is meaningless in the face of state will, but those responsible for impressment can congratulate themselves that the action is not one of enslavement since there is payment in exchange: both of wages and belonging in a national cause. Masters, mariners, and boys on these ships were paid daily wages for their service, sometimes even receiving a regardum—additional weekly payment—for extra work.[48]

The particulars of the experience of impressment are outlined in *The Autobiography of Joseph Bates*,[49] who was impressed into the British navy during the War of 1812. Bates describes how his "American protections,"

Cultural Impressment

or documents proving American citizenship and exemption from British impressment, were disregarded by the press-gang which overran the boarding house where he was staying in Ireland. Upon receipt of the "king's shilling," he found himself divested of the ability to leave, but otherwise in possession of the same benefits held by volunteers: the same rations, the same accommodations, and the same hardship of duties belonging to any member of the ship. But the navy did find some motivational literature necessary, and Bates's brief mention of this is important to note, lest the associations between impressment and culture seem too much of a stretch. He recounts: "when we had a few leisure moments from ship duty and naval tactics,

> we were furnished with a library of two choice books for every ten men.... The first book was an abridgement of the life of Lord Nelson, calculated to inspire the mind to deeds of valor, and to teach the most summary way of disposing of an unyielding enemy.... The second was a small Church-of-England prayer book, for special use about one hour on the first day of the week.[50]

It is noteworthy that along with the physical force which prevented their leaving the service, Bates and fellows in impressment were offered works of English writing which glorified service to the imperial crown. They were provided with the very book which the Church of England used to unify the nation under a single form of worship in a single language, and an example of one man's perfect service to the glory and defense of Britain. Both books emphasize subsuming individual will to the will of the nation, for the greater good of all. This convergence of action and motive in both military and cultural force demonstrates how closely the two can go together.

FOOD FOR POWDER

Whether or not use of the concept in nationalist writing was intentional, or even something of which the writer was conscious, this use of military force existed alongside a use of representation of people who were colonized, or targeted for colonization, as serving the empire. Shakespeare's image of Ireland, Scotland, and Wales happily serving the interests of the English crown is a fairly imaginative construction. As shown above, literature of the period, most notably Spenser's *View*, demonstrates that these countries were such a pervasive problem for English imperialists that suggested measures for subduing them were desperate enough to become frighteningly brutal. Henry V's officer-coterie of Celts would certainly seem harmless by comparison as a form of imperialism, but such measures are connected, and these neighboring cultures are represented as loyal servants of the empire without their acquiescence. Even enlisting a people in the service of the empire by employing their representations in a work of nationalistic writing is cultural impressment. The term "cultural impressment" then allows for a description of such representation which is not otherwise available.

If an empire is engaged in a project of self definition that promotes dominance and the right to rule, then a group of people targeted for colonization and rule must be represented in such a way that the group assists by providing a fall guy—a domain that needs the rule of the empire. Shakespeare's cultural impressment of the Irish can be located in characters who embody stereotypical Irish characteristics and serve the English nation-writing interests of a play. It can also be located in structures that close with English characteristics triumphing over Irish ones in a represented trajectory of British history, such as in the history plays. Representation of the Irish in Shakespeare covers a wide spectrum between the conspicuously literal and the metaphorical. The most easily recognizable is MacMorris, serving Henry V as the Irish one of a small coterie of captains, each from a different Celtic part of the empire. Many would argue that *The Tempest* holds the most recognizable instance of the "other," but while certainly the Irish have identified themselves as Caliban, so too have other "others." The island is most frequently identified as being the New World, rather than part of the Old World, of which Ireland, while exoticized, was most certainly a part. Prospero's island has been well trod by scholars of post-colonialism and cultural materialism. This study's seeming avoidance of the play owes more to the fact that the relationship between colonizer and colonized is simpler in *The Tempest* than it is in other plays—the invasion of the island and the enslavement of the native are so directly represented in that play that the nature of how those things are accomplished is no longer ground which is open for extensive investigation.

Ireland itself figures literally into the Shakespeare canon in interesting ways, most of them negative. Two instances in the history plays alone depict it as baggage, and as a breeding ground for rebellion. Richard II confiscated Bolingbroke's inheritance in part to finance wars in Ireland, and it is while he is there putting down rebellion that Henry takes opportunity to act. In *2 Henry VI,* York returns from Ireland with the force with which he will fight the crown.

It is also characters whose mysticism and idealism make them incapable of ruling as effectively as pure specimens of English pragmatism in which Irish writers have located "Irishness," regardless of the stated nationality of the characters themselves. Idealism and mysticism belong not only to the early modern English conception of the medieval period, they belong as well to the early modern English conception of any "less civilized" place. In both Barnaby Riche's and Edmund Spenser's constructions of Ireland, it is the absence of pragmatism in the Irish which makes English rule of them necessary. Just as in Riche's dismissal of the Irish "misuse" of the "hubbub," there is plenty of room in the construction of the Irish for dissident reading.

CREATING THE HUBBUB

Certainly a construction of the Irish as further behind the English in cultural and social progression qualifies under Greenblatt's framework as an imperialist society justifying its force against an othered society by representing that society's ideology as being false and in need of correction. Such a representation provides more than a justification for violence, it provides validation of the imperialist society as well; the backwardness of the other validates not only the force of the imperial society, but the qualities of the imperial society itself. The imperial society then not only writes its own justification for physical violence, but in an act of cultural violence represents another society as a means of self-definition. The imperialist society inadvertently provides inclusion for the othered society, despite the fact that it can record that other with any degree of dismissiveness it chooses.

However, as Jonathan Dollimore points out, once the dominant power has recorded the other, it has made the eternal error of having represented that society and identified its opposition. Once done, that othered society, having been identified, can now self-identify, and once the othered society has self-identified it can never be erased. Dollimore also argues that all plays contain subversive elements—that no work can exist without them—because whatever elements stand victorious at the end of the work do so at the expense of those which have been determined to deserve losing, and that tragedies of the sixteenth and seventeenth centuries were written with precisely this in mind. But as Dollimore argues, the closure of a play with the dominant ideology in power nevertheless cannot "control what it permits" and once a subversion is represented, "ideological erasure" cannot be guaranteed, as closure cannot act retrospectively.[51] The cultural impressment of Ireland in the early modern British empire's national writing could not control what it permitted, and Ireland, in being put to service, was never erased.

Terry Eagleton reports that "in 1900, the *United Irishman* described Shakespeare as a 'Celt born in England.'"[52] Ireland was struggling in its own nationalist movement with the challenge to free itself from provincial status without losing its "unique identity" and the relationship with English culture was inevitably a primary issue in the struggle. Eagleton grapples with the complicated matter of the Irish "interest in the English Elizabethan and Jacobean periods" and finds in Yeats and Synge a reverse reading of Spenser's take on Ireland as a previous England: "Indeed Ireland comes to figure not just as the other of Britain but as its origin, the very image of the integral past from which it has declined."[53] Certainly there was a resurrection of the Gaelic language, and texts were written in it, but these would necessarily have a limited audience. While English writings may have served for inspiration in the Irish reimagining of itself, Eagleton points out that "to use English to give voice to non-English experiences, in the manner of colonial and post-colonial writing, is then to drive a dangerous wedge between signifier and signified."[54] That wedge is the essence of language reappropriation, since the Irish would be describing their oppressed, colonized experience through the language of the terms which had justified English invasion. It wrests the terms out of exclusive English control. It does not, however, hand exclusive control to the Irish either. To use English, however subversively, reinscribes the dominance of English. To use the language for their own self-description, however, confutes the terms through which they had been described by the English.

The Irish were experts at reading definitions and expectations of themselves and alternately inhabiting and refusing them as occasion arose. It became part of the Irish stereotype to destabilize previously inscribed positioning of themselves in the empire and in the language of the empire. Declan Kiberd writes that "The British professed themselves baffled by the twists and turns of Irish political history. They complained that whenever they seemed close to solving the Irish question, the Irish had a dreadful habit of changing the question."[55]

The Irish were perhaps able to be seen as evading the question because their position of "our other" resists resolution. The Irish found themselves contending with, and sometimes accepting for expediency, images of themselves which they had no part in constructing, but the construct itself keeps the "Irish question" going. Kiberd opens *Inventing Ireland* with the statement that "If Ireland had never existed, the English would have invented it; and since it never existed in English eyes as anything more than a patch-work quilt of warring fiefdoms, their leaders occupied the neighbouring island and called it Ireland." The construction feeds itself. Kiberd continues, saying that Irish writers learned to "decode those texts which presumed to decode them."[56]

The place of Shakespeare in that decoding is implicitly questioned in Kiberd's statement that the "Irish young people who studied English literature at the end of the nineteenth or beginning of the twentieth century found themselves reading the story of how they had been banished from their own home."[57] This banishment failed in the long term, of course, in Ireland as elsewhere, as the sharp minds of those native to the colonized lands leapt through and over English texts and stubbornly insisted on reading those texts in terms of their own experience, in terms of the very culture that the English had subordinated but never totally eradicated, but with the additional ammunition provided by the culture forced upon them. Irish references to Shakespeare and their reappropriations of his work contain a paradoxical mixture of reverence and resentment. His work is both a means of their oppression and yet still their own inheritance—their cage and yet their key. Kiberd also lauds "their capacity to reformulate the culture which had been used as an instrument to 'civilize' them."[58] This is dissident reading of a complicated kind.

Because they find themselves included in the definition of Britain, given great "British" works to read, they inevitably read themselves in the definition. They, as members of the British empire—however lesser members they may be beside the English members—have access to, in fact are required to access, the works which those governing the British feel are indicative and representative of British greatness. The sailors who were impressed by the British navy and forced to join the roster of a ship may have found themselves unable to leave, but they were accorded the same rations as the rest of the lower shipmates. Just as those sailors were given the *Book of Common Prayer* and a *Life of Nelson* to read as examples of behavior models for good British sailors, the Irish found themselves in possession of great works of British culture, from which they were to discern what made British culture great. So when the Irish writers sought to rediscover their own discourse, they found themselves in conversation with Shakespeare.[59]

LINGUISTIC MUTINY

To enter into the struggle with the empire, Irish writers entered into a struggle of definitions and mastery of the language in which they had been told to give up and assimilate. But victory is not possible, since there is no way to wrest themselves from a past which they may access only through the reality of their colonial existence. The result for Irish subjects is an identity suspended between unstable definitions which are written in the master's language. Edward Said describes the upper-class English education he received while living in Egypt—an education that enabled him to enter a larger and more public world but which divided him from a connection to his cultural origins:

> My whole education was Anglo-centric, so much so that I knew a great deal more about British and even Indian history and geography (required subjects) than I did about the history and geography of the Arab world. But although taught to believe and think like an English schoolboy, I was also trained to understand that I was an alien, a Non-European Other, educated by my betters to know my station and not to aspire to being British.[60]

Rather than living "suspended" between his fragmented selves, he found that his contrapuntal identities required that he be engaged in all simultaneously. The point of his work became, not to resolve his disputing existences, but rather to engage in them with "a greater transparency" and to write in a way that expressed himself clearly and firmly.[61] It is in inhabiting many identities that he is able to, literally, choose his own terms.

Just as other colonial subjects, the Irish were taught in English in National Schools, where they learned English texts and English history. When they learned about their own land in British geography, it would have been with English names for towns and rivers.[62] Speaking English at school and in any official discourse, they quickly learned both English and that it was the "proper" language. Caught between the language of the empire and the language they identified with their own origins, Irish writers who wished to reach a broader-than-Irish audience wrote in English, and they did so with ferocity.

To ignore English—its grammar, its forms, and its greatest masters—would be to ignore that which they had been given as colonial subjects and that which had separated them from something entirely their own. Unable to dismiss it, they worked defiantly within it. Unable to steal it away from the masters without acknowledging them as masters, Irish authors set themselves up as the new masters who can best contend with the old. In order to culturally impress the Irish into imperial service by depicting them as succumbing to it, the empire cast them in an role constructed of fragmented identities. The empire must insist upon Irish difference to authorize its own control and must also insist upon a common identity with Ireland in order to authorize including it. Unable to resolve the fragments of the marginal identity, Irish writers made the fragments the point and starting place for their writing. They understood that they were within a structure over which they could not take control, but, unwilling to let the English win, Irish writers fought back in English and used their fragmentation to confute English dominance, winning neither battle nor war, but at least preventing the empire from winning either.

Cultural Impressment

The positioning of Ireland as "our other" created for England and Ireland a contest of ideologies from which neither would ever escape. The cultural impressment of Ireland in service to the question of "What is Britain?" made that question eternally unanswerable. It forcibly provided access for those impressed into its service to cultural ammunition with which to resist total consumption in the empire: an understanding of themselves as outsiders. The very image that Shakespeare created for the Irish permanently confutes any depiction of Britain as a resolved and cohesive entity.

Chapter Two

Macmorris and the Impressment of the Irish Servant

In Act 1, scene 2 of *Henry V*, the king asks the Archbishop of Canterbury: "May I with right and conscience make this claim?" (line 96). The question regards whether the king may claim France as part of the British lands and follows a reading of the king's ancestral lineage so lengthy, convoluted, and dry that even the archbishop performing the reading is able to make an ironic statement about its "clarity." In fact this reading of lineage and placement of Henry as the rightful master of Britain is the center of more than the opening of the play; it echoes throughout the following acts as Hal slowly backs up paper with prowess, claiming in fact, and blood, what has been claimed before in theory.

Alan Sinfield writes in *Faultlines* that *Henry V* "can be read to reveal not only the rulers' strategies of power, but also the anxieties informing both them and their ideological representation."[1] Henry is certainly anxious about holding on to the crown, an anxiety he inherited from his father, along with very good reasons to be anxious. Hal formulates a strategy, also inherited from his father, to consolidate his power in his own country by invading another. He follows the recital of his heritage with this question that reorganizes what might otherwise be a simple history play and problemitizes the panegyric: "May I with right and conscience make this claim?" He is assured that he may. "Right" and "conscience" are then played out through a depiction of the essence of the greatness of Englishness and the fallibility of other nationalities. His play follows three others in which his father grapples with the rightness of having taken the crown. Hal, in proving his claim to other lands, in essence proves his claim to his own. The anxieties to which Sinfield refers are not only those which lead to the invasion of France in order to bring his people together as a "band of brothers." They are also the anxieties of who is to be included in that band. In pitting Henry/England against France/NotEngland, the play investigates the essence of what it means to be English (and superior, since England, of course, wins). But it also investigates what is English about those who band together to fight with Henry—those who join not only his cause but the cause of Britain. The play impresses not only France into English service by representing its fall to a superior English force, it also impresses the Celtic surroundings of England (Ireland, Wales, and Scotland) by placing them in the service of Henry/England. They must be demonstrated to be non-English or the greatness of English impressment will not be clear. They must be recognizably Celtic. But they must not have distinctions which might disfigure them as rightful belongings of the empire.

Successful invasion will solidify a kingdom; successful formulation of a national character will create a myth. Shakespeare's *Henry V* subsumes into a national figure Hal's own personal character which has developed over the course of the previous two history plays. It is important to recall that, along with his character, Hal developed an uncanny ability to play a role for the benefit of his own ambition. By becoming all that is perfectly Britain, Henry can consolidate his own kingdom. His dialogic use of power and his claim to France are connected issues. By viewing himself as an extension of his kingdom, he constructs around his kingship a mythology that is national rather than personal. His myth is solidified by his claim to France and he enlists his entire kingdom in the cause. If he can get others to agree that he is the rightful heir to France, it would seem to follow naturally that he is rightfully king of England.

Hal, leaning on his legacy, not just in the vocabulary of lineage, but in practice, follows the example of his grandfather and the advice of his father. John of Gaunt, through his speech creating an association of himself with England as a nation, serves as an example for the someday-great national hero Hal would become. Bolingbroke's advice to his son, to keep insurrection at bay by distracting his people with "foreign quarrels" (4.5.214), actually fits with Hal's re-imagined kingship. Hal constructs his myth not around a man's right to a crown, but a nation's right to invade another nation.

Henry IV justified taking the crown after Richard II interfered with the rights of inheritance, and afterwards an aptitude for governance must be proven over and over to maintain the right to the crown. Bolingbroke had initially returned to England from exile with the statement that his homecoming was for no more than to take back "his own:" Richard had taken advantage of Bolingbroke's absence at the death of his father and had confiscated the Lancaster lands to finance his own royal excesses, including maintenance of control in Ireland (see Chapter Three). Richard had reinscribed his authority through the rhetoric of kingship, but once that rhetoric was demonstrated to be empty in the face of an angry Bolingbroke and a host of rebellious nobles bent on revenge, rhetoric alone would never again be enough to keep the court in line. Inheritance was no longer enough—a ruler had to demonstrate ability to govern fairly, as Bolingbroke, now Henry IV, learns when his previous cohorts find him failing in what they perceive to be appropriate treatment of the nobility.

While Henry IV demonstrated less than perfection in this area, his son and heir is more successful. Hal as King Henry V is brave, wise, cautious, fair, merciful to the fallen and harsh to traitors. The virtues his father lacked—the capacity to listen to those he rules and a graciousness to those near him in power—the new King Henry has in abundance. The second tetralogy wraps up a series about pragmatism triumphing over inherited right with a final play which begins by justifying invasion through inherited right. Pragmatism is the ultimate English virtue, and those who serve Hal as well as those who fall to him are inevitably portrayed as lacking the solid pragmatism Hal has in such measure. Hal's followers are generally a rag-tag bunch who need his stout assurance and his charismatic rhetoric of unity in order to stay on task. The French, particularly the Dauphin, are reckless, feckless, and arrogant. They strut in their defiance while ineptly underestimating the determination of the English force. Character is tied to origin and origins not only begin the play, they will continue to guide it.

While the French may have been the greatest problem for the English while Henry V was king, the Irish were the biggest problem while *Henry V* was flourishing on Shakespeare's stage.[2] Henslowe's *Diary* first records a performance of "harey the v" on 28 November, 1595, and the Diary records receipts for another nine performances before the end of May, 1596.[3] Andrew Hadfield and Willy Maley write that the rebellion of Hugh O'Neill which began in 1594 and was also called the Nine Years' War, was "the most threatening event of Elizabeth's last decade."[4] This had been preceded by the 1585 revolts of the Earl of Baltinglass and the Earl of Desmond, the latter being famous for the brutality with which it was put down.[5] Alan Sinfield posits that

> Ireland was the greatest problem—the one Essex was supposed to resolve. The population was overwhelmingly Catholic and liable to support a continental invader, and resistance to English rule proved irrepressible, despite or, more probably, because of the many atrocities committed against the people—such as the slaughter of all the six hundred inhabitants of Rathlin Island by John Norris and Francis Drake in 1575.[6]

The extent to which the English feared Irish Catholicism should not be underestimated. Many of the Irish rebellions were either instigated or funded (or both) by the Catholic church. The Earl of Desmond had invoked the papal bull which excommunicated Elizabeth at the outset of his rebellion,[7] and, as shown in Chapter One, writers such as Barnaby Riche blamed Irish misbehavior for the most part on priestly misguidance. England's constant battling with other Catholic nations, notably Spain and France, made Ireland the location of potential invasion for Catholic monarchs who could have found the Irish willing to submit to another master who did not wish to eradicate their Church.

If there was a fear that the atrocities of physical violence could drive Ireland to seek protection from, and connection to, a fellow Catholic nation, cultural impressment offers a fine alternative. It is not physically violent, it provides a sense of unity and harmony—despite its culturally violent tendencies, which are psychological and perhaps not readily apparent, certainly not in the pit of the Globe which would have been filled with English citizens. The English would have seen the Irish as needing a cultural lift which citizenship in Britain would provide. Sinfield continues that

> The assumption that the Irish were a barbarous and inferior people was so ingrained in Elizabethan England that it seemed no more than a natural duty to subdue them and destroy their culture. Indeed, at one level, their ideological containment was continuous with the handling of the disaffected lower-class outgroup. . . .

The ideological containment Sinfield is talking about is a part of cultural impressment—it is inclusion with the purpose of reaping the resources they have to offer while containing their dangerous differences. If they are barbarous, and they will always be inferior, they can nevertheless be less barbarous if they are Anglicized. They are the inferior, but they are made an inferior part of the great nation of Britain. They are just like the lower class of English (except that they are even lower, of course) in that they are privileged to serve. And serve they shall. Sinfield points out that:

> But much more was at stake in the persistent Irish challenge to the power of the Elizabethan state, and it should be related to the most strenuous challenge to English unity in Henry V: like Philip Edwards, we see the attempt to conquer France and the union in peace at the end of the play as a re-presentation of the attempt to conquer Ireland and the hoped-for unity of Britain. The play offers a displaced, imaginary resolution of one of the state's most intractable problem.[8]

That imaginary resolution is an imagined community, an idea best codified by Benedict Anderson. Sinfield is talking about the presentation of an imagined community—an imagined Britain—to demonstrate the hoped-for reality at stake. Shakespeare creates that hoped-for reality in the collection of captains—the cheerfully serving Celts who are all there to fight for the expansion of Britain and the glory of England.

Assisting Hal in his invasion of France are captains representing nations already invaded by England. They are so neatly arranged that the representation is obvious. Captain Fluellen is Welsh, Captain Jamy is Scots, and Captain Macmorris is Irish.[9] They serve alongside the English captain Gower. These four captains serve equally in Hal's service. If Hal is the nation of England or Britain, then these captains are the parts of that nation, and they encompass the different national legacies of the British Isles, and the different "races" that are being unified through the structure of the dramatis personae.[10]

Part of the confusion of distinguishing a difference between "England" and "Britain" is the fact that the two seem interchangeable here, yet Gower represents the English alongside the other represented nations making up Britain, and yet Henry is lauded as being all that is best of the "English." England, Scotland, Wales, and Ireland are depicted serving equally as captains to Britain, and yet that Britain is also synonymous with one of the serving nations.[11] This is key to understanding the relationships between Britain and its subservient nations. The king of Britain is not the king of equally represented nations—he is England, he is Britain, and the two are the same thing despite the fact that other nations make up Britain. England is Britain, and Britain is England, and yet Ireland, Scotland, and Wales are also part of Britain. They are, therefore, part of England, but are not England. Stephen Greenblatt points out in *Shakespearean Negotiations* that

> by yoking together diverse peoples—represented in the play by the Welshman Fluellen, the Irishman Macmorris, and the Scotsman Jamy, who fight at Agincourt alongside the loyal Englishmen—Hal symbolically tames the last wild areas of the British Isles, areas that in the sixteenth century represented, far more powerfully than any New World people, the doomed outposts of a vanishing tribalism.[12]

This sets up a permanently subservient relationship. England can be interchangeable with Britain, but the others will always be "parts." They are parts which serve and are rewarded with belonging but not with equality.

The Irish response to *Henry V* is not as obvious or easy to trace as it is to other plays. The name of the king and the situation itself does not recur in Irish nationalist literature as do the names of Hamlet and Richard II. The play does not appear to set up a recycling of situation or theme. But *Henry V* does contain the most obviously Irish character: Macmorris.[13] Declan Kiberd writes in *Inventing Ireland* that the English writers, knowing that they were "the lords of language" in their own imperial situation, rarely "considered, even for a passing moment, that the Irish might have a case for their resistance. Henceforth, Ireland would be a sort of absence in English texts, a utopian 'no place' into which the deepest fears and fondest ideals might be read." He continues that the "two major Irish stereotypes on the English national stage embody those polarities of feeling" and he describes them as "the threatening, vainglorious soldier" and the "feckless but cheerily reassuring servant." They were first, however, "soothingly conflated in the sketch of Captain Macmorris in *Henry the Fifth*."[14] Complicating any patent dismissal of the Irish in this conflated sketch, however, is the fact that Macmorris is a much better servant to king than the English personal friends whom Henry must discard for faithlessness. Unlike the impressment of Irish characters discussed in subsequent chapters, this case is more clear and simple. Macmorris is undeniably Irish, but he is a willing, even passionate, servant of Henry. Whereas characters in other plays are forcibly deprived of their own autonomy by the superior pragmatist, Macmorris is glad to serve Henry and the goals of England.

SERVANTS AND THE BODY POLITIC

Hal begins a transformation of himself from man to king at the end of *1 Henry IV*, but the transformation is not complete at the beginning of *Henry V*. It must continue, as Henry sheds personal companions and replaces them with an abstract—an assortment of embodiments of Britain's holdings. In this, Henry trades the personal king's body for the state king's body and trades a set of separate nations for an empire. The personal disappears as those who serve Henry are pressed by the play into the service of Britain. The conflict between the king's two bodies is resolved by the elimination of the personal. Even when Henry woos Katherine, he woos her not as a man wooing a woman but as Britain wooing France, struggling with the French language and finally shifting the dialogue completely into the English Katherine has begun to learn and will now speak forever. That is only the final capping of Henry's progress towards total embodiment of the state. By the end of the battle, Henry has no remaining personal companions. His tavern mates are dead or cast aside and his friends of aristocratic upbringing are executed for treason.

Pitted rhetorically against Cambridge, Scroop, and Grey as a trustworthy band of officers, Gower, MacMorris, Fluellen, and Jamy are hardly able to do less than shine. The metaphor digs deeper than simply two groups of officers, one of which turns on the king. The first group is all English, all noble, and all real and longtime friends of the king (Scroop especially). Henry disproves his own initial gauge of a good officer in his rant against Scroop:

> O, how hast thou with jealousy infected
> the sweetness of affiance! Show men dutiful?
> Why, so didst thou. Seem they grave and learnèd?
> Why, so didst thou. Come they of noble family?
> Why, so didst thou. Seem they religious?
> Why, so didst thou. Or are they spare in diet,
> Free from gross passion or of mirth or anger,
> Constant in spirit, not swerving with the blood,
> Garnished and decked in modest complement,
> Not working with the eye without the ear,
> And but in purgèd judgement trusting neither?
> Such and so finely bolted didst thou seem.   (2.2.126–137)

The merits on which Henry estimated the value of a good friend and officer were very much based on aristocratic birth and wealth. These qualifications, by the way, do not describe his former friend Falstaff, whom he dismissed upon gaining the throne. Falstaff, the Vice character who directed the mischief of Hal's dissolute days, may have aspired to the position of Lord Chief Justice, but, since Vice cannot take the place of Justice in the administration of a king who will restore not only order, but also dignity, to the throne, Falstaff was cast aside. The list of virtues Hal expects in a friend do not in any way describe Falstaff. Having now surrounded himself with people who fit the bill, Henry finds that the list provides no guarantee of loyalty. Duty, nobility, piety, stoicism, modesty, and wisdom can be bought, apparently, for a decent sized purse of foreign gold. But lest the Cambridge plot and the dismissal of personal and noble friends appear to be the only necessary sloughing off of personal obstacles, we are given our old tavern fellows to review.

The comparison with Henry's former associates is highlighted by the juxtaposition of scenes. The unveiling of the traitorous group in the Cambridge plot sits between two scenes of the slow death of Falstaff, attended by Nym, Bardolph, Pistol, the Boy, and the Hostess.[15] Nym, Bardolph, and Pistol will follow Henry to France, and will prove, as can be expected, no more trustworthy than the nobles. Sinfield points out that "Despite the thorough dismissal of Bardolph, Nym, and Pistol, Henry V does not leave the issue of lower-class disaffection. If those characters must be abandoned because they were unworthy or incapable of being incorporated into the unified nation, others must be introduced who will prove more tractable."[16] Slowly, Hal comes to know them not, just as he did Falstaff.

Sinfield is correct when he argues that Shakespeare depicts Henry as discarding his tavern fellows, once and for all, as Nym, Bardolph, and Pistol, like Falstaff before them, fail to fit Henry's new vision of a king's companions. Just as Falstaff, the embodiment of Vice, could not take the role of Lord Chief Justice which his ambition led him to request, the other roustabouts of the tavern cannot be Britain's representatives of imperialism. Shakespeare first forces Henry to discard his aristocratic fellows. One does not see these childhood friends in the previous two plays, but Henry berates Lord Scroop, saying, "Thou that didst bear the key of all my counsels,/ That knew'st the very bottom of my soul, . . ." (2.2.96–7). Henry's "princes" and "noble peers" (2.2. 84) are no better companions for the king than the men of the tavern.

Scroop, Grey, and Cambridge, not knowing that they have been found out, continue (in Henry's trick to trap them) to act as though they are on the side of the state, advising Henry what to do with a man who has committed sedition in having "railed against" the king's "person" (2.241). They offer what Stephen Greenblatt calls "salutary anxiety" in a true example of hegemonic muscle-flexing when Grey suggests to Henry: "Sir, you show great mercy if you give him life/ After the taste of much correction" (2.2.50–51). But Grey, as the king and the audience already know, is ill-fit to administer or advise justice, and will "taste of much correction" himself soon enough.

The exposé of the Cambridge plot, in which close friends and nearly peers in aristocratic upbringing "should, for a foreign purse sell/ His sovereign's life to death and treachery," is sandwiched between two tavern scenes of Nym, Bardolph, and Pistol and the death of Falstaff. Falstaff was, of course, the first to be discarded, but the emphasis on service to the crown is set when the first of these two tavern scenes begins with Bardolph and Nym addressing each other, not as fellow roustabouts, but as officers: "Well met, Corporal Nym" and "Good Morrow, Lieutenant Bardolph" (2.1.1–2). Despite their place as officers in the king's army, however, their squabbling, so inappropriate in those whose focus should be on the state, is instead on brawling out their own unresolved disputes. The bickering is temporarily quieted when the Boy enters to announce Falstaff's fatal illness, presumably death of a broken heart from having been abandoned by Hal. Bardolph is then able to resolve the argument between Pistol and Nym, saying, "We/ must to France together. Why the devil should we/ keep knives to cut one another's throats?" (2.1.90–91).

The second scene is a brief and humorous group elegy for Falstaff, remembering his vices and bemoaning the lack of remuneration they found in his service. It ends in harmony, with Pistol addressing the others as his "yokefellows" or companions, and the men leaving to meet the king in Southampton. The scene of the Cambridge plot, inserted between these two tavern scenes, dramatizes the downfall of Henry's traitorous aristocratic companions. Shakespeare shows treason being followed by Pistol and company leaving to join the king in a seemingly patriotic brotherhood of service and, after scrapping the upper-class friends, momentarily offers Hal's old carousing pals in their place. The reunion is not to last.

Their departure is immediately followed with a scene in France and a demonstration of what is at stake. When the French king asks Exeter what will happen should France resist the British invasion, Exeter answers with the coldest and most frightening possible answer: "Bloody constraint; for if you hide the crown/ Even in your hearts, there will he rake for it" (2.4.97–98). In successful invasion, all must be turned over to the victorious, including personal ambition, agency, and dreams. The absorption of person into state continues. In 3.0, the Chorus tells the audience that Katherine has been tendered, with some "unprofitable dukedoms" as part of a cease-fire offer (considered by the British too petty an offer to be accepted). Henry's future marriage is already one of lands rather than people. But Hal and Katherine are not the only humans being understood as state property. State persona applies to those who serve the state in lower and more dangerous capacities as well. In 3.1, with the siege of Harfleur, Henry shouts the famous: "Once more into the breach, dear friends, once more,/ Or close up the wall with our English dead!" (1–2). The soldiers, instead of being people who sacrifice their lives, are now stones to "close up the wall." Their humanity is denied in a patriotic act of either breaching the fortress or rebuilding its fortifications through their deaths, although their deaths are not mentioned as such but are rather translated into inanimate objects. Their service is to the state, through their lives or through their fall, and it doesn't seem to matter which, as long as the state is served. They are abstracts now, like the abstractions of the Celtic nations which the captains like Macmorris represent. All are pressed into service to the empire as less important entities than the superiority of the state. Even Henry's humanity disappears further when he lists himself in the things to fight for, alongside England and the symbol of England, with the closing shout: "God for Harry! England and St. George!" (3.1.34). The shout suggests a new trinity, not including the Almighty but rather blessed by him—a trinity of the state.

EVEN IN YOUR HEARTS

The last trade of individual persona for state persona begins in the next scene, 3.2, when we meet for the first time the Captains Fluellen, Gower, Macmorris, and Jamy. When Henry's last remaining personal companions, the tavern fellows, are caught by Fluellen while electing to stay out of "the breach" into which Henry has ordered them, we find the beginning of the end for personal will against state will. It is Fluellen who first catches the tavern fellows shirking their duty at Harfleur, calling: "Up to the breach, you dogs!" in a less eloquent reiteration of the king's words. The Boy, who moments earlier would have given all his "fame for a pint of ale and safety" (3.2.13) now, in a lengthy and far more articulate speech than any we will hear from the other tavern men now speaks an individual indictment of each of the others' failures, their absences in abiding the law, and the petty-criminal life they would lead him into: "which/ makes much against my manhood, if I should take/ from another's pocket to put into mine, for it is plain/ pocketing up of wrongs." He leaves them to "seek some better service" (27–52). Avoiding prescribed service to the state apparently will not do.

His exit comes with the entrance of Gower, followed by Macmorris and Jamy. Fluellen is interested only in "the disciplines of war" in a silly obsession with traditional Roman science of war. Macmorris's failure to adhere to these marks him for Fluellen as a poor soldier and leader, but in fact brings Henry the success he wants. What follows is a flurry of ridiculous accents arguing military strategy and the best way to serve the British goal of victory and expansion. When Fluellen, disdainful of all that is not English (presumably excepting himself), picks an argument with Macmorris over differences in perception of service, Macmorris wants to get back to the battle, but Fluellen insists that they first "discourse" upon the merits of Roman military discipline. Gower the English captain is silent on the matter, but Jamy the Scots captain is eager to hear the debate. Macmorris furiously declines.

The dispute over the Roman "science of war" is an interesting topic for debate amongst captains representing the holdings of Britains empire. Rome was the glorious example of empire for Britain and an ancestor in the imperial mythology of the Renaissance. Rome also demanded allegiance to the empire over local allegiances, and it is here that irony collects in the scene: Fluellen wishes to debate Roman military science, Macmorris keeps his focus on the battle, and when Fluellen presses the issue and begins a sentence with "not many of your nation . . .," he gets a tirade. Macmorris responds:

> Of my nation? What ish my nation? Ish a
> villain, and a bastard, and a knave, and a rascal? What
> ish my nation? Who talks of my nation?   (3.2.121–123)

The question marks confuse the potential meaning. The delivery of this speech would determine whether Macmorris is dismissing his nation or defending it. Is he responding with an angry conjecture that Fluellen is insinuating that Ireland is "a villain, and a bastard, and a knave, and a rascal?" Or is Macmorris, more interested in his service to Britain (as he certainly is at this moment, with "throats to be cut, and work to be done" waiting for him in Harfleur) than he is in his Irish origins? When he demands, "What ish my nation?" is he demanding an explanation for an insult, or denying a nationality separate from Britain?

The interpretation could be dependent upon performance and inflection, but positioned in the context of his demanding to be free from an entangling exchange that prevents his dutiful service in the king's siege, his question indicates that, as far as he is concerned, "his nation" is the one battering the gates of the embattled French town. His nation may be Ireland, but it is also Britain, and his service to Britain does not, for him, conflict with his Irish nationality. The denial of a separate identity performed in a clearly colonial accent confuses his meaning. By giving Macmorris an identity that has nothing to do with personal differences and everything to do with an Irish abstraction serving Britain, Shakespeare creates for his definitively Irish character an identity that refuses individuality while insisting upon difference. The difference, his accent, is used to serve the king as it demands to leave the verbal battle and fight the military one. The exchange is immediately followed by the complete and utter surrender of Harfleur, after the king warns the town's governor "to our best mercy give yourselves" or he "will not leave the half-achievèd Harfleur/ Till in her ashes she lie burièd" (3.3.3, 8–9). With this king of Britain, there is no partial surrender, there is no "half-achievèd" invasion, there is no place—even in one's heart—to hide a sense of autonomy which complicates one's total service.

The king the French call "Harry England" must himself devote his own body and heart to that greater body of the nation. *Henry V* increasingly disposes of the king's Body Natural in favor of the Body Politic—a move which erases personal flaw and imperfection in inheritance, and a feat which his father, Henry IV, was never able to accomplish. Yet, despite a shift which grounds Henry's desire to place himself irrevocably on the throne, and ties him through the immortal Body Politic to an unshakable right to the crown, the Body Natural continues to surface, both in Henry's self-doubting tour of the camp and, ironically, in the marriage of his body to Katherine's in a move that is the essence of the Body Politic in its use of the king for national ends.

The concept of the "king's two bodies" has been an issue in criticism since Ernst Kantorowicz's investigation of the history of the concept.[17] And just as every conflict a monarch experiences eventually makes its way through the ranks of society, so too will this one, as the demands of service to the state are built to cover imperfections in authority and in personal ability in the monarch. The duality of the Body Natural/Body Politic relationship holds the two to be the same, but, due to the "immortal" nature of the Body Politic, privileges that body over the Body Natural. This, of course, holds true in the relationship between king and subject, and can deny the interiority of the individual, the agency and wishes, while still holding claim to the service to be rendered by the individual body.[18] Kantorowicz's study applies to cultural impressment through the consideration of the erasure of individuality by public interest. The people whom the monarch claims to be represented by the Body Politic are subsumed by it and subject to its demands. Although its identification is as much with the body of subjects as it is with the body of the monarch, it is the body of the monarch which makes those demands. Monarchial use of the plural personal pronoun "we" in official state documents and dialogue to represent not just the crown but those who are ruled by it is a form of imagined community as the monarch's conceptualization of those included in the "we" ignores their personal differences through rhetorical inclusion. The monarch as "we" speaks for self and all subjects—impressment in the "we" is expected and understood.

That service in Macmorris's case, however, is service to a king with whom the audience never sees him converse, with whom he shares no stage time. At the moment Macmorris demonstrates his dedication to the imperial master in a definitively Irish accent, that master is off-stage. Macmorris is unable to fully articulate his difference—a statement of what ish his nation—when asked, but his answer's being made in heavily accented English makes the point for him. He serves an English master, but has not been English-ized. He has been British-ized, impressed into the empire through the representation of supporting the concerns of the crown through an accent of difference. It is that difference which makes his impressment meaningful to the empire, and the very thing which makes total inclusion of him impossible.

WE HAPPY FEW (WHO ARE PRESSED INTO SERVICE)

The violent inclusion present in the plural personal pronoun "we" in official state documents and dialogue represents more than a collection of people—it represents an understood unified body which takes on a persona of its own. When "we" want a certain action to be taken or when "we" find a person guilty of treason or sedition or simply petty theft, the "we" represents the accused as much as it does everyone else because it demands inclusion in a collective thought. "We" is the state, and, as a demanded inclusive, any divergence from "we" is not a divergence from the personal perspectives of a monarch, it is a divergence from the better wishes of the state. A divergent perspective is then placed in a position of conflict with more than "the state" as a separate institution; it is in a position of conflict with a body to which it is assumed to belong. It is the difference between an enemy and a traitor: an enemy is a combatant from another group, but a traitor is a combatant against a group in which he or she is assumed to belong. The enemy fights from elsewhere, but the traitor fights from within by refusing the demanded inclusion.

Shakespeare complicates the unity of Britain as, while those unwilling to toe the state line—the Cambridge plot nobles and the tavern fellows—are discarded by the text, the group of captains which structurally replaces them have demonstrable differences in language. Each has a distinct accent, which, if inaccurately depicted, nevertheless provides for each character a decided link to home and culture separate from the others. One purpose for this depiction is perhaps the opportunity to poke fun at their speech, something done before Shakespeare and certainly well after, but the captain best situated as an object of humor is Fluellen, who is overtly ridiculous enough in his manner without accent playing a part in it. The arrangement of captains accomplishes the goal of representing the image of English occupied territories as serving cheerfully the ambitions of a king who is England itself and is done through the representation of their names and their accents. Recognition of the ethnicity of a name and an accent is an implicit recognition of a separate culture, and of that culture's separate history.

Shakespeare, by recording the linguistic differences of Henry's captains, records, acknowledges, if seeking to contain, the cultural differences of the captains. The ideal model of unity, the "we" towards which the play works, is an impressment in terms of behavioral compliance—agreement in the "we." And the captains do agree. When Henry as Britain speaks, he speaks for the captains, and the captains as Servants of Britain carry out his orders. While *Henry V* creates a new myth of inclusion, however, the captains' differences in language suggest different ontologies, and it is here that Shakespeare creates the potential for dissident readings to which the peoples represented in those captains may cling.

In *Faultlines,* Alan Sinfield offers the captains of Britain as the "tractable citizens" Shakespeare sought. Sinfield points out that "The issue of the English domination of Wales, Scotland, and Ireland appears in the play to be more containable, though over the centuries it may have caused more suffering and injustice than the subjection of the lower classes. The scene of the four captains (3.3) seems to effect an effortless incorporation. . . ."[19] Despite Hal's insistence upon raking in the heart to eliminate personal conflict with the interests of the crown, in an unreserved service to the nation, these meticulously, if ridiculously, depicted accents suggest a level at which incorporation cannot be fulfilled. Herein lies what Sinfield would call a "faultine:" in order to depict Macmorris's otherness and glorify the depth and breadth of British unity, his difference must be demonstrated; however, once his difference has been demonstrated, it permanently disrupts the total unity for which the play strives.[20]

Despite the fact that Macmorris is given very little stage time, his scrappy and combative yet servile character resonated with Irish audiences. He is certainly not the only such character to appear in a long tradition of Irish stereotyped characters, but his defining question, "What ish my nation?" makes him accessible for Irish writers in the surge of twentieth century Irish nationalism who were seeking to investigate and overturn the stereotypes under which they labored. When Declan Kiberd points out that the "threatening and vainglorious soldier" and "feckless but cheerily reassuring servant" were conflated in Macmorris, he points out that those character types survived in the "modern period in such identifiable forms as [Sean] O'Casey's Captain Boyle and Joxer, or Samuel Beckett's Didi and Gogo." He continues that "In Shakespeare's rudimentary portrait are to be found those traits of garrulity, pugnacity and a rather unfocused ethnic pride which would later signalize the stage Irishman."[21] O'Casey's and Beckett's comic pairs do not simply take on the insulting characteristics of type in order to rework the tradition. They prove themselves descendants of Macmorris the servant, because they too are defined by questions of origin.

PRINCIPLES DON'T PAY THE SHOPKEEPER

Shakespeare's stage Irishman is there to serve the British ideal, and so must, at whatever cost to himself, belong. Macmorris would not be the last traitor to their self-respect the Irish would ever find on an English stage. The clichés of the servant are rampant still, although they began to take on more tragic qualities in the twentieth century. The servant must be read through the master, since it is through the master that the servant finds identity. Personal agency is erased by serving the agency of the master.

An Irish playwright working to rehabilitate the cliché stage Irishman would preferably erase the master and privilege the narrative of the servant, but in the tradition in which he or she writes, there are many gaps to fill. The two playwrights whom Declan Kiberd points out as creating descendants of Macmorris chose to reinscribe the servant/master relationship, but take advantage of the master's absence. Macmorris ardently serves a master who is off-stage during his strongest articulation of service. An abstract representation of his own nation, his impressment is to an empire identified only in the abstract. O'Casey and Beckett respond by exploring that relationship and distancing the master to an entity the servant cannot identify, and so cannot identify with. O'Casey's Boyle and Joxer and Beckett's Didi and Gogo are servants of masters they never see. They do not, however, reduce the service. The servant narrative takes place center stage, but, as a critic of *Juno and the Paycock* wrote in a 1925 review of the play, the servant is still a servant and the master is still in control: it "is as much a tragedy as *Macbeth,* but it is a tragedy taking place in the porter's family."[22]

Christopher Murray writes in his introduction to O'Casey's *Three Dublin Plays* that it is possible to see these as history plays; that O'Casey "was a great admirer of Shakespeare's history plays" but that these three "were not written as a cycle and that they were written to illustrate just the opposite of Shakespeare's histories: unredeemed disorder ('chassis') rather than order, democratic man rather than kingship, decentered impotence rather than centralized power."[23] Indeed, all three demonstrate the bleak and joyless lives of those in the Dublin tenements, and each manages to kill off or irredeemably discourage those few characters who at the beginning had hope for better lives.

The two perhaps greatest exceptions to this rule, however, are Captain Boyle and Joxer Daly from *Juno and the Paycock,* who are almost precisely the same at the end as they are at the beginning: unending powerlessness seems to go hand in hand with unending apathy and consequent drunkenness. Boyle and Joxer are very ugly descendants of Macmorris—the Shakespearean Captain's inept but duty-bound service to the British crown translates into an inept and duty-bound service to shiftlessness—the worst stereotype of the tenement bum who lives off of others in order to drink. Boyle and Joxer are a comic version of that stereotype. They are lazy, irreverent, drunken slobs who would do anything to avoid work: Mrs. Boyle shouts to Boyle, "It ud be easier to dhrive you out o' the house than to dhrive you into a job."[24] Despite bellicose chants about their national pride, Boyle and Joxer are less driven by any sentiment than they are by immediate needs—each is the happy servant of whatever authority is in front of him at the time. But because they are so easily swayed from each other, they lose the chummy and sympathetic humor of the standard comic pair—they engage in bantering that becomes not just squabbles, but outright betrayal of each other. Removed from overt service to any known or tangible master, Boyle and Joxer are rootless and wayward.

Their depiction is as much an indictment of Ireland as it is of England—O'Casey, though once a follower of Pearse and O'Connell himself, was eventually sick of the inevitable simplicity and sentimentality of nationalism. In *Juno*, service to the state is no clear matter when the state could be either one of two entities—Mrs. Tancred, on her way to her son's funeral, finds a mutual loss with her neighbor: "An' I'm told he was the leadher of the ambush where me nex' door neighbour, Mrs. Mannin,' lost her Free State soldier son. An' now here's the two of us oul' women, standin' one on each side of a scales o' sorra, balanced be the bodies of our two dead darlin' sons."[25] These events drive the plot and inform the characters, but because such events are inescapable in O'Casey's Dublin, they are not what the play is about. This is not a play about the Irish civil war any more than *Gone With the Wind* is a book about the American civil war. *Juno* is the story of a small group of Dubliners, and there is nothing sweeping about it. The sense that the master is still in control pervades the despair and lack of assurance of their lives. In *Heathcliff and the Great Hunger*, Terry Eagleton describes O'Casey's characters as people who "gabble colourfully away while just beyond the door their destinies are being determined for them by a history which is always elsewhere."[26] The history is being determined by a metropolis far away. The master is absent, and that absence may give the characters some sense of control over their own lives, but when push comes to shove, they find that the master, though elsewhere, is still in control.

When O'Casey tells the story of "the porter's family" by painting the national narrative of Ireland into the backdrop of a domestic narrative, the set becomes a slum and the characters become unable to experience the private narrative with which they are finally provided. The set is a single room, and the absence of privacy is apparent, even when the characters leave the set. The community of the tenement is a claustrophobic, if not close, one—everyone knows everyone else's business, and most of the characters help themselves to the Boyle's hospitality whether welcome or not (Mrs. Boyle says bitingly to her husband's crony: "Pull over to the fire, Joxer Daly; people is always far more comfortabler here than they are in their own place."). Eagleton notes that "O'Casey's typical room is part of a tenement building with a good deal of toing and froing, and so hovers between a private and a communal space in the way that an Ibsenite or Chekhovian living room does not; nobody in

O'Casey ever seems to knock at the door."[27] Their not-very-private community is hardly a community at all in the midst of civil war.

Despite the setting, however, not one character in *Juno and the Paycock* seems to have existed prior to the Easter Uprising only a few years before. Their history appears to have begun at the siege of the Post Office. These people understand themselves only through a history that is just a few years old, and with no apparent knowledge, certainly no mention, of the life before it that the uprising sought to change. For Eagleton, O'Casey's characters are doomed to aspire to only a domestic sort of heroism to which the women may occasionally succeed, but the men inevitably fail. All of them, however, find that they exist in a moral vaccuum, and the only practical thing they can cling to is the money they need to survive. That money is dangled in front of them, and they squander it because they have never had enough money to understand how to handle this currency that determines everything. As Mrs. Boyle says in response to Mary's striking on "principle," "Principles don't pay the shopkeeper." This should be alleviated when Captain Boyle is promised a fortune in an unexpected inheritance.

Captain Boyle has no principles, and he will never pay the shopkeeper, because the inheritance he has been promised will never arrive. His greatest failure comes in his complicity with being duped. The trick comes from a very English seeming teacher-cum-lawyer whose failure to adequately draw up a clear will results in Boyle's inheritance going astray. That teacher/lawyer is named Mr. Bentham, a name irrevocably associated with the English due to the fame of Jeremy Bentham,[28] and it is unclear whether Mr. Bentham failed from honest inattention or careless neglect. He also leaves the Boyle's daughter Mary pregnant and abandoned, a situation Mrs. Boyle considers "worse than consumption."[29] Bentham, who has left, appropriately, for England, is nowhere to be found. The Boyle family collapses, financially, socially, and structurally, as Mrs. Boyle prepares to leave with Mary and the son Johnny is killed by his "Die-Hard" cohorts for having betrayed the Tancred boy to the "Staters."

Captain Boyle is left with Joxer to continue the life they led before the money and the failure. The play ends as a starker version of how it began, with the two coming into the now empty flat, drunk and philosophizing about Ireland and their plight. As Joxer thickly whines out one of the patriotic songs that become meaningless in his shallow and drunken voice, Captain Boyle, whose patriotism also grows with intoxication, once again re-imagines for himself a more heroic role in the recent history which has brought him nothing new or good:

> Boyle: If th' worst comes . . . to th'worse . . . I can join a . . . flyin' . . . column . . . I done . . . me bit . . . in Easther Week . . . had no business . . . to . . . be . . . there . . . but Captain Boyle's Captain Boyle!
>
> Joxer: Breathes there a man with soul . . . so . . . de . . . ad . . . this . . . me . . . o . . . wn, me nat . . . I've l . . . an'!
>
> Boyle: (subsiding into a sitting posture on the floor) Commandant Kelly died . . . in them . . . arms . . . Joxer . . . Tell me Volunteer Butties . . . says he . . . that . . . I died for . . . Irelan'![30]

But Boyle ends the play with his more general philosophy, one now much more true for him than it was at the opening of the play, when he at least had his family and the prospects of work: "I'm telling you . . . Joxer . . . th'whole worl's . . . in a terr . . . ible state o' . . . chassis!"[31]

Ireland is falling apart around him, but no more so than it was when the play opened. His own domestic tragedies can be distinctly traced to the entrance of Bentham and the promise of an inheritance. Like many Irish figures, Boyle must wait for what he wants, and he will wait interminably. He believed in the inheritance, put his trust in Bentham, and collected debts on the surety that the money would come. Bentham's errors are Boyle's undoing, but it is Boyle's own fault that he spent a fortune promised by a stranger. The general tragedies of his country are reflected in the events caused by his own errors in judgement, as those errors ruin him and demolish his family. Here, Boyle fulfills Declan Kiberd's description of the feckless but cheerily reassuring servant; like Macmorris, Boyle participates freely in what the empire has handed him. Unlike Macmorris, Boyle has been given nothing concrete in which to participate—there is no glory in the available service and so he serves no one. O'Casey's version of the Irish servant of the empire is a servant who is gone astray.

O'Casey's remarks on Ireland's cultural inheritance, also gone astray, are found in Boyle's criticism that Mary's loss of virtue comes from having read too many books ("nothin' but thrash, too"—Ibsen, in fact) and in Boyle's and Joxer's only real sense of community being found in the local pub. More cutting is the fact that Boyle's own imaginative flights of fancy are interrupted and cut off by the prosaic call of the coal-vendor whose merchandise Boyle needs but can hardly afford:

> Boyle: An,' as it blowed an' blowed, I ofen looked up at the sky an' assed meself the question—what is the stars, what is the stars?
>
> Voice of Coal Vendor: Any block, coal-blocks; blocks, coal-blocks!
>
> Joxer: Ah, that's the question, that's the question—what is the stars?[32]

The tenements are more than the setting; they intrude upon the action in O'Casey's reinscription of the Irish servant's narrative. Boyle's stories may be exaggerated or wholly concocted narratives of his history, but they are appreciated by the willing audience of Joxer. The telling of the story is punctuated by the interruption of everyday need and so the play's audience, rather than seeing an uplifting look at the life of people usually playing supporting characters, are treated instead to a story of how easily exigencies can keep those characters out of the limelight.

While O'Casey's strategy for reclaiming the private demonstrates how despairing and intruded upon those private lives are, Samuel Beckett acknowledges the total loss of the private for those permanently exposed to the elements of someone else's will. Instead of the community, however false, of the slums, Beckett sets his exercise in the "feckless but cheerily reassuring servant" in a wasteland that has no recognizable geography and strips his comic pair of any knowledge of how they got there. Their history is erased even to themselves, and, unlike Captain Boyle, they cannot reimagine or enlarge it.

Norman Vance writes that "most of Beckett's protagonists, having once got away, keep clear of Ireland and hardly mention the place," but that "Even so, the place left its mark on him."[33] Beckett's desire to escape the sectarianism of his home and his impatience with nationalist poetry do not necessarily indicate an ability to shed frustration with the situation of the Irish and the writing tradition in which they found themselves. To insist that Beckett freed himself by moving to France and writing in French is to ignore his preoccupation with the English in his works. The very fact that he escaped to France and abandoned both the language of Ireland's oppressor and the language which the Gaelic league attempted to recapture as native is either an example of the studied neglect of the cultural victim or an inventive way to attempt to reread his own narrative. Beckett's famous reply to the question, "Are you English?" with the French "au contraire" is as cleverly packed with intellectual diversion (both in the humorous and slight-of-hand senses) as are his plays.

En Attendent Godot may not have situated itself clearly in a dialogue, in fact it refuses to participate coherently in any dialogue, but its threads include references to the English.[34] Estragon, in one of the play-long series of abortive actions, begins to tell a joke: "An Englishman having drunk a little more than usual proceeds to a brothel. The bawd asks him if he wants a fair one, a dark one, or a red-haired one. Go on."[35] The joke, of course, is never completed. Like everything else in Beckett, however, the ending is not the point. The fact that the joke attributes to an Englishman the same drunken and bawdy behavior indictingly used to stereotype the Irish creates something of a reversal, but Estragon cannot complete the joke. He doesn't know the ending. The Englishman in the joke is given assembled women of diverse ethnic ideals from which to select one for the paid degradation of prostitution, but his selection goes unknown, and so the action is not completed. Both the Englishman's action and the subversion of the joke are halted in their tracks by Estragon's inability to articulate the punchline.

NOTHING TO BE DONE

Estragon and Vladimir will not complete any action, and incompletion becomes the animating force of the play in which they are trapped. The great misfortune of cultural impressment is that the representation set up by the master dooms the impressed servant to participate forever. The servant, once represented, must eternally play out the part, even in rebellion. There is no escape from the narrative, and there is no removing oneself from the act of representation. All attempts to rebel against the controlling national narrative in which one finds oneself represented result in either recapitulation or a studied neglect. Either way, the narrative remains a controlling factor, but where open rebellion will not work, subversion can—twisting from within. Here is the ability to re-read with an eye for non-complicity, and to do so is the job of the writer who, in his or her own construction of the relationship between tradition and individual talent, chooses to rehearse the roles but casts a new narrator. Left to Beckett, that narrator is incoherent.

Macmorris's "What Ish My Nation" is repeated in Didi and Gogo's attempts to reconstruct their history. Their total inability to function because they don't have all the information about themselves leaves them vulnerable to the plans of the elusive Godot. Absence of history means absence of autonomy. Macmorris sets a dangerous representational precedent: if participating in the present means denying the past, one must deny one's past or be left out of the present. Like O'Casey's Boyle and Joxer, Didi and Gogo experience absence of origin along with servitude, making them descendants of Macmorris. They cannot remember the beginnings of anything, much less of themselves.

They do not know where they came from, they know only that they are. They do not know for what it is they wait. They just wait. It is the very essence of paralysis, and it comes from absence of context. If they knew where they were or what day they were living, they might be able to make choices that lean on that knowledge. As it is, they spend much of their time attempting to reconstruct the history that they need in order to understand the present. They do not realize at each moment that they are lost, in fact, they tend to stubbornly insist that they are not lost, but they have no idea where they are. In their attempts to reconstruct themselves, Didi and Gogo ask each other "What did we do yesterday?":

> ESTRAGON: In my opinion we were here.
> VLADIMIR: (Looking round) You recognize the place?
> ESTRAGON: I didn't say that.[36]

They are impaired by absence of their own narrative. Perhaps Macmorris's questionable service at Harfleur is related to the absence of nation for which he is so famous. Absence of nation would then be the same as absence of narrative. In *Godot,* not only is it absent, it has been dropped along the way and they can not find it. Didi and Gogo are waiting for narrative as much as they are waiting for anything else. Its absence is the reason that they obsessively engage in absurd dialogue which attempts to reconstruct history, so that they have something to go on and continue. The narrative is too quiet to be heard. According to Kiberd, Didi and Gogo are

> presented as characters without much history, who are driven to locate themselves in the world with reference to geography. But the world in which they live has no overall structure, no formal narrative: instead, it is a dreadful place in which every moment is like the next. Unable to construct a story of the past, the tramps learn nothing from their mistakes, because they can make none of the comparisons which might provide the basis for a confident judgement. Beckett's characters all know the longing to turn their lives into narrative . . . and, by this second look at their history, to free themselves of it; but the trick is not so easily done. Even those who think that they 'possess' their past on a tape recording or on a page find that the present invariably flavours it, emphasizing the near-impossibility of entering into a dialogue with their own history.[37]

Kiberd also reports that "When a friend complained to Beckett that the tramps at times talked as if they possessed doctorates, he shot back 'How do you know they hadn't?'" And Kiberd adds to this that "Their self image is certainly that of an educated class, even if they are leading the life of the hobo."[38] They are tramps, and like most tramps, are seen only in the moment of their bad times. The shabby clothes of the classic tramp figure have a higher class origin, but are worn and torn with wear and hard times. Didi and Gogo have an air of better times gone wrong. Surely they have origins, even if they are unable to articulate them for the audience or even for themselves.

What Beckett does is take a seemingly simple and certainly dead-end situation—two guys who don't know where they are or what they are doing—and dramatizes it so that the audience is able to experience the materiality of the paralysis. The general bleakness that comes from not understanding their situation is experienced again in microcosmic levels—they are incapable of completing any action, however small. Each small stop, from trying to remove a boot to finding a carrot to eat, results in the recognition that there is "nothing to be done."

While the play enacts an absence of context in what Norman Vance calls Beckett's "obsession with elegantly meaningless rituals," we are not to understand that Didi and Gogo are entirely without instructions.[39] Indeed, Godot does exist, as is attested by the Boy who enters just to tell them that Godot will meet them another time. Vladimir assesses the situation and comes to the conclusion that "What we are doing here, that is the question. And we are blessed in this, that we happen to know the answer. Yes, in this immense confusion one thing is clear. We are waiting for Godot to come—." Even totally absent, Godot is totally in control, and Didi and Gogo are left to congratulate themselves on how well they serve this absent benefactor. Stood up again and again, they are left with Didi's attempts to make remarkable their situation: "We have kept our appointment and that's an end to that. We are not saints, but we have kept our appointment. How many people can boast as much?" Gogo answers: "Billions."[40]

Estragon, trapped just as much as Vladimir in the circular nothingness of their situation, is less hopeful. Strangely, Estragon is the one with faintly better memory, who at least recognizes that time is passing and the location has not changed, but he is angrier that he has "never stirred" from the "muckheap" where he finds himself.[41] Vladimir is the hopeful one, the one who continually attempts to resolve the situation, who says to himself "Vladimir, be reasonable, you haven't yet tried everything. And I resumed the struggle."[42]

Vladimir's consistent attempts to complete an action are evident in his attempt to sing at the beginning of Act Two. This is perhaps the most obviously literary attempt of all their actions, and it too is thwarted. The circular song epitomizes Didi's doomed attempts to escape the closed system of incomplete actions:

> A dog came in the kitchen
> And stole a crust of bread.

> The cook up with a ladle
> And beat him till he was dead.
>
> . . .
>
> Then all the dogs came running
> And dug the dog a tomb
> And wrote upon the tombstone
> For the eyes of dogs to come:
> A dog came in the kitchen
> And stole a crust of bread. . . . [43]

Vladimir's attempt to console himself through singing results in a song that he will never finish, and one that concerns itself with a doomed attempt to find sustenance. It is a continuous story of recording and reliving transgression and punitive action. The dog is endlessly resurrected by the writing on the tomb to steal the bread and be killed for it. Vladimir is stunted by the song, befuddled by its lack of ending and beginning, and he wants it to end, but the circular nature of the song prevents him from closing it. It is a creative version of the circular action in which he and Estragon find themselves, and his frustration with it leads him to move "feverishly about the stage" he cannot seem to leave.

Since the end is not something Didi and Gogo can bring about themselves, they are trapped in this narrative because they need something from Godot (they don't remember what) and until he appears, they cannot leave. Having gone to Godot at some point (they don't remember when) with "a vague supplication," they must wait until he makes a decision—but Godot put them off with evasive rhetoric which is probably very familiar to anyone bringing a "vague supplication" to someone in a position of power:

> ESTRAGON: And what did he reply?
> VLADIMIR: That he'd see.
> ESTRAGON: That he couldn't promise anything.
> VLADIMIR: That he'd have to think it over.
> ESTRAGON: In the quiet of his home.
> VLADIMIR: Consult his family.
> ESTRAGON: His friends.
> VLADIMIR: His agents.
> ESTRAGON: His correspondents.
> VLADIMIR: His books.
> ESTRAGON: His bank account.
> VLADIMIR: Before taking a decision.[44]

Macmorris and the Impressment of the Irish Servant

Trapped in a position of supplication and waiting, Didi and Gogo have surrendered already to the will of Godot. This itself is perhaps Beckett the self-exile's clearest indictment of the supplicating joiner, and the place where Didi and Gogo establish the ultimate pitfalls of being Macmorris's descendant. Becoming supplicants to Godot has eliminated their autonomy. Just as Boyle and Joxer willingly participate in the small, marginalized world of the tenements which they have inherited as their home, Didi and Gogo willingly participate in the rhetorical nightmare of their own marginalized existence as servants to an absent master. As Macmorris's descendants, they look no further than the place they have been allotted, and that place dooms them to serve another's vision. Answering Estragon's question, "We've lost our rights?" Vladimir answers, "We got rid of them." There is nothing to be done, but wait.

Chapter Three

Richard II, Irish Exiles, and the Breath of Kings

It is a terrible shame that, as W. B. Yeats points out, Richard II is not the wiliest king. But Yeats insists that Richard's command of language is the greater of the two contending characters, that Richard's story is tragic because this wonderful man who is king is not, in fact, a wonderful king, and he argues that there should be sympathy for the tragedy of that circumstance rather than joyful divestiture of Richard's crown. When the dispossession of Richard's crown renders him a subject of the kingdom he once ruled and of a man who was once his subject, he famously attempts to recreate through language a new subjectivity for himself—a new identity as ruled rather than ruler—and to take control of that new identity with the same force he had used to inhabit his previous role as king.

Shakespeare, unsatisfied, apparently, merely to dramatize the historical accounts he found in Hall and Holinshed, chose instead to ascribe to his characters radically different approaches to government in an investigation of functional rule. Had he wanted merely to depict a very successful upstart in Henry, depriving Richard of an inherited throne, he could have given Henry both action and a command of language. Shakespeare chose instead to pit action and language against each other. Action wins the crown, but language wins the sympathy of the audience.

By the time Shakespeare got to his second tetralogy, his use of history had taken on properties of larger things—history was there to teach social and political lessons, but other genres were there to expand those lessons onto a larger cosmic stage. Jonathan Dollimore writes in *Radical Tragedy* that "It is true that some of the most intriguing plays of the period do indeed rehearse threats in order to contain them. But to contain a threat by rehearsing it one must first give it a voice, a part, a presence—in the theatre, as in the culture." But Dollimore points out here that the very representation of that which must be contained constitutes a challenge in itself. He writes that it is "not a vision of political freedom so much as a subversive knowledge of political domination, a knowledge which interrogated prevailing beliefs." Dollimore calls this interrogation "intellectual vandalism" because it marks the status quo as being under threat from some outer or interior force.[1]

The status quo under threat here is the stability of Britain, and Shakespeare impresses the Irish into service to British state interests by attributing to Richard's character Irish stereotypes and their inadequacy for effective rule. But while that threat must be "disempowered" by the end of the play, in order to reestablish the status quo and end with the hope of order which Elizabethan tragedy demands in its generic function, a complicated play, a good and interesting play, will attribute to the losing representation some quality which makes its downfall pathetic. After all, the play is not the tragedy of the winner. It is the tragedy of the loser. And for the loss to be tragic, there must be some redeeming feature to the eliminated threat.[2] While Shakespeare certainly had what Terence Hawkes calls an "industrial-strength Englishness,"[3] the location for sympathy in *Richard II* lies in Richard, and his downfall both eliminates and eulogizes his unfitness to rule.

Richard's redeeming feature does not truly appear until he is left crownless and a subject of the cousin who once bowed to him. Richard, having once exiled Henry temporarily, finds himself exiled from his throne permanently, and it is in his nature to examine as well as bemoan. Cut off from the trappings through which he once understood himself, he constructs a new identity through words, and that identity is that of an exile in his own country.

THE EXILE

Edward Said writes in "Reflections on Exile" that we miss the truth of exile when we consider it in literature.[4] While it may be "strangely compelling to think about," the fictional account of exile, even the written account of a single artist who experienced exile, in fact misses the agonizing displacement of unwritten millions that "exile" has meant in history.[5] I put the word in quotations, though he does not, because his juxtaposition of romanticized artistic exile and the truth of countless, unrecorded refugees necessitates a distinction between over-use of the word as a literary motif and the unwritten people it represents. The two are connected, and the written representation of a character in exile does allow the reader (or, when performed, the viewer) to experience on some level the practice of exile and the dis-identification that is at the heart of the condition. Indeed, Said points out that "To see a poet in exile—as opposed to reading the poetry of exile—is to see exile's antinomies embodied with a unique intensity."[6] Many are represented by the one, and the one wanders far from home with a baggage that carries the representation of millions along with a few portable possessions. An exile reads the exile's story with that representation in mind.

When identity is at stake in a text, there is no better wedge between identity-unexamined and identity-under-scrutiny than the dispossessed. This is the crux of Said's argument about the relationship, and, in fact, the cause-and-effect, between exile and nationalism. Having discussed briefly the conditions and dispossession endured by Faiz Ahmad Faiz, Eqbal Ahmad, and Rashid Hussein, Said aggregates their experience with the statement that "These and so many other exiled poets and writers lend dignity to a condition legislated to deny dignity—to deny identity to people."[7]

Exile is the denial of dignity. Words are the means through which an exile can find a new dignity—even if that dignity has the worn edges of a forced effort to ennoble a patently undignified condition. Deprived of the given identity, the exile creates a new identity which is based on its very disconnection from the usual means of identification: home, family, location, language, community. These inherited entities are replaced by something self-made, and the dignity, perhaps, lies in that achievement, but the achievement is forced and informed by the loss. Said writes that "the interplay between nationalism and exile is like Hegel's dialectic of servant and master, opposites informing and constituting each other."[8]

The truth of this is even more clear when the exile is consciously writing on behalf of others. A new community is formed through the writer's words—one which is constituted by the communal loss. The ties of the new community are formed through the articulation of a mutual history, even if that history must be constructed. In Chapter Two, in the Irish reappropriation of *Henry V,* this is accomplished by reinscribing the role of servant and master so that the master is absent and the servant, while still under that absent thumb, nevertheless has room to navigate and consider his condition, and that navigation is done in a search for history.

Richard II is another matter. Unlike Macmorris who is as obviously Irish as Shakespearean characters go, Richard has no stated ties to Irish character. He is, in fact, opposite the Irish in a number of ways: an historical English king who works, during the play, to subjugate Ireland and who non-violently hands his authority over to another (whether or not under duress). But Irish writers working in nationalist literature in the early 20th century read Richard as themselves, and perhaps their sympathy with him lies in his dispossession, something they understood very well. Their manor houses had been appropriated for English owners, many absentee. The Irish found themselves under the direction of strangers who valued the land, while Anglicizing the place names, but thought the people ethnically inferior or, in some cases, a blot on the beautiful landscape.[9] Said writes of politically forced physical exile, legal and literal separation from one's own land and the forced existence in a country not one's own. The experience of the Irish exile in the early twentieth century is not precisely parallel here because those who left were forced to leave by economic hardship and those who stayed were able to enjoy no legal right to their own land. Irish revolution included the attempted recovery not only of their country and its lands, but also of self-determination and even of the original language. The Irish sense of dispossession of the early twentieth century is one in which the land they occupy belongs to someone else and their physical inhabitancy of it is contingent on their acquiescence to subjection and their acceptance of the master.

Yet the emotional condition of which Said writes is the same, because the inherited entities are now separated from the would-be beneficiary, and the replacement must be self-made. The Irish, separated from their own inheritance of land and authority over themselves under the law, deprived of the inheritance of their own language and the eminence of their own literature in national schools, are exiles in their own country. They make their own replacements for the dignity which they have been denied by attempting to reconstruct themselves in a way which overcomes the invader's culture. Said writes that exile "is fundamentally a discontinuous state of being," in which exiles are "cut off from their roots, their land, their past." Their attempted reconstruction takes a cultural or ideological form because it was the dignity attached to the roots, the land, and the past from which they have been separated that gave those things meaning in the first place: "They generally do not have armies or states, although they are often in search of them. Exiles feel, therefore, an urgent need to reconstitute their broken lives, usually by choosing to see themselves as part of a triumphant ideology or a restored people."[10]

The Irish attempt at reconstruction, however, must include acknowledgment of the force which brought about the exile. Their self-made replacements of the loss are informed by the new master, and so they reconstruct their history either in the English they have been forced to learn or in an Irish they must unearth through an archeological search for their original language. Those replacements provide them with a new, if refurbished, version of the old identity. This is, as in the reappropriation of Macmorris in Chapter Two, a system of master and servant, but here, the servant was once his own master and the master of others—the king has become the subject—and reversal frees neither side from the inevitability of the relationship.

By deploying Irish stereotypical characteristics in his depiction of Richard in order to posit Richard's incompetence, Shakespeare impressed the Irish into service as representational opposites of what makes the stalwart and pragmatic English the natural masters of empire. Richard's loss is sad, but the play leaves little doubt that Henry will be the more capable ruler. "Uneasy lies" his head, perhaps, but he has zero tolerance for the corruption and exorbitance that was rampant under Richard, and his attempts to bring order and the restoration of a system that protects inherited right must necessarily deprive Richard of his inheritance. Richard finds himself crownless in his own kingdom, and cut off from the inherited entities through which he had previously understood his identity. Forced to form a new identity, Richard takes on the task which makes his character the sympathetic tragic figure for which he is famous—Richard forms, through words, the new identity of the exile in his own land.

RICHARD AS IRELAND?

In Shakespeare's history plays, excursions to Ireland end badly for English kings. Already in the second tetralogy (the first one written), York has returned from Ireland with a force to overthrow Henry VI. Richard II learns not to be away when Henry of Bolingbroke is the mouse who will play with nobles afraid of being deprived of their lands by an extravagant and greedy king. The massive expense of keeping the Irish rebels under control leads to Richard's idea to confiscate the Lancastrian estate; Richard's complaints of the need to "farm our royal realm" in order to fund the excursion are interrupted by Bushy's news of the demise of Gaunt. Richard's first thought is that "The lining of his coffers shall make coats/ To deck our soldiers in these Irish wars" (1.4.61–62). John Julius Norwich writes in *Shakespeare's Kings* that

> Most of the summer of 1394 Richard spent in mourning for his wife; then, towards the end of September, he left for Ireland. The visit was, he knew, long overdue. In 1368 and again in 1380, all those English lords possessing estates in Ireland had been ordered either to return to them or to make proper provision for their defense; but the order had proved unenforceable and with every year that passed the administration had become more chaotic, with the local Irish kings and chieftains penetrating deeper and deeper into the lands of the English absentees. In 1379 Edmund Mortimer, third Earl of March, had been appointed Lieutenant

and had done much to retrieve the situation in Ulster; but in 1381 he was drowned crossing a ford in County Cork, and his immense estates had passed to his seven-year-old son Roger. In the following year, with the situation growing increasingly desperate, Richard had appointed his uncle Gloucester as Lieutenant, but had subsequently changed his mind for reasons unexplained; and it was by now clear not only that he must go himself, but that he must do so at once. If his visit were to be any longer postponed, all Ireland—and its revenues—would be lost.[11]

Shakespeare did not invent the Irish problem for Richard; the problem was one of historical record and was, in fact, a serious drain on the treasury (in large part because Richard's personal excesses were also a drain on the treasury and not much was left for fighting). The fact that Richard's problematic involvement in Ireland was part of the perceived ineptitude of his rule associates him with that country in a very unflattering way.

In addition to medieval characteristics, Shakespeare gave Richard some of the fundamental flaws stereotypically associated with the Irish: he is unpredictable, easily led by malicious people, unreliable, and impractical (see Chapter One). Both are drains on the English coffers, and the exchequer was in the red even before Richard needed to raise money to put down the Irish rebels. By positioning Richard as a figure with Irish characteristics, Shakespeare is able to depict not only Richard falling to Bolingbroke, but also Ireland falling to England in a vision of the greatness of English pragmatism.

Richard's court was sumptuous, and perhaps even decadent by standards of the time. Certainly it was extravagant, but money was his to spend and the kingdom was his to rule. While his grandfather, like kings before, justified rule through prowess on the field, Richard saw no reason to justify his placement on the throne. His coronation was enough. Richard's belief system appears to be inherited along with his crown. Henry's interruption of that inheritance and the belief system that goes with it appears to be a new and novel idea. Henry's pragmatism comes in as a new way of getting and justifying a crown. In a play which revolves almost entirely around inherited right, the two sides need to function as not only opposites, but as inherited tradition versus innovation.

Shakespeare's telescoping of issues, as well as time and place, serve in this play to sharpen the differences between Richard and Henry, and the information which was left out serves as a keen guideline to finding what Shakespeare felt was important to the story he sought to tell. Henry was by no means the only, or even the first, to attempt to divest Richard of his crown, or at least limit the power he enjoyed in it—others had previously attempted to do this, including the Duke of Gloucester, who threatened Richard with "ancient statute and recent precedent" allowing parliament to remove him from the throne if he did not meet his obligation to call the body together once a year.[12] Gloucester was bluffing. Parliament itself attempted administration reform in 1386, creating a council to take control over royal seals and finance, and greatly limiting the king's powers. Richard, in that case, successfully operated against it. Richard even managed to hold on to power through a lengthy battle with parliament over ultimate sovereignty in 1388.[13] Certainly his power was under attack long before Henry of Bolingbroke arrived on the English shore to threaten Richard's hegemony.

Shakespeare's representation of Richard did lean heavily on popular perceptions and cultural memory of the king. Norwich writes that while Richard at first showed promise of becoming a "more than passable king," from the time of his marriage onward, "it rapidly became clear that he would be nothing of the kind." Norwich's description of Richard's faults sounds like typical characterizations of the Irish: "Already he was showing signs of a quite alarming arrogance, self-indulgence and irresponsibility; any attempts to remonstrate with him threw him into a towering rage, provoking streams of insults and abuse that did little to increase the dignity which he was always so anxious to preserve."[14]

It is difficult to establish Henry as "entering" with something new, since by the time he in fact "re-enters" he has already had plenty of opportunity to set up his own characteristics for the audience, but it is only with his re-entry that he appears as an alternative ruler with something new to offer. He appears so to Northumberland and his allies as well as to the audience. Charles R. Forker writes in the introduction to the Arden edition that

> Richard's essentially feudal world, a world of oaths and codes of honour, of titles and of fixed identities, of ritual solemnity and ceremonial beauty, puts heavy stress on the seriousness and potency of words. Bolingbroke, who challenges and overturns that world, brings to bear a more modern, relativistic, sceptical and less comely understanding of how meaning is generated.[15]

Forker is elaborating on an earlier point that "Richard, the man of words, postures and ceremonial dignity, is defeated by Bolingbroke, the man of actions and pragmatic realism. A new spirit of assertive individuality seems finally to dissolve the settled harmonies of medieval tradition and hierarchical order."[16] Yet Joseph Papp points out in his introductory remarks for the Bantam/David Bevington edition of the play that while Richard "may lose in politics, he unquestionably wins in the theater—for in Shakespeare the character who controls language is the character who controls the play."[17]

TO LOOK SO POORLY AND TO SPEAK SO FAIR

Richard is reluctant when it comes to action, so much so that he changes his mind at the last minute after deciding that Henry of Bolingbroke and Mowbray should resolve their dispute through combat. Resorting to his power of language, he exiles them, and their acquiescence to language is revealed in their answers. Mowbray, exiled for life, responds with an acknowledgment of his own muteness:

> Within my mouth you have enjailed my tongue,
> Doubly portcullised with my teeth and lips,
> And dull unfeeling barren ignorance
> Is made my jailer to attend on me. (1.3.166–169)

Bolingbroke's answer is more clear in its awareness of the king's power of language. When Richard reprieves Henry's exile by four years out of pity for Gaunt's grief, Henry answers: "Four lagging winters and four wanton springs/ End in a word; such is the breath of kings" (214–215). As becomes typical in this play, Richard's power through language is immediately tempered by someone's awareness of its limitations. Gaunt, still grieving for the loss of his son, points out to Richard that, while Richard can shorten Gaunt's life by imposing losses, he cannot conversely add to Gaunt's life just by stating that he "hast many years to live" (225). Richard attempts to maintain control through language, even as he begins to understand its fallibility. Returned from Ireland in 3.2 to find Henry in arms, Richard proclaims his authority. The more famous line, "Not all the water in the rough rude sea/ Can wash the balm off from an anointed king" is followed by the less famous, but more telling of Richard's belief in language: "The breath of worldly men cannot depose/ The deputy elected by the Lord" (54–57). Richard calls the angels to join him in his fight, but, interrupted by the entrance of Salisbury, asks immediately: "Welcome, my lord. How far off lies your power?"(63). Unfortunately, Salisbury has no force with him, as the Welsh he was to lead heard that Richard was not returning, and they fled to Henry.

The next scene underscores the growing power of action over words in gaining political ends. Henry's force gathers menacingly before Flint Castle, and Richard "appeareth on the walls" with the Bishop of Carlisle, Aumerle, Scroop, and Salisbury. In a play heretofore dominated by small groups of characters battling in a flurry of words, the visual discrepancies of this scene would be startling. Henry and a large number of cohorts and soldiers are arrayed on the stage in front of Richard and four supporters standing on the battlements (presumably played in the balcony). Yet Richard's rhetoric only grows stronger, berating Henry and the others for their treasonous acts against the crown:

> Tell Bolingbroke—for yon methinks he stands—
> That every stride he makes upon my land
> Is dangerous treason. He is come to open
> The purple testament of bleeding war. (3.3.91–4)

Despite his vulnerability and absence of support, Richard is still in control of the dialogue, because, speaking as an authority to a misbehaving subject, he forces Northumberland to respond as a supplicant:

> The King of Heaven forbid our lord the King
> Should so with civil and uncivil arms
> Be rushed upon! Thy thrice-noble cousin
> Harry Bolingbroke doth humbly kiss thy hand;" (101–4)

Northumberland, of course, can proclaim all day long that Henry is there for no other reason than to beg "humbly" for the return of the Lancaster lands, but he is still there as part of a large force that has not budged. Richard is aware that he may be in control of his words, but his words are not in control of his political reality, and he says so to Aumerle: "We do debase ourselves, cousin, do we not,/ To look so poorly and to speak so fair?" (127–8). Once he agrees to descend, literally, to the "base court," he know that it is over, and he is aware of the significance of the descent. Richard makes no pretense of the reality of the situation, although Bolingbroke continues to insist that he is there for no more than "his own" (196). Richard agrees to make Bolingbroke his heir. Richard does not have the physical might, the fighting force, that Bolingbroke does, and he finds that the water in the rough, rude sea might may not wash off the balm of an anointed king, but it might take his crown and his power to control if it is rough and rude enough. Richard's language is empty in the face of his pragmatic opponent. Richard's visual shift from master to servant may begin when he descends to the base court to negotiate with the rebels, but the shift is inevitable from the first moment Bolingbroke proves that the breath of kings, unsupported by physical force, is vulnerable.

There is one scene between this one and the famous deposition scene. It is a post-lapsarian Eden scene of the Queen in the Duke of York's garden, in which she laments to the gardener, "old Adam's likeness," the "black tidings" he brings her of Richard's fall. The deposition scene, 4.1, opens with a strangely funny episode in which a number of men argue over the murder of Thomas of Woodstock (the Duke of Gloucester)—the very argument that got Henry and Mowbray banished at the beginning of the play. The humor comes from the continuous throwing down of "gages," or gauntlets, in calls to duel. First Aumerle throws down his gage in response to Bagot's accusation, followed by Fitzwater throwing his down in allegiance to Aumerle, followed by Percy throwing his down against Aumerle. Aumerle picks up Percy's, but "Another Lord" throws down his own gage against Aumerle, and Aumerle picks that one up as well. When Surrey throws down his gage against Fitzwater, Fitzwater picks it up, but then throws down either it or his own against Surrey. Despite the fact that he is already holding two people's gages, Aumerle "borrows a gage [from Fitzwater] and throws it down" against Norfolk, who is absent.

By the time Henry intervenes, Percy, Another Lord, and Surrey are without gages, Fitzwater has one and Aumerle has two. It is a ridiculous representation of quarreling men of action, and would never have happened in Richard's ceremonious court. Henry, however, judiciously declares that the argument will hold until Norfolk can be brought back from exile to take his own part in the argument. That will be a long time, apparently, as this declaration is followed by the news that Norfolk is dead.

This bizarre scene of barely controlled chaos leads into the deposition of the "divinely anointed" king. Richard enters, and with him comes his most shrill, but perhaps most impressive, display of his awareness of words. Clever before, Richard now falls into sarcasm:

Alack, why am I sent for to a king,
Before I have shook off the regal thoughts
Wherewith I reigned? I hardly yet have learned
To insinuate, flatter, bow, and bend my knee.
Give sorrow leave awhile to tutor me
To this submission. (4.1.163–168)

Asked to resign his "state and crown" to Henry, Richard does so, but then creates an argument about what it is he is resigning. In 4.1, Henry asks if Richard does not give some of his griefs along with the crown, but Richard, too clever by half, responds that his griefs are his own. Bolingbroke says to him: "Part of your cares you give me with your crown" (195). But Richard latches on the word and demonstrates his wit:

> Your cares set up do not pluck my cares down.
> My care is loss of care, by old care done;
> Your care is gain of care, by new care won.
> The care I give I have, though given away;
> They 'tend the crown, yet still with me they stay. (196–200)

Henry asks if Richard is "contented to resign the crown," and Richard cleverly confutes his willing surrender of the crown with the answer, "Ay, no; no, ay; for I must nothing be" (201–2). The line means less in writing; in speech, "ay" can be "yes" or a personal pronoun. One must say it out loud to reveal its layers of meaning. It would sound like: "I? No. No, I, for I must nothing be." Or, "I, no. No I (an abbreviated—there is no 'I'), for I must nothing be." Or, "yes, no. No yes (there is no 'yes') for "yes" must nothing be." The possibilities are many. Did he willingly yield his crown? He is pointing out that, in practicality, Henry is already king, so yielding the crown is ceremonial only. Faced with the inevitabilities of action, he uses words to confute the action he is forced to take. Richard acknowledges the ambiguity of the situation his is about to enter—his identity is being removed from him and his exile from his own inherited understanding of his place in the world is beginning. There is no "I" indeed.

THIS PRISON WHERE I LIVE

There is no "I" left for Richard, because that which gave him an understanding of himself is gone and belongs to another man. Having grasped the world through eyes beneath a crown, without that crown Richard is left without the guideposts through which he interpreted his existence. But he still has words. Despite being a man with situational ethics, Richard is consistent in his determination to construct his reality through words, however difficult it may be to do so. In 5.5, Richard's prison is more than the walls of Pomfret Castle. It is the prison of the exile: left with nothing to cling to, Richard attempts to create for himself a new reality through words, but without his inherited identity, those words allow him only a variety of empty identities. His thoughts have become "fortunes' slaves" and they work feebly and at the mercy of harsh reality:

> Thus play I in one person many people,
> And none contented. Sometimes am I a king;
> Then treasons make we wish myself a beggar,

> And so I am. Then crushing penury
> Persuades me I was better when a king;
> Then am I unkinged again, and by and by
> Think that I am unkinged by Bolingbroke,
> And straight am nothing. (31–8)

It is not long after this that Richard is killed. And should Shakespeare's point about the importance of command of language have been less than clear, Richard's death underscores it. Henry, now king, spoke cryptically of wishing to be rid of the threat Richard poses while living. Just as someone had interpreted Richard's fury against Thomas of Woodstock as an encoded assassination order, Henry's imprecise words lead Exton to assume that the king is requesting for someone to take Richard's life.[18] Richard uncharacteristically takes action to defend himself physically, and kills two of his would-be assailants, but still poetically asks that his soul mount "on high" while his body dies.

Language has fallen to pragmatism, and language alone will never again control the kingdom. Richard's flaws are obvious, and Henry will probably be the better king—he will, at least, not divest his subjects of their property to fund his own excesses, nor will he allow sycophants to control him. But the single scene which follows the death of Richard is brief and painful. Exton carries Richard's body to King Henry, and the king is shaken by the suggestion that this murder took place at his bidding. Exton's explanation that "From your own mouth, my lord, did I this deed" leads to the exile of Exton at the end of the play. Henry, the first exile of the play, was sent away in an acknowledgment of the power of the breath of kings. Upon his return, he proved that power empty by demanding the end of his own exile and the beginning of the exile of Richard from court. Now Henry, the author of Richard's murder however directly or indirectly he suggested it be done, reinforces his own and Richard's exiles with the banishment of Exton: "With Cain go wander thorough shades of night,/ And never show thy head by day nor light" (5.6.43–44). Henry, who could not wash the balm off the anointed king, announces that he will travel to fight in the crusades to "wash this blood off from my guilty hand." The scene, haunted by Richard's absence, is one of few words. While the play begins with criticism for Richard's flaws, it ends acknowledging that the "untimely bier" carried offstage bears in it something remarkable.

THE VESSEL OF PORCELAIN

The fall of Richard had a strange effect on two Irish writers in England in the early part of the twentieth century. W. B. Yeats and George Bernard

Shaw both found themselves confused by what they understood to be an English glorification of Henry and a dismissal of Richard. Yeats was frustrated by what he saw as an English failure to see that remarkable man for who he was—was frustrated with a glorification of Henry and a dismissal of Richard. Yeats's assessment of Richard is well-known enough to be included in introductory material to the play, and David Bevington writes in the play's introduction that "In William Butler Yeats's fine maxim, Bolingbroke is the vessel of clay, Richard the vessel of porcelain. One is durable, and utilitarian, yet unattractive; the other is exquisite, fragile, impractical. . . . Yeats himself characteristically sided with beauty against politics."[19] What Bevington misses is that for Yeats, beauty and politics were related, and he fought to reinstate what he understood to be inherent Irish beauty as part of the political process of reinstating Irish self-rule. Yeats's failure to attach to Henry is not a relegation of politics—it is an embracing of Irish politics. His re-reading comes from his understanding of what is truly preferable.

It is here that Dollimore's "intellectual vandalism" comes into play for the Celtic writer. Declan Kiberd points out in *Inventing Ireland* that "Hidden in the classic writings of England lay many subversive potentials, awaiting their moment like unexploded bombs. So the young Irish man and woman could use Shakespeare to explore, and explain, and even perhaps justify themselves."[20] Kiberd goes on to apply this to Yeats, writing that, for him, "the failure of Richard the Second was due not to bumbling ineptitude but to a sensitivity and sophistication in the man far superior to the merely administrative efficiency of Bolingbroke" and that, in Yeats's reading, the play was "the story of England despoiling Ireland."[21]

Yeats's "At Stratford-on-Avon," which Bevington quoted, was written in 1901 and works to rehabilitate Richard from what Yeats saw as an English Victorian misunderstanding of Shakespeare's construction of character. He writes critically of the 19th century Shakespearean critics who

> grew up in a century of utilitarianism, when nothing about a man seemed important except his utility to the State, and nothing so useful to the State as the actions whose effect can be weighed by reason. The deeds of Coriolanus, Hamlet, Timon, Richard II had no obvious use, were indeed, no more than the expression of their personalities, and so it was thought Shakespeare was accusing them, and telling us to be careful lest we deserve like accusations. It did not occur to the critics that you cannot know a man from his actions because you cannot watch him in every kind of circumstance, and that men are made useless to the

State as often by abundance as by emptiness, and that a man's business may at times be revelation, and not reformation."[22]

Yeats's sympathy for Richard reveals a sympathy for one who had "no obvious use" to the state, but who was instead a person of unrealized potential. His attack on critics who see Richard II as a justly deposed monarch continues into a full scale exoneration of a fellow man of words. He compares the harsh criticism of Richard to what "schoolboys do in persecuting some boy of fine temperament, who has weak muscles and a distaste for school games."[23] Apparently, the critics Yeats had read dealt too lightly with Richard's charisma and placed too much emphasis on Henry's lauded pragmatism. Yeats goes on to suggest that the vulnerable "fine temperament" is connected with Ireland.

Yeats's first close comparison of Richard with Ireland comes when he rehearses some of the history of criticism which had preferred Henry V to Richard II—bemoaning the tendency to laud Henry V as "Shakespeare's only hero." Yeats mentions Professor Dowden's work on Henry V, and writes that Dowden "meditated frequently upon the perfection of character which had, he thought, made England successful." But Yeats first places Dowden as having "lived in Ireland, where everything has failed." Henry V's character was his father's magnified—pragmatic, physical, determined, and straightforward in language. He was successful. Richard was not. Yeats's comment that in Ireland "everything has failed" positions Ireland to be like Richard— the opposite of England and that which succeeds. Yeats's frustration with Dowden is clear: Dowden, rather than looking to his own country, finds instead that it has failed, and looks to the ultimate Englishman for a recipe for success. Yeats goes further in his exoneration of Richard and insists that "To suppose that Shakespeare preferred the man who deposed his king is to suppose that Shakespeare judged men with the eyes of a Municipal Councillor weighing the merits of a Town Clerk."[24] He is confident that Shakespeare did not mean to dismiss Richard and prefer Henry.

Yeats's invective against Edward Dowden says as much about Yeats's interpretation as it does about Dowden's. Dowden's treatise of Shakespeare's characters from the history plays certainly posits Henry V as far superior to Richard II. While Dowden does not strongly suggest a national association for either character, he does write of Richard's character in the worst possible terms.[25] Dowden writes that "it is clear and unquestionable that King Henry V. is Shakespeare's ideal of the practical heroic character" and describes Richard II as "a failed, a hectic, self-indulgent nature, a mockery king of pageantry, and sentiment, and rhetoric."[26] Dowden does not consider the history plays to be Shakespeare's greatest investigations of "manhood"—that distinction goes to the tragedies. But Dowden does consider the history plays to be "an inquiry into the sources of power and weakness, of success and of failure in a man's dealing with the positive, social world."[27]

Dowden aligns himself with the powerful in that "positive, social world" and celebrates Henry for "his glorious practical virtues, his courage, his integrity, his unfaltering justice, his hearty English warmth, his modesty, his love of plainness rather than of pageantry, his joyous temper, his business-like English piety." All these qualities make Henry "the ideal of the king who must attain a success complete, and thoroughly real and sound."[28] Perhaps Yeats was merely responding as a rational man to the saccharine diatribe of Dowden's praise, but as a writer seeking the essential and powerful nature of the imaginative Celt, Yeats would have been even more affronted with the all-powerful all-Englishness of Dowden's argument. And Dowden is not finished.

Giving a separate section to further discuss Shakespeare's history plays, Dowden separates them into groups of "kingly weakness" and "kingly strength." Richard II, it should come as no surprise, falls into the "weakness" category. Calling Richard a failure who is more show than substance in nearly every paragraph on the subject, Dowden suggests that Richard does have a slight charm and a way with words, despite his being wholly without authentic patriotism or piety. Dowden will not even allow him the traditional soubriquet "poet-king," but writes instead that Richard's rhetorical abilities are not directed towards actual art and are amateurish and "unformed."[29] Dowden writes that Richard's words about his home soil upon returning from Ireland are "a graceful incident in the play of Richard's life, but can hardly compensate the want of true and manly patriotism."[30] For Dowden, Richard's participation in his own life, certainly in ruling his kingdom, is no more than inauthentic spectacle and sentimentality.

Dowden's further commentary on Henry V is notable only for its ability to continue lauding him without running out of energy. Separation between the two rulers, which Dowden himself sets up early in the book as the examples of best and worst among the history-play kings, is one of such polarized separation of ability and sensibility that they mark Dowden's own ideas about the realities of power and of success or failure with it. It is to this coronation of Henry as the successful pragmatist in a world made for pragmatists that Yeats, ever ready to rehabilitate the imaginative Celt, responds. Yeats's statements against Dowden, and others, argue that the English are entirely missing Shakespeare's point and suggest that only the Celt could understand Shakespeare accurately. He does not flinch in taking to task previous writers who dared misinterpret the dramatist he felt he understood implicitly. Kiberd describes Yeats's reading in these terms: "Yeats's Richard was no peripheral victim, but the centre of meaning, moral and poetic, in Shakespeare's play: if Bolingbroke epitomized the failure of triumph, then Richard embodied the triumph of failure."[31] Yeats's focus is on Shakespeare's, and here specifically, King Richard's, extraordinary command of language and the pity of his exile from the state to which he was born.

Yeats, however, was not the only Irishman who traveled in England and found his own understanding of Shakespeare to be at odds with the interpretations of the English. George Bernard Shaw made a career of ridiculing English aristocracy on stage, but also wrote in prose his rejections of the idea of English superiority in art and culture. Shaw is a paradox—a writer who lived and worked in England but who understood himself to be an Irishman to the core. His play *John Bull's Other Island* begins with a preface in which Shaw expounds upon the "good deal more to say about the relations between the Irish and the English than will be found in my play."[32]

Shaw characterizes *John Bull* as "uncongenial to the whole spirit of the neo-Gaelic movement, which is bent on creating a new Ireland after its own ideal, whereas my play is a very uncompromising presentment of the real old Ireland."[33] Lest this be taken to mean that Shaw does not identify himself as an Irish writer working against the English, the remainder of the prefatory essay is a tirade against the English in which he mercilessly attacks them for stupidity, idolatrous patriotism, wastefulness, hyper-sentimentality, and "intellectual laziness," a term he uses frequently throughout.

While Shaw may have been a socially privileged Anglo-Irishman, he identifies himself with absolute clarity as an Irishman who is against English rule of Ireland and who attributes much of Irish poverty and unrest to British subjugation. In the segment subtitled "What is an Irishman?" Shaw clarifies his nationality for any who might be uncertain as to both it and the allegiance which Shaw feels that it demands:

> When I say that I am an Irishman I mean that I was born in Ireland, and that my native language is the English of Swift and not the unspeakable jargon of the mid-XIX century London newspapers. . . . I am violently and arrogantly Protestant by family tradition; but let no English Government therefore count on my allegiance: I am English enough to be an inveterate Republican and Home Ruler. It is true that one of my grandfathers was an Orangeman; but then his sister was an abbess; and his uncle, I am proud to say, was hanged as a rebel.[34]

His English, we can note, is the English of Swift. He identifies English as his native language, but it is an English spoken by another Anglo-Irishman whose work became included in the British canon (an inclusion Shaw notes with sly disdain at times in the essay). He is "English enough to be a Republican and Home Ruler," and here again he uses his convoluted wit to argue that since the English have self-government, then to be Irish and want self-government is to be "English."

Shaw's primary objection to the English character is excessive sentimentality, particularly of a patriotic nature, and an unshakable belief in their own practicality. Time and again he ridicules the English for mistaking the privileges which come with economic success for a natural superiority inherent in Englishness. Contrasting the two main characters of his play, the English Broadbent and the Irish Doyle, Shaw concludes that, while English critics of the play attributed all of the two characters' success in their business venture to Broadbent's character, in fact Broadbent's "special contribution was simply the strength, self-satisfaction, social confidence and cheerful bumptiousness that money, comfort, and good feeding bring to all healthy people." Broadbent, while a relatively likeable character, is charming despite his Englishness. He is cursed with every charge that Shaw can make about the English, and yet believes himself the more practical. Shaw, however, believes that a better kind of practicality belongs to the Irish Doyle: "Doyle's special contribution was the freedom from illusion, the power of facing facts, the nervous industry, the sharpened wits, the sensitive pride of the imaginative man who has fought his way up through social persecution and poverty."[35] Shaw, like Yeats, attributes imagination to the Irishman. Yet while Yeats attributes actual practicality to the Englishman, Shaw is less kind: he attributes to the Englishman a false sense of practicality, an inflexibility of mind, and a gross sentimentality that does not pass for artistry. Broadbent is less so than the average Englishman Shaw describes in this preface, but Shaw declares that his somewhat more gently drawn Englishman is not someone he wants as a master: "Much as I like him, I object to be governed by him, or entangled in his political destiny."[36] All of the disdain with which he wrote the Englishman Broadbent also appears in Shaw's critiques of English actors attempting to interpret Shakespeare.

In several of his theatre critiques, Shaw pilloried an actor who preferred the character of Henry V to Richard II, an actor who failed to satisfy Shaw's own interpretation of Shakespeare's work in general and *Richard II* in particular.[37] Shaw successfully removes all of Richard's famous arrogance in what amounts to an exoneration of Richard while attacking Beerbohm Tree's performances of Shakespeare (or, "Shakespear," as Shaw preferred to spell it). The play in question in this review (from 1905) is *Much Ado About Nothing*, but Shaw vents his fury at Tree's record of unsatisfactory performances by reciting their history. His attacks on Tree's misinterpretations of *Richard II* demonstrate, by opposite, what Shaw feels were Shakespeare's intentions. He first writes of Tree in general:

> Among the managers who are imaginative and capable enough to count seriously, Mr. Tree is the first within my experience for whom Shakespear does not exist at all. Confronted with a Shakespearean play, he stares into a ghastly vacuum, yet stares unterrified, undisturbed by any suspicion that his eyesight is failing, quite prepared to find the thing simply an ancient, dusty, mouldy, empty house which it is his business to furnish, decorate, and housewarm with an amusing entertainment. Totally insensible to Shakespear's qualities, he puts his own into the work. When he makes one of Shakespear's points—which he does extremely seldom—it is only because at that particular moment Shakespear's wit happens to coincide with his own.[38]

Tree, apparently for Shaw, lacks the wit not only to understand Shakespeare's intentions, but to care that Shakespeare had intentions. Shaw, on the other hand, posits himself as the authority. According to Shaw, Tree sees a play which needs embellishment rather than a complete text which it is his job to illuminate for the audience. Tree is caught up in show. Shaw is caught up in the words. After having demonstrated so completely and bitingly that this English actor/manager has it completely wrong, he allows us to see what the most awful misinterpretation of *Richard II* could be:

> You remember Richard the Second, though moved only to futile sarcasm by Bolingbroke's mastery of him, turning away with a stifled sob when his dog deserts him and licks Bolingbroke's hand. You remember, too, how Richard munches sweetmeats whilst his peers are coming to blows in his presence, and how, after his disgrace in Westminster Hall, instead of making the conventional pathetic exit, he clasps his hands affectedly behind him, cocks his chin pettishly in the air, and struts out, not as an accomplished actor would go out, but—he convinces you—as Richard himself probably did go out on that occasion.[39]

What is missing from Tree's performance that grates so on Shaw is Richard's command of the rhetoric of the situation. Tree's Richard, in Shaw's description, over-indulges in emotion when stoicism is called for but lacks emotion when the text requires it. Richard's sarcasm may be futile in the face of his inevitable loss, but it can be cunning and cutting and he uses it to put other characters on the defensive. Shaw is bemoaning the loss of Richard's mastery of language.

Shaw was so disturbed by Tree's mishandling of Richard that he brought it up again in another piece written later for a collection of memoirs for Tree.[40] Again, he brings up the dog, which he is careful to point out this time "does not appear among Shakespear's dramatis personae." Again he brings up the walking out of Westminster Hall after the abdication, but this time, Shaw recounts other errors, including an egregious one of depicting on stage the entry of Bolingbroke and Richard (post-deposition) into London. Shaw proclaims that

> Shakespear makes the Duke of York describe it. Nothing could be easier with a well-trained actor at hand. And nothing could be more difficult and inconvenient than to bring horses on stage and represent it in action. But this is just what Tree did. One still remembers that great white horse, and the look of hunted terror with which Richard turned his head as the crowd hooted him. It passed in a moment; and it flatly contradicted Shakespear's description of the saint-like patience of Richard.[41]

Shaw's interpretation here is interesting, because the play does not actually contain a description of "saint-like patience." Richard is at times pettish and petty and irritable. He does not demonstrate a saint-like patience while hoping Gaunt will go ahead and die so Richard can confiscate his lands. Shaw's reading of Richard is one which focuses on Richard's qualities rather than flaws, but the greatest of those qualities is language, and Shaw has no mercy for Tree when the performance lacks the rhetorical panache Shaw feels it deserves:

> Turn now to the scenes in which Shakespear has given the actor a profusion of rhetoric to declaim. Take the famous 'For God's sake, let us sit upon the ground, and tell sad stories of the death of kings.' My sole recollection of that scene is that when I was sitting in the stalls listening to it, a paper was passed to me. I opened it and read: 'If you will rise and move a resolution, I will second it.—Murray Carson.' The late Murray Carson was, above all things, an elocutionist; and the scene was going for nothing. Tree was giving Shakespear, at immense trouble and expense, and with extraordinary executive cunning, a great deal that Shakespear had not asked for, and denying him something much simpler that he did ask for, and set great store by.[42]

Shaw is justified in his dismissal of Tree's inept portrayal of the magnitude of Richard's plight by the unexpected support from an elocutionist—not an actor, not a fellow writer, but a man whose primary accomplishment is the superior speaking of other people's words. Shaw's representation of Carson's ability to anticipate and expect his own frustration with the sadly bad acting allows Shaw to demonstrate his own reputation for high standards and what he feels to be the accurate understanding of how it should be done. As far as Shaw is concerned, Carson sent the note to him, therefore Carson must have known Shaw to be someone of similar high standards and true understanding of the accurate interpretation of Shakespeare. Shaw's ambiguous words suggest that, as far as he is concerned, there is an accurate interpretation, and it is his own. His use of Carson to back him up demonstrates that he feels his own "accurate interpretation" is recognized by another worthy audience member.

Shaw writes that "the scene was going for nothing." He does not go into great detail about exactly what Tree was doing that so terribly missed the mark, only that Tree was giving an inadequate rhetorical rendering of a great speech. The reader can assume that Shaw is not referring to a too subdued performance, as he writes that Tree was giving Shakespeare a great deal that he "had not asked for." Shaw does not cease spearing Tree on the point of his pen and continues to demonstrate this poor actor of Richard and his inability to understand the language that is crucial to Shakespeare. Later in the same review, Shaw cuts to pieces Tree's Malvolio, writing that while Tree was able to get great laughs with prat falls and physical humor, he failed to deliver even the simplest lines: "But when he came to speak those lines with which any old Shakespearean hand can draw a laugh by a simple trick of the voice, Tree made nothing of them, not knowing a game which he had never studied."[43]

As far as both Yeats and Shaw are concerned, they have studied the game and understand it much better than the English with whom they are frustrated. It is remarkable how these two Irish writers—one a poet, but both playwrights and essayists—claim superior knowledge and understanding of Shakespeare over that of the English. For Yeats and Shaw, theirs, apparently, is the true reading, and the English have simply got it wrong. The English are missing the point of *Richard II,* and the main point they are missing is the true majesty of this fallen king and his imaginative and rhetorical superiority to the pragmatic Henry. Shakespeare attributed to Richard a superior command of rhetoric, and for Yeats and Shaw this is clear evidence that Shakespeare implicitly preferred Richard to Henry. The lauded pragmatism with which Henry accomplishes the throne is so completely associated with the English character that Yeats's Professor Dowden examines it as a way to learn how the English manage to be great—he studies it as an example of how to succeed. But Yeats and Shaw, writers who are successful at re-visioning their Irish origins while inserting themselves into English culture, are far more interested in examining how the porcelain vessel manages to be so poetic.

Their frustration at the English failure to appreciate Richard's poetic superiority is something very like an Irish frustration at the English failure to appreciate the poetic nature of the Celt. That this poetic superiority functions in an English play as falling to a superior English man-of-action demonstrates how the winner, the pragmatist, can be read against the poet. But other writers can identify with the "triumph of failure" and relocate the tragedy for themselves. The "breath of kings" may prove, against action, to be no more than breath, but its power can be reappropriated—if only to re-write one's relationship to the kingdom.

Chapter Four
Hamlet and Other Kinds of In-between-ness

There is an old adage that "The problem with the Irish Question is that the Irish seem to keep changing the question" and like the Irish, Hamlet's specialty seems to be changing the question. Not ruthless enough to slaughter his way to the throne, he is nevertheless ruthless in his questioning. The only character with more verbal agility than Hamlet is the grave digger, a representation of the death which is Hamlet's only inevitability. No other character can rhetorically pin the down the clever and questioning prince, but the freedom Hamlet seeks eludes him. A cautious guard of the purity of his own motives, Hamlet cannot overturn that pragmatist king who popped in between his expectations and the crown except at the expense of either his innocence or his own life. His imaginative flexibility with language therefore brings him the freedom only to describe and subvert the royal administration under which he finds himself. Just as in *Richard II*, the conflict in *Hamlet* is one between an idealist and a realist, between a character marked for his rhetorical flexibility and a character marked for his pragmatic grasping of power. *Hamlet* presses the idealist into service to the victory of pragmatism by demonstrating the impossibility of a successful revolt.

Hamlet appears with frequency in Irish literature, rarely as a protagonist, but frequently in titles, referential frameworks, or quotes that appear only long enough to deepen or confute meaning and then disappear again. Turned into a supporting character by the Irish, Hamlet has a continual walk-on part in Irish literature. He is the lash occasionally but persistently used to whip the English for what they have done. The English put *Hamlet* into Irish classrooms and on Irish stages as evidence of English superiority; the Irish, separated like Hamlet from their own throne, took him gladly as their own.

81

Hamlet was Yeats's hero. Declan Kiberd writes that Yeats felt style was escaping his fellow writers, but that "England once upon a time had known style, in the 'heroic self-possession' of Hamlet, who could teach a nervous Irish youth how to play magnificently with hostile minds."[1] He is in Seamus Heaney's "Whatever You Say Say Nothing," when Heaney, frustrated by yet another journalist's question about his "views/ On the Irish thing" is driven to write that "The times are out of joint"—and Heaney, like Hamlet, cannot "put it right" any more than any other Irish person can.[2] Ciaran Carson's collection *Belfast Confetti* includes "Hamlet," a poem about boundaries, time, death, and ghosts. The poem uses the frameworks and the tragedy of *Hamlet* to characterize the futility of resolving the conflict in that embattled Northern Irish city. One of the poem's ghosts is a legendary tin can that folk-lore says can be heard rattling down the street "any night that trouble might be/ Round the corner,"[3] any time that someone will die in the hopelessly unending street-by-street battles of Belfast. That ghost, like the ghost in *Hamlet,* is a herald of the rotten state of things. Carson hints at his own Irish literary inheritance in his metaphor for the Northern Irish attempt to piece together their own history though collective memory: "Like some son looking for his father, or the father for his son,/ We try to piece together the exploded fragments."[4]

The situation of separated father and son is one packed with problems for inheritance and lineage. The archetype of the father and son seeking to be reunited is Homer's *Odyssey* and it is most famously recycled in Joyce's *Ulysses,* which seeks to put back together the father and son figures of Odysseus/Bloom and Telemachus/Stephen. In the original epic, Odysseus wanders the Aegean sea attempting to get home while his son, Telemachus, seeks news of his father in his own coming-of-age voyage to a neighboring island. The issues at stake are reinforced throughout the epic through references to the fate of Agamemnon—a fellow leader in the Trojan war who returned home too late. Upon his arrival, Agamemnon was killed by his faithless wife and her lover, who had taken over control of his kingdom. When the son reached adulthood, he avenged his father by killing his mother and her lover and restoring the kingdom to order. With Agamemnon's misfortune in the ever-present background, the importance of Odysseus's imminent return to suitor-beseiged wife and teenaged son is reinforced. The parallels with the story of *Hamlet* are remarkable, with the primary difference being that Hamlet does not succeed the throne even after the deaths of his mother and stepfather. But Joyce's use of *The Odyssey* as an overarching framework to tell the story of wandering father and son figures places an essentially Irish story into a referential structure resonating with the parentage issues of both

The Odyssey and *Hamlet*. In the most straightforward convergence of the two, the novel tries to reconcile the Shakespearean father and son called Hamlet in the chapter "Scylla and Charybdis."

As in nearly all of his plays, Shakespeare took the essential plot of *Hamlet* from already existing sources. The story of Amleth, a Danish boy-prince who had to spend the years of growing into adulthood hiding his coming revenge against his uncle for killing the king, had already been adapted into a play in which the story was tweaked and the name changed to Hamlet.[5] What knowledge remains of this earlier play, which was written during the vogue of the more straightforward revenge tragedy, leads us to believe that Shakespeare's changes, while not large, were substantial in meaning. Shakespeare's *Hamlet* is not only deeper and richer and more "lifelike," which we would expect, but also more subversive in his intents and motives and in his careful manipulation of the order of his uncle's shaky hold on power.

Hamlet is more than a clever subverter of order—he is a man surrounded by uncertainties who questions his surroundings and his own identity most of all. That in itself might lead Irish readers questioning their own identity to see *Hamlet* as the story of themselves, but Shakespeare also left clues that Hamlet's experience was an Irish one—by redrawing the areas of certainty and uncertainty in terms that refer to Ireland, and surrounding Hamlet with uncertainties which he must navigate and comprehend. While Hamlet may become a metaphysical navigator, he will not become king of his country—his revenge leads to his own doom and re-inscribes his being closed out from the throne. An outsider will step in to put Elsinore to rights—a quick and decisive, pragmatic and level-headed soldier will take his place on the throne which lineage, if not destiny, meant for the poetic prince. Once again, Shakespeare dramatizes the colonial mystic as alluring, and yet not meant to rule his own destiny. Once again, Shakespeare culturally impresses the Irish into service to the empire by showing them closed out from their own seat of authority, and, in this case, without any recourse that does not lead to their own destruction.

However, Shakespeare creates for this thwarted character more intense audience sympathy; by giving Hamlet the most introspection and the richest inner life, Shakespeare give the audience more glimpses into Hamlet's soul, and so makes Hamlet the primary location of the play's sympathy and the most interesting character in the Shakespeare canon. Despite his remarkable qualities, Hamlet is nevertheless doomed to fail. He will never, no matter his actions or character, gain control of his destiny. Small wonder that the Irish decided Hamlet was an Irishman. The reason behind Hamlet's frequent cameos in Irish literature may lie in the extensive room Hamlet's character is given to move in the play. The space between the moment of his becoming a clearly subversive force against the usurper and the moment his inevitable doom comes to fruition is quite large and gives an audience like the Irish plenty of text in which to find themselves. There are also stronger pointers towards the space for a dissident Irish reading—Hamlet is given deep associations with Catholicism and Ireland through the ghost of his father. Claudius is a Protestant/English figure using pragmatic ruthlessness in murdering the very Catholic king of Denmark and taking the throne. Stephen Greenblatt asks: "But why would Shakespeare . . . have given the Protestant position to his arch-villain in Hamlet? And why should his Ghost . . . insist that he has come from a place where his crimes are being burned and purged away?"[6]

Greenblatt's answer is that Shakespeare was demonstrating the frustrating emptiness of Protestant rites for the dead in a contentious religious conflict over church corruption and charges of heresy, but the over-arching effect of the extremes Shakespeare sets up function to show the doomed nature of a Catholic-inspired revolt against a Protestant regime. The impressed Catholic Irish, given more sympathy in this play than in any other, are still enlisted into British service in a dramatic show of the inevitable failure of rebellion. Hamlet, whom Greenblatt calls "the prince of the inward insurrection," is, like Richard II, a poetic sort, and Hamlet acts on the directions of a ghost who is given deeply Catholic, and specifically Irish, associations, in both a potential pun on the fact that he is a "ghostly father," and his theatrical origin in the Purgatory under the stage's trap door.

GHOSTLY FATHERS

According to early modern stereotypes, like the ones appearing in the writings of Riche, Spenser, and Sidney, the Irish are subversive by nature. Riche prefaces "A Short Survey of Ireland" with the statement that he seeks the cause of "that miserable & wretched Realme of Ireland, where so many good people of all sorts are so continually seduced and abused by the Popes factors."[7] They are misled by "ghostly fathers" into being excessively pious and emotional.[8] They act mad and cause disturbances. They disrupt otherwise orderly events. They cannot be trusted by state officials. They challenge authority and think they should be in charge of their own place.

Hamlet, like the Irish, can "put an antic disposition on." Rather than blindly conforming as Ophelia does, he questions everything and so his inwardness, his incessant pondering of everything, is subversive in its essence. His ghostly father is more than a metaphor, it is an actual ghostly father. Hamlet's madness, manifested in his "antics," causes great disturbances and is purposefully done in order to subvert the silence surrounding his uncle's scheming coup d'etat. Hamlet disrupts the court by becoming a cause of concern and, more openly, disrupts the play with his subversive tricks. As for challenging authority and thinking he should be in charge of his own place; that is, after all, the center of the play's plot. The very means that Hamlet uses to subvert his uncle's usurpation of the throne are positive versions of Irish stereotypes, which work in the play as a doomed, if sympathetic, example of how one is shut out from his or her destined place.

Kept from his rightful ascension in the chain of being, Hamlet is perhaps the most aware of all the characters of the connections between levels in the chain of being—of the trickle down effect of leadership and justice. Claudius seems to have no sense of the "unweeded garden grown to seed" and instead lives and thinks almost entirely inside Elsinore. Laertes is too busy debauching at school or lecturing his sister at home to notice the delicate balance of structure and power and righteousness that has been shaken and threatens to collapse completely. Hamlet and Horatio are the only ones who seem aware of not only palace intrigue, but of a kingdom in danger. Claudius, the man of action, grabs the crown, but Hamlet, the thinker, is aware of the crown as a metonym for something much larger and more expansive.

Claudius sets the court on a collision course to disaster. The events he puts in motion must inevitably lead to the deaths of many. What thought he gives to his plan is focused on its cleverness and not on its dangers and potential detours (it truly never occurred to him for even a moment that the queen or anyone else might drink from the poisoned cup? Or that the poisoned sword might get into the wrong set of hands?). And while it may be possible to think of Fortinbras as a usurper who pops in at he last minute to live off the scraps, it is actually a good thing that he appears when he does. By the end of the play, Fortinbras is the only living person with any claim at all to leading the kingdom and he appears in time to step over the corpses of those in line ahead of him and set to rights the little that remains of the Danish throne. He remarks that Hamlet was "likely, had he been put on,/ To have proved most royal," but that comment may or may not be a part of handling his default-victory sportingly, since at that moment it could not make the slightest difference whether or not Hamlet would have been a good king. Hamlet will never be king, and could never be king from the moment his uncle eliminated the rightful king and stepped into his place, interrupting the rightful succession and corrupting the throne with the greed and ambition of an outsider.

Like Richard II, Hamlet has been separated from the throne that is rightfully his. Richard is removed from a throne he ascended upon his grandfather's death, and Hamlet is prevented from ascending because he is away in Wittenberg when his uncle snatches the throne. A king is naturally fatherless, as it is the loss of the antecedent that makes ascension possible. What the two different situations have more in common is the interruption of the throne's natural progression of antecedents. Richard's line has been interrupted, and Hamlet senior's line has been interrupted. Both thrones have seen the expected and natural succession interrupted by a power-grabbing relative, but while Richard is separated from the means through which he identifies himself, Hamlet is the heir in waiting—unable to identify himself through a place because he has not yet taken, nor will he, the place for which he is meant. While Macmorris understands his place through his service to Henry V, and Richard understands his place through the rule he is denied, Hamlet is given an understanding of his place through the direction given him by his father, the ghost.

The ghost of Hamlet's father is one of the more difficult obstacles of the play, in part because it is tied to Hamlet's "madness."[9] Stephen Greenblatt reports that modern readings do not understand the ghost as it was meant and that an "overwhelming emphasis on the psychological dimension, crowned by psychoanalytical readings of the play in the twentieth century, has the odd effect of eliminating the Ghost as ghost. . . ." In forgetting or misunderstanding the theologically conflicted atmosphere of early modern England, we succeed instead in transforming the ghost "into the prince's traumatic memory or, alternatively, into a conventional piece of dispensable stage machinery."[10] While the modern reader might be tempted to think of the ghost as Hamlet's hallucination, we must remember that the guards saw the ghost first, and ghosts were acceptable realities on stage, to be taken for what they presented themselves to be, not as figures of the characters' imaginations. More troubling, once the ghost has been accepted as an actual ghost, is the ambiguity with which he charges Hamlet with revenge.

The ghost of Hamlet's father does give him a direct course to follow, with deceptively specific details on what to do with Gertrude, but leaves the general method to Hamlet: "If thou didst ever thy dear father love—[. . .] Revenge his foul and most unnatural murder" (1.5.24, 26). His instructions regarding Gertrude are:

> Let not the royal bed of Denmark be
> A couch for luxury and damnèd incest.
> But, howsoever thou pursues this act,
> Taint not thy mind nor let thy soul contrive
> Against thy mother aught. Leave her to heaven
> And to those thorns that in her bosom lodge,

> To prick and sting her. Fare thee well at once.
> The glowworm shows the matin to be near,
> And 'gins to pale his uneffectual fire.
> Adieu, adieu, adieu! Remember me. (1.5.83–92).

The directions given Hamlet are: Revenge the murder and do not let the rulers of Denmark be corrupted with an incestuous marriage. Leave Gertrude to Heaven and her own pangs of guilt. Make all this happen in one way or another, but without specific directions how. The ghost, creating immense room for confusion, leaves Hamlet to decide "howsoever thou pursues this act." The clearest instruction throughout is "Remember me."[11]

Hamlet takes this as the overarching goal of the enterprise and speaks of it as not only an instruction but as a course of action: "So, uncle, there you are. Now to my word:/ It is 'Adieu, adieu! Remember me.' / I have sworn't." (1.5.111–112). The most immediate sense of the word "remember," when speaking of someone who is dead, is to think about and to commemorate, but Hamlet understands it as the focal point of the task that lies ahead. To remember his father, to think on and commemorate him as a person, is to cling to the previous king and the past. It is also to realign himself with the ruler from whom Hamlet directly receives his inherited right to the throne, rather than Claudius's stated attachment of Hamlet to the line of succession. The ghost is the past, and by holding to his past and refusing the current and villainous oppressor, Hamlet can fulfill his vow to his father and his own origins.

The ghosts's directions are designed to reinforce the father's hold, and therefore the past's, on Hamlet. Not only is Hamlet to eliminate the one who eliminated the father, and to spare his mother, he is directed by the ghost to "Remember Me." Hamlet is operating, for the majority of the play, upon the directions of his ghostly father, a decidedly Catholic image, who has come from Purgatory, another decidedly Catholic image, to set Hamlet against the man who has taken the throne of Denmark. Claudius is a pragmatist: like Bolingbroke, he is an opportunist who is ruthless in taking what he wants when the chance comes around, but wants to be a good and stable ruler when he gets there. Perhaps his plea to keep Hamlet in Denmark and away from school is an attempt to keep his friends close and his enemies closer, but Claudius does name Hamlet his heir (small joy to Hamlet, who should by all rights should have inherited the throne from his own father, and not from the man who interrupted his claim). Claudius may also be trying to create a family for himself, a family unit of which Hamlet is a part.

This, too, is similar to cultural impressment of the Irish—they are prevented from their own autonomy, but renamed a part of the new family.

It is a similar violent inclusion. It is announced to Hamlet that he is, rather than the ruler of his own kingdom, now a subservient part of a family he had no interest in creating. In just the same way, it is announced to the Irish that they are a new and subservient part of a unit which they had no interest in being a part of. The past to which they cling will direct them to a doomed attempt to avenge the wrong done them. The extremes of fatherhood in Hamlet are extremes of a passionately vengeful, ghostly father come from Purgatory and the past against a ruthless and opportunistic pragmatist of the present. These opposites in position, barely a hint in *Henry V,* and somewhat more developed in *Richard II,* are openly pitted against each other in Hamlet. The losses of the poetic mystic are sad, but the pragmatist ruler must win. More developed, too, than in Richard II is the lesson that to fight the inevitable victory of the pragmatist will bring destruction. According to the English (see Riche in Chapter One) the Irish priests, the "ghostly fathers" of the Irish, set the conflicted but possibly otherwise rule-able Irish people against the Protestant interlopers and doom them to inevitable destruction of not only self, but the kingdom they are trying to cleanse. In *Hamlet,* the direction to attempt rebellion against the interloper comes from the ghostly father of Hamlet, a ghost given deep associations with Purgatory and, therefore, Ireland.

THE PATRON SAINT OF IRELAND

Circulating legends about Purgatory made their appearances in both theological tracts and in histories, and one of the more prominent was the belief that Purgatory, unlike other destinations for the dead, could be reached by the living through an entryway. That entryway could be found in Lough Derg, in County Donegal, Ireland, according to several medieval stories, most particularly the twelfth century Latin prose text, *Tractatus de Purgatorio Sancti Patricii,* or *Saint Patrick's Purgatory.*[12] The story is of a knight named Owein, or Owayne, who travels through the tortures of Purgatory to emerge into bliss and thereby pre-emptively cleanses himself of earthly sin and guarantees his entry into heaven once his life was over. The story grew enormously popular and led to many similar stories and a thriving tourist/pilgrim trade in County Donegal. Holinshed's Irish Chronicles carried a version of it, as did writing of many genres in England and on the Continent.[13]

The church grew uneasy with the traffic to Donegal, after a number of people who traveled there found nothing wondrous and began to question the doctrine of Purgatory in general, and on Saint Patrick's Day in 1497, "the pilgrimage site at Lough Derg was destroyed on orders of the pope,

Alexander VI." The pope and the church acted in vain. Legend and the attractions of a reachable entryway persisted anyway and so "the demolition was only temporary: the office of Saint Patrick was introduced in the Roman missals in 1522, and pilgrimage resumed, at a slightly different location in Lough Derg, in the sixteenth century." The pilgrimages became a thorn in the side of Protestants and dismissive remarks about belief in Purgatory led to the inclusion of Lough Derg in the "repertory of Irish jokes."[14] The association would have been well known, and Shakespeare need not have emphasized it.

He did emphasize it, however, by giving Hamlet a line which brought Ireland on stage not by hint but by direct utterance. Hamlet swears by Saint Patrick in an unusual, whole oath (not a "zounds" or a "s'blood") to Horatio after conversing with the ghost:

> HORATIO: There's no offense, my lord.
> HAMLET: Yes, by Saint Patrick, but there is, Horatio,
> And much offense too. Touching this vision here,
> It is an honest ghost, that let me tell you. (1.5.141–144).

Hamlet speaks hastily, as he will in fact spend the next few acts determining whether or not the ghost is "honest," but his oath by Saint Patrick is telling. For the moment, at least, Hamlet understands the ghost to be a spirit truly come from Purgatory, even while he plans to act out madness in order to confirm the ghost's story. The oath, if only for a moment, calls on the patron saint of not only Purgatory, but of Ireland, and trots him right out onto the stage.

Indeed, Hamlet would seem to have visited the site himself after having spoken with the ghost. Shakespeare gives him, in 1.2, a melancholy disposition, but the charges that his mourning is excessive come, we must remember, from his father's murderer and from his mother who remarried with indecent haste. Wearing black and grieving for his father within a couple of months after the death hardly seems excessive in a time when mourning for immediate family could last more than a year.[15] After his encounter with the spirit from the realm of Saint Patrick, Hamlet puts his antic disposition on, and his melancholy grows. And as it does, his words describing his state sound more and more like one who cannot shake off the experience. Early modern stories of pilgrimages to Lough Derg report marked changes in the temperaments of some pilgrims. One account includes that statement that a pilgrim, although he need never enter Purgatory again, spent the remainder of his living days as though "never shall nothing in this world please him that he shall see nor he shall never be joyous nor glad nor shall not be seen to laugh. . . ."¹⁶ He was unable to leave the encounter behind, and so was trapped in a kind of Purgatory of the mind. The earth became a permanent Purgatory for him.

When Hamlet greets Rosencrantz and Guildenstern, he does so in his guise of madness. His words may be part of that guise, but they are strikingly associative with the Purgatorial experience of one of Saint Patrick's pilgrims. Hamlet describes his existence as a sort of lingering Purgatory:

> I have of late—but
> wherefore I know not—lost all my mirth, forgone all
> custom of exercises; and indeed it goes so heavily with
> my disposition that this goodly frame, the earth,
> seems to me a sterile promontory; this most excellent
> canopy, the air, look you, this brave o'erhanging
> firmament, this majestical roof fretted with golden
> fire, why it appeareth nothing to me but a foul and
> pestilent congregation of vapors. (2.2.296–304.)

Here, Hamlet describes something very like Purgatory—despite his dwelling in a beautiful earth, he is unable to enjoy it, but rather is trapped in a vision of it that consists of a "pestilent congregation of vapors" in a "sterile promontory." The language of Purgatory to describe his current state of mind suggests that he has not shaken his encounter with his father's ghost, and it echoes the story of the pilgrim who "shall never be joyous nor glad" after his Purgatorial encounter. Whether Hamlet is feigning madness or experiencing authentic grief, the prompt for his language is his meeting with the ghost from Purgatory who reminds him of the past. Not only does the ghost hint with all the transparency Shakespeare could afford in a Protestant kingdom that he comes from Purgatory, but Hamlet himself exists in a kind of Purgatory—a place of not one thing and not another, where his destiny is delayed by an interrupting king and his surrogate direction, given by his ghostly father, will have an uncertain outcome.

PURGATORY AND IN-BETWEEN-NESS

Hamlet, who is denied his father, his faith in his mother, and his rights to the throne, has been cut loose from his means of self-identification. He has also been denied his wish to return to school after being importuned by his mother and the king (whom he legally cannot deny) to stay in Elsinore, where he must constantly face his own wandering. The play immediately offers him some occupation in the form of his father's ghost charging him with revenge. Greenblatt points out that this is no ordinary revenge tragedy—Shakespeare has radically expanded the distance between the "first motion" and "the acting of a dreadful thing" in order to expand the area in which the character's inner life can be exposed.[17] Like the Purgatory from which the ghost comes to charge Hamlet with his duty, the space between revelation and action is a place of uncertainty and fear, and it lasts for nearly all of five acts.

Greenblatt focuses his chapter on *Hamlet* in *Will in the World* around not only Shakespeare's loss of his own son and the expected loss of his father, but also in the loss of the beliefs and rituals which the then-illegal Catholicism had once provided the bereaved. Having already established the likelihood that John Shakespeare was a recusant, as well as the likelihood that Shakespeare himself was one of many who occupied a middle ground between the religious extremes of the period, Greenblatt examines the inadequacy of Protestant funeral ceremonies to comfort parents of a dead child.[18] One of those comforts, which had the downside of also being fearful, was the idea of Purgatory, in which souls neither saintly enough to immediately enter heaven nor sinful enough to be denied salvation wait in agony while Purgatorial fires (like those of hell) burn away any sins of the unshriven. The fearfulness came in the hell-like fires, but this middle ground between heaven and hell also offered a place not yet so removed from life that the dead were irrevocably beyond reach. Purgatory had clear Catholic associations; one of the great struggles for Protestant reformers was to dispel the idea of Purgatory and to limit the destinations of souls to Heaven or Hell. Greenblatt writes in *Hamlet in Purgatory* that "the notion of an intermediate place between heaven and Hell and the system of indulgences and pardons meant to relieve the sufferings of souls imprisoned within it had come to seem, for many heretics and orthodox believers alike, essential to the institutional structure, authority, and power of the Catholic Church."[19]

Greenblatt also writes that "Though the rituals of the everyday life centered on the intimate and familial, they encoded the sense of a larger bond as well, linking the living with the souls of countless previous generations." He continues that "Purgatory forged a different kind of link between the living and the dead, or, rather, it enabled the dead to be not completely dead—not as utterly gone, finished, complete as those whose souls resided forever in Hell or Heaven."[20] Purgatory has the essence of a link to the past because it offers a past not completely gone or out of reach. The past, as it is embodied by Purgatory, is a reachable past which can still speak and direct one's path.

Purgatory, then, is a place of in-between-ness, a space between certainties and a place between action and resolution. It is not only the cosmic space between hell and heaven, it is also the space between earthly action and spiritual resolution. Hamlet fears it, and with good reason. The ghost could not utter the place's actual name (the name brought with it Catholic baggage and would have sent the Master of the Revels' censors into a frenzy).[21] Instead, Shakespeare gives the ghost lines which depict Purgatory in terms clear enough to get the idea across, but also to clarify the nightmarish quality of the awful place in which he has found himself. Given only the single witching hour in which to walk the earth, the ghost must return to "sulfurous and tormenting flames" (1.5.3). Although that description gives the audience a clear indication of the Purgatorial state from which the ghost comes, is not enough for Shakespeare. The ghost continues:

> I am thy father's spirit,
> Doomed for a certain term to walk the night,
> And for the day confined to fast in fires,
> Till the foul crimes done in my days of nature
> Are burnt and purged away. But that I am forbid
> To tell the secrets of my prison house,
> I could a tale unfold whose lightest word
> Would harrow up thy soul, freeze thy young blood,
> Make thy two eyes like stars start from their spheres,
> Thy knotted and combinèd locks to part,
> And each particular hair to stand on end
> Like quills upon the fretful porcupine.
> But this eternal blazon must not be
> To ears of flesh and blood. (1.5.10–23)

The ghost, having set up a punishing uncertainty for himself, echoes the uncertainty Hamlet has already expressed about life and his own situation, and prefigures the means through which Hamlet will begin to describe his own existence as a "prison."[22] The ghost is "forbid" to tell more details of Purgatory and instead contents himself with describing the expected reaction he would get from Hamlet were he free to tell. Rather than focusing the speech on himself, he focuses it on Hamlet, directing the audience's attention to the prince instead of on the ghostly king. He also manages to describe Purgatory without details that would give away its mystery. Having sufficiently set up his own place of uncertainty, he will now send Hamlet spinning uncontrollably into his own: "List, list, O, list! / If thou didst ever thy dear father love—/ [. . .] Revenge his foul and most unnatural murder" (23–26). Charged with an action, Hamlet is now in the Purgatory of space between direction and resolution.

The ghost of Hamlet senior comes to Hamlet from Purgatory, a place of not one thing and not another, but the torture of Purgatory is more complicated than that—it is a state of not -something. It is a place for the not damned and not yet cleansed. It is not hell, but it is not yet heaven. It is not entirely anything. The sinner is trapped in a place of fire, like hell, but the time there is limited by the potential for salvation from sin, and once the sinner has been cleansed by the fire, he/she may enter heaven. An in-between-things place—a realm of static existence held together by, and holding together, certainties—Purgatory can be understood only through the certainties that surround it and its meaning comes from the strange space it inhabits between them. To attach Ireland to Purgatory is to attach it to a place of tortuous uncertainty, and to the effects of cultural impressment—a state which exists between identifiers. The focus would ordinarily be on the identifiers, the things that can be seen and understood and pointed to. For Shakespeare, however, and, later, for Joyce, certainties were not where the real story lay.

THE POET AND THE SEA OF TROUBLES

Like King Richard in *Richard II,* Hamlet is the character with the power of words. Hamlet's long speeches are magical moments of introspection and philosophy. Although Hamlet humbly remarks that he is not a good poet, he speaks at length to himself and others in densely packed poetic language, and he has also written poems to Ophelia and composes an insert for "The Murder of Gonzago."

The increasing complexity with which Shakespeare constructs characters with Irish characteristics is, in part, a shift in genre, and that shift—from history to tragic history to tragedy—complicates the impressment. In a history play, Macmorris is "historically" a part of Henry V's campaign. Richard, who must be shown as having flaws that make him unfit to rule England, is given Irish characteristics, although he slowly becomes a sympathetic figure and so complicates the impressment. Hamlet, too, is given Irish characteristics and a very uncertain existence, characteristic of any colonial subject who is at the mercy of an invader's administration, but while he tragically falls, he so completely governs his own play and his fall is so terribly tragic that the playwright's impressment of the Irish here is far more problematic. Elsinore is taken over, at the end, by an pragmatic outsider who will put all to rights. While Fortinbras will probably make a better king than Bolingbroke did, there is less opportunity to take comfort in the rule of the pragmatist because the loss of the poet is far more tragic. Shakespeare had long been dealing in extremes, but by widening his extremes in *Hamlet,* Shakespeare extends the area of uncertainty between them. Then he makes uncertainty the whole point.

The most famous speech from *Hamlet,* from Shakespeare, and perhaps the English language, is an articulation of uncertainty. With Purgatorial uncertainty in mind, specifically the Purgatorial uncertainty of one who is trapped between acquiescence and a doomed rebellion, the speech becomes less a contemplation of suicide, which is the traditional interpretation, and becomes instead a consideration of action versus inaction. Hamlet has, in fact, already ruled out suicide as an option in 1.2 with the wish "that the Everlasting had not fixed /His canon 'gainst self slaughter!" (131–132). But in order for self-slaughter to be a sin, it must need to be an immediate act, since Hamlet can still consider actions which could lead to death at the hand of another. Hamlet seems to understand, in the great "To be, or not to be" speech, that action taken to redress the wrongs done his father and himself will bring an untimely and unpleasant end. "The question," which by itself could be understood only as whether or not "to be," is followed by further illustration of the problem Hamlet must solve for himself:

> Whether 'tis nobler in the mind to suffer
> The slings and arrows of outrageous fortune,
> Or to take arms against a sea of troubles
> And by opposing end them. (3.1.57–61)

Hamlet's question then becomes a question of whether or not to act: is it better, more noble, to take it on the chin, or to rise up against the source of the problem and eliminate it? The answer would seem obvious (to end the problem) except that Hamlet, in further consideration, recognizes that the penalty for rebellion might be death. At first thought, death might be preferable to earthly oppression:

> —and by a sleep to say we end
> The heartache and the thousand natural shocks
> That flesh is heir to. 'Tis a consummation
> Devoutly to be wished. (62–65).

His ensuing contemplation of death is the recognition that while death may seem preferable to earthly suffering, the fearful uncertainty of what comes "in that sleep of death" (67) prevents action. His characterizations of suffering are of the sufferings of one who is disinherited and thwarted from his destiny. He asks "who would bear the whips and scorns of time . . ."

> Th' oppressor's wrong, the proud man's contumely [abuse],
> The pangs of disprized love, the law's delay,
> The insolence of office, and the spurns
> That patient merit of th' unworthy takes, . . . (71–75)

Might he end those troubles with self-destruction? He asks "Who would fardels bear,/ To grunt and sweat under a weary life" when there is an alternative? The list of wrongs one must suffer is condensed in the words of "fardels," or burdens, and "a weary life," but it is noteworthy that the list contains one specifically romantic ill ("disprized love") and five that are directly or indirectly related to politics and an oppressed community. There are many reasons to act, but the one good reason not to completes the question:

> . . . the dread of something after death,
> The undiscovered country from whose bourn
> No traveler returns, puzzles the will,
> And makes us rather bear the ills we have
> Than fly to others that we know not of? (79–83)

Hamlet, of course, has met a traveler returned from that undiscovered country of Purgatory in the ghost of his father, but that encounter is hardly likely to set anyone at ease about the nature of the place. The ghost was clear that he can walk the earth in his deathly form for only a certain time before being called back to the Purgatorial fires. Since the uncertain prison of the world is preferable to the uncertain "prison house" of Purgatory, "conscience does make cowards of us all" and "enterprises of great pitch and moment/ With this regard their currents turn awry/ And lose the name of action" (87–89). Despite suffering under oppression, abuse, insolent officials, thwarted legal remedy, and rejection by the unworthy, the misery of actual Purgatory may be worse, and so great movements toward redress of wrongs that might end in death will be done in hesitation and will be derailed. The "name of action" is lost.

To redirect the speech's focus on the choice between an earthly Purgatory or a post-mortem one, Hamlet, spying the entrance of Ophelia, addresses her in terms the audience would have immediately connected with the Catholic practice of intercessory prayer: "Nymph, in thy orisons/ Be all my sins remembered" (90–91). Orisons are prayers, and Hamlet is asking for Ophelia to pray for the mediation and forgiveness of his sins. Catholics prayed for the forgiveness of sins of those who had died so that the dead might be spared a long time in Purgatory. Bequests to Catholic orders for the saying of masses was for the purpose of intercessory prayer—in the belief that souls trapped in Purgatory, in order to have their sins cleansed by suffering and fire, might find their sins, and so also their time in Purgatory, lessened by the prayers of the living. Hamlet's internal monologue which we receive in soliloquy is his personal working-out of the choice between a familiar earthly Purgatory or a frightening and unseen spiritual one. By asking someone to pray for his sins so that the time his spirit spends in the unseen Purgatory will be lessened, Hamlet states his choice. Frightened of Purgatory but frightened also of the potential for his conscience to make a coward of him, Hamlet chooses certain doom in action.

That choice is short lived, or at least delayed, by what he calls his need to "unpack" his "heart with words" and so he must sharpen again and again his "almost blunted purpose." Perhaps Hamlet does not give himself enough credit, since it is, as often as not, through words that Hamlet sharpens his senses and accomplishes the goals he can meet. Although Hamlet is a man of words like Richard II, perhaps he is even more so than the "poet king" from whom we have no poems, since Hamlet does actually write. When he writes, he writes about certainties and uncertainties. His love poem to Ophelia—"Doubt that the stars are fire . . . ," etcetera—is about the uncertainty of earthly things but offers his own certainty in the line, "But never doubt I love" (2.2116–119). We have no way of knowing which are the "dozen or sixteen lines" which Hamlet set down for the Players to insert into "The Murder of Gonzago," but that masque "of a murder done in Vienna" is itself is a lengthy exchange of promises of certain faithfulness between man and wife, king and queen. However, most of Hamlet's words are spoken words and it is through speech that he investigates and navigates the uncertain world in which he lives and dies. The fearful existence of being in-between things motivates Hamlet. Even in the short time between poisoning and death, Laertes quickly absolves Hamlet and himself of their last sins: "Mine and my father's death come not upon thee,/ Nor thine on me!" (5.2.332–333). Hamlet twice says to Horatio "I am dead"—between life and death, Hamlet is doomed but still able to articulate his existence (or non-existence) in a statement Greenblatt points out is more appropriate to a ghost: "It is as if the spirit of Hamlet's father has not disappeared; it has been incorporated by his son."[23] The revenger has become a ghost, a marker of the past, who speaks from a place of unstable existence between life and death.

HAMLET, DANE OR DUBLINER

Hamlet's unstable existence did not end with his death. Stephen Daedalus refers to Hamlet as "Dane or Dubliner" and in doing so, points not only to Hamlet's "universality," but also to an Irish sense that Hamlet's experience is an Irish one. Declan Kiberd writes that "The strategy of the revivalists thus became clear: for bad words substitute good, for superstitious use religious, for backward say traditional, for irrational suggest emotional." The "positive aspect" of this strategy was that "it permitted Irish people to take many images which were reflected by English society, occupy them, reclaim them, and make them their own." The "negative aspect," however, "was painfully obvious, in that the process left the English with the power of description and the Irish succumbing to the pictures which they had constructed."[24]

There is something even more slippery about Hamlet, and Kiberd's answer is an incomplete one. The Irish response to Shakespeare's cultural impressment of the Irish through Hamlet is more complicated, because the play is more complicated than the others which appear in Irish writing. Shakespeare's development as a writer over his career was one of increasing complexity of character, and so while Macmorris is a man without a country, and Richard is a man without a throne, Hamlet is both and something more. Hamlet is not defined by the thing he is operating without, he is defined by what he substitutes for it. For loss, Hamlet substitutes a richer inner life for himself. Separated from the certainties he had before his father's death, Hamlet instead begins to investigate the space between certainties, in a Purgatory of his own existence.

The story of a poet separated from his inherited rights and, in his attempt to uncover the perpetrator and enact revenge, is doomed to death, is much like the story of Ireland, and Irish writers in the early twentieth century found it swimming on the surface of their consciousness as they attempted to write their way into self-determination. But when Joyce reappropriated and wrote against *Hamlet,* he predictably confused mediums of self-understanding. The result of Joyce's grafting of *Hamlet* into *Ulysses* is that the space between certainties in Shakespeare's *Hamlet,* and the barren and corrupt landscape of widely separate identifiers, becomes a claustrophobic meshing of overlapping identities. In *Heathcliff and the Great Hunger,* Terry Eagleton situates Joyce's work in a context of contending cultural identities, writing that "If contending cultures can converge anywhere, it is in the pages of *Ulysses* and *Finnegan's Wake;* but this fruitful exchange of idioms can happen only in the non-place of exile, or a book."[25]

For Joyce, Ireland was a location for his fiction but not for himself, and he left Dublin for the Continent in a self-imposed literal version of the figurative exile of the Irish at home. The middle-ground he then discovered came from his escape from the pulls of life in Dublin—Eagleton writes that Joyce, in choosing Trieste over London, "bypassed the culture of the metropolis as surely as the nationalists he despised, who by turning backward to ancient Ireland, and forward to a nation yet to be born, hoped to squeeze out the history of British sovereignty which intervened between them." If Joyce wanted to explore the present, he would be forced to leave a place too focused on the past and the future, but "the free play of the signifier which results from Joyce' literary scavenging has as its referent (Ireland) a place where such freedom is largely absent. Hence the 'free state' of his fiction, in which a ceaselessly mobile discourse moves within a cyclical enclosure."[26] The relationship between fathers and sons, images of past and future, is an in-between place of existence, and Joyce investigates that place as it relates to historical and literary pasts and futures in an argument that Shakespeare is the father of Hamlet and the father of all.

Stephen's theorems on Shakespeare's ghost, spoken to other Irish literati in the Irish National Library, pivot on the relationship between father and son and the nature of being each. Joyce conflates family relationships with national and imperial relationships in a confusing engagement of belonging. Terry Eagleton tries to untangle this engagement, describing the relationship between England and Ireland as a "matter of some unthinkable conundrum of difference and identity, in which the British can never decide whether the Irish are the antithesis or mirror image, partner or parasite, abortive offspring or sympathetic sibling." He echoes images of overlapping identities in *Ulysses* with the statement that "If Britain is the source of authority, then it is the parent and Ireland the child; but if both bow to the jurisdiction of the crown, then the two nations instantly become siblings, recomposing their relationship" and creating a "puzzle of which we have a microcosm in *Ulysses:* are Stephen and Bloom brothers or father and son, and if father and son then which is which?"[27]

Ulysses, already arranged to point us to father/son relationships through the Ulysses/Telemachus figures of its governing narrative structure, reaches in "Scylla and Charybdis" into its own literary origins to reposition opposites as locations of multiple meaning. Stephen's speech creates an overlapping of the episode's recurring relationships of father/son and creator/creation, and serves to destabilize extreme positions. It has been on Stephen's mind from the beginning of the novel: the Englishman Haines, who equates the tower where they live to Elsinore, asks Buck to tell him about Stephen's theory of *Hamlet.* He asks, "Is it a paradox?" Buck replies, "We have grown out of Wilde and paradoxes. It's quite simple. He proves by algebra that Hamlet's grandson is Shakespeare's grandfather and that he himself is the ghost of his own father."

Haines, horrified, asks: "What?[. . .] He himself?" Buck, in his typical levity, responds only with an address to Stephen: "O, shade of Kinch the elder."[28] Buck mockingly confuses Stephen's theorem and Stephen, saying that "it is too long to tell," refusing then to sort it out. It is in "Scylla and Charybdis" that Stephen will expound his theory of the identity of the paternal ghost.

Far from Buck's deliberately confused characterization of Stephen's argument as an illogical and chaotic recasting of relationships, Stephen's theory of biographical identification, while presenting overlapping identities, still creates opposite positions between which identity is uncertain and disorienting. By setting the discussion in the framework of the extremes of Scylla and Charybdis, Joyce sets Stephen's attempts to contend with Shakespeare's genius in a situation of dangerous extremes Stephen must explore for his own ambition as an artist.

Stephen, despite his admiration for the Bard, still charges Shakespeare with complicity in the oppression of Ireland. Stephen comments that "Twenty years he lived in London and, during part of that time, he drew a salary equal to that of the lord chancellor of Ireland."[29] The lord chancellor was the officer in charge of managing Ireland and keeping it subdued through the constant elimination of Irish custom and the insertion of English custom in its place. He was the officer in charge of "civilizing" (read: "Englishizing") Ireland. Shakespeare's office of playwright for the Lord Chamberlain's Men, who performed his plays like *Hamlet*, is compared with the lord chancellor's office of subduing Ireland by separating it from its own identity—and found similar. Stephen finds that "the note of banishment, banishment from the heart, banishment from the home, sounds uninterruptedly from *The Two Gentlemen of Verona* onward till Prospero breaks his staff, buries it certain fathoms in the earth and drowns his book."[30] Stephen will banish certainties when he posits Shakespeare as the ghost of Hamlet's father, disinherited brother, and "father of all his race," and posits Hamlet as Shakespeare's child Hamnet, as his brain-child, and as Stephen himself.[31]

Stephen articulates the difficulties of being an Irish writer under an English stranglehold by picking up on the father/son paradigm in *Hamlet* and exploiting it to make his own points about the asphyxiating experience of writing in the shadow of an all-powerful English writer. Vincent John Cheng writes of Joyce's use of fathers and sons in *Finnegan's Wake* that "to Joyce, the influence of 'fathers' was at once indelibly shaping and insufferably suffocating." He explains that: "All his life he struggled with the paternal powers in himself: John Joyce, Dublin and the fatherland, the Church Fathers, the Jesuits, God the Father, and his literary masters, such as Ibsen, Dante, and Shakespeare." But while "Joyce sees himself as a filial figure, a disciple to an old master, an Icarus to a Daedalus," Joyce's choice of last name for one of his allegorical characters, Stephen Daedalus, is telling: "he always has that desire to shake off the wings and the guiding influence of the parent, and to fly on his own—he himself aspires to be the creator-father figure."[32]

"Scylla and Charybdis" is situated in the Irish National Library, a place for the collection of texts important to the Irish, but more specifically, in a reading room where Irish writers and thinkers may study and conduct discussion. The location is, for Stephen, one appropriate for a response to cultural impressment because it is a location for the development of Irish writing, something to which Stephen is failing to actually contribute. The setting then creates an atmosphere of what Stephen should be doing there, as opposed to what he does; Hugh Kenner writes that, in this location, "a poet who spends his day not writing" has a "place appointed as though by Aristotle, in which conspicuously not to fulfill his function." Stephen spends his time talking about writing, but not actually contributing anything tangible to the literary revival of which the other literati are a part. His absence of location-appropriate occupation creates a "certain decentering," which highlights his disconnected experience while separating him from his fellows.[33]

The writers and thinkers present are the librarian Mr. Lyster, John Eglington, Russell, Mr. Best, and Stephen, and they are joined by Buck Mulligan. Haines, the Englishman who serves throughout the novel to frustrate Stephen's ambitious thoughts and provide, symbolically, an English presence to thwart him, has here symbolically absented himself to go purchase a copy of Hyde's *Lovesongs of Connacht*. The discussion, predictably amongst these writers, ranges widely through a very narrow topic: their own writings, great Irish writers, associations between them, Irish publications, and idle social marginalia of the literary world, strung together by the thread of the aim of literary contribution. The lightness with which they banter over great Irish writers and with which they drop the names of publications and fellow writers serves to trivialize their pursuits instead of emphasize their importance. There seems to be no unity in their literary force—their trade seems scattered. They themselves trivialize their own aims. In the midst of the discussion, Buck teases Stephen:

> —The tramper Synge is looking for you, he said, to murder you. He heard you pissed on his halldoor in Glasthule. He's out in pampooties to murder you.
>
> —Me! Stephen exclaimed. That was your contribution to literature.[34]

Stephen, frustrated with the false comraderie, mocks their discourse in his own internal monologue:

> Young Colum and Starkey. George Roberts is doing the commercial part. Longworth will give it a good puff in the *Express*. O, will he? I liked Colum's *Drover*. Yes, I think he has that queer thing, genius. Do you think he has genius really? Yeats admired his line: *As in wild earth a Grecian vase*. Did he? I hope you'll be able to come tonight. Malachi Mulligan is coming too. Moore asked him to bring Haines. Did you hear Miss Mitchell's joke about Moore and Martyn? That Moore is Martyn's wild oats? Awfully clever, isn't it? They remind one of don Quixote and Sancho Panza. Our national epic has yet to be written, Dr Sigerson says. Moore is the man for it. A knight of the rueful countenance here in Dublin. With a saffron kilt? O'Neill Russell? O, yes, he must speak the grand old tongue. And his Dulcinea? James Stephens is doing some clever sketches. We are becoming important it seems.[35]

Stephen juxtaposes conversational drivel with ambitions of importance, inanity with dreams of genius, imagination with commercialization, and verse in English with ideas of Irish language and national literature. The result is a biting representation of the sort of empty talk which surrounds and impoverishes what he feels to be true literary ambition. In case Stephen seems to be too harsh, or exaggerating to the point of falsifying, his monologue is followed by a conversation that validates his frustrations. When Stephen gives Russell a letter he is submitting for publication, the response is: "—Synge has promised me an article for *Dana* too. Are we going to be read? I feel we are. The Gaelic league wants something in Irish. I hope you will come round tonight. Bring Starkey."[36]

Stephen's mocking thoughts, followed by Russell's earnest response, illustrates what Hugh Kenner points out about this episode: that while the scene appears to be dominated by Stephen, whose voice we get much of here, the truth is that much of Stephen's talk is interior, and his interior monologues comment on and inform the actual conversation in which he is taking part. In a discussion of literary contribution, Stephen's open contribution to the discussion is one which sets up a literary father for them all, and that father is not Irish. Kenner writes that "his intricate talk is of paternity: the father a playwright, the offspring a brainchild."[37] Stephen's external and internal utterances operate in the context of a rhetorical landscape of Irish writers seeking prominence. Stephen's fellows are deeply concerned with the absence of an Irish national epic. Against this persistently intrusive backdrop,

Stephen's suggestions of literary parentage encoded in a discussion of Shakespeare as the ghost, father, and past create a crowded space of identifiers for an Irish writer.

The absence of an epic comes up several times—beginning with John Eglinton's comment at the beginning: "—Our young Irish bards, John Eglinton censured, have yet to create a figure which the world will set beside Saxon Shakespeare's Hamlet though I admire him, as old Ben did, on this side idolatry."[38] They discuss Shakespeare at length, usually on this side idolatry, but with an important insert by the facetious Buck Mulligan. Finally joining them in the library, Buck is told that they are discussing Shakespeare. His response is one of dismissive humor: "Shakespeare? he said. I seem to know the name." After a moment he adds to this: "To be sure, he said, remembering brightly, The chap that writes like Synge."[39] Immersed in discussions of their writing and the writing of literary masters, they adjust and replace writers' importance while trying to insert themselves within the literature they value. To compete, they write in English. To find literary origins that are not English, they write in Gaelic. To write in what Stephen calls "lean, unlovely English" is to write within a tradition they have inherited through cultural impressment.

Their words indicate that they understand the possibility of reading Hamlet as being a representation of Ireland. Stephen calls Hamlet "Dane or Dubliner," and John Eglinton asks if anyone has suggested in criticism that Hamlet could be read as Irish. He tells the others: "Judge Barton, I believe, is searching for some clues. He swears (His Highness not His Lordship) by saint Patrick."[40] They have picked up on the play's most overt Irish reference. Within this rhetorical landscape, Stephen's contention that Shakespeare is the ghost in Hamlet sets up a literary ontology from which there is no escape. His own inserted references to Purgatory are all interior, and they bring together remembrance and the past as a father with which they must all contend.

GHOSTS AND FATHERS—A NECESSARY EVIL

Stephen subliminally equates Hamlet's father with his own mother—who, too, asked a son to "remember" her in prayer by praying for her soul, but he refused. Burdened by guilt but certain of the rightness of his choice, Stephen rejects the past and is highly sensitive to its appearances. He will have a visitation from his own parental ghost later, in "Circe," but confines himself in this episode to a single reference. After speaking of Anne Hathaway, older than Shakespeare, as one who saw Shakespeare "into and out of the world," he presents an image of Anne laying pennies on Shakespeare's eyes "to keep his eyelids closed when he lay on his deathbed." Stephen's internal monologue interrupts with: "Mother's deathbed. Candle. The sheeted mirror. Who brought me into the world lies there, bronzelidded, under few cheap flowers. *Liliata rutilantium.* I wept alone."[41] Through most of his dialogue, Stephen is concerned with Hamlet's having to face his own lost origins:

> —What is a ghost? Stephen said with tingling energy. One who has faded into impalpability through death, through absence, through change of manners. Elizabethan London lay as far from Stratford as corrupt Paris does from virgin Dublin. Who is the ghost from *limbo patrum,* returning to the world that has forgotten him? Who is king Hamlet?[42]

Stephen goes on to present Shakespeare as the king, "a ghost by absence, and in the vesture of buried Denmark, a ghost by death, speaking his own words to his own son's name."[43] Stephen correlates the ghost to Shakespeare, Gertrude to Anne Hathaway (whom Stephen accuses of an adulterous affair that drove Shakespeare to live in London and to write of betrayal), and Hamlet to Hamnet Shakespeare.

Stephen's reading of the father/son relationship is one which exposes difference as well as overlapping identities. The difference between them makes them rivals: "his growth is his father's decline, his youth his father's envy, his friend his father's enemy."[44] Despite this, the two are connected through a lineage of words: "He is a ghost, a shadow now, the wind by Elsinore's rocks or what you will, the sea's voice, a voice heard only in the heart of him who is the substance of his shadow, the son consubstantial with the father."[45] The son, hearing the words of the father, carries and so becomes what is left of the father, and so the son who follows this past-parental guidance keeps the father alive in himself. If Shakespeare is, then, the ghost of Hamlet's father, then Shakespeare continues to exist within the character of Hamlet, whoever Hamlet might be. If the Irish find themselves represented in Hamlet, then the Irish, in following a Shakespearean lead, are keeping Shakespeare alive within their own pursuit. Shakespeare/the ghost's words are to "Remember Me." Certainly Stephen is remembering Shakespeare through his diatribe, and so, according to his own syllogism, becomes a writer in whom Shakespeare survives.

Stephen is not, of course, finished confusing the roles. Wandering into religious doctrine, Stephen suggests that, since the Father and the Son are the same deity although they have different parts, father and son are the same:

> He Who Himself begot, middler the Holy Ghost, and Himself sent Himself, Agenbuyer, between Himself and others, Who, put upon by

> His friends, stripped and whipped, was nailed like bat to barndoor, starved on a crosstree, Who let Him bury, stood up, harrowed hell, fared into heaven and there these nineteen hundred years sitteth on the right hand of His Own Self but yet shall come in the latter day to doom the quick and dead when all the quick shall be dead already.[46]

The begetter and the begotten are the same, and so the child is the father and the father is the child. Eglinton sums up Stephen's remarks: "The truth is midway . . . He is the ghost and the prince. He is all in all."[47] What this means for Stephen's positioning of himself as Hamlet is that this literary father, Shakespeare, whose words Stephen not only carries but uses with facility, is a rival, but also simultaneously the same as himself. Kenner views Stephen's response as quite conventional. According to Kenner, Shakespeare had dominated literary discussions for decades and that it was typical of the time to "create a Shakespeare in one's own image." Stephen's "Shakespeare in middle life is wounded, driven; moreover, his plight rhymes with Stephen's own," but Stephen creates Shakespeare in his own image in part to contend personally with the writer who towers over him and in part to lift himself in the eyes of the other Irish writers in the discussion.

Kenner argues that "Part of Stephen's desire is to astonish, part of it to parade his knowledge of how genius works, knowledge those present—Dublin's senior *litterati*—are to understand he has by birthright."[48] Stephen wants to be the inheritor of Shakespeare's genius, an idea he encodes cryptically even in his interior monologue. Mr. Best, in his patronizing but kindly way, tries to agree with Stephen but gets it wrong: "Yes, Mr Best said youngly, I feel Hamlet quite young. The bitterness might be from the father but the passages with Ophelia are surely from the son." Stephen responds internally, "He has the wrong sow by the lug. He is in my father. I am in his son."[49] Stephen is in "his son," meaning he is in Hamlet. Shakespeare is the father instructing Stephen to "remember me." By openly presenting Shakespeare as the ghost/father, and keenly encoding himself as the inheriting son, Stephen sets himself up as the inheritor of Shakespeare's genius. In a discussion among the literarily ambitious, these are strong words indeed. Joyce, characteristically, then confuses the structure his alter ego character has spent nearly a whole chapter setting up. Asked by John Eglinton: "Do you believe your own theory?" Stephen answers: "No," but in his own internal monologue he says, "I believe, O Lord, help my unbelief. That is, help me to believe or unbelieve? Who helps to believe? *Egomen*. Who to unbelieve? Other chap."[50]

Stephen still believes, or, at least Joyce still creates the possibility for him to believe. Joyce is about to offer Stephen a father—a ghost of a man who has lost the fidelity of his wife and the life of his son. Buck, leaving the library with Stephen, points out Leopold Bloom in the shadows. Bloom is suddenly cast in the role of Hamlet's father in a similar description to the ghost wandering for a "certain time" at the gates of the palace of Elsinore:

> A dark back went before them. Step of a pard, down, out by the gateway, under portcullis barbs.
> They followed.
> Offend me still. Speak on.[51]

Within moments, Stephen ceases his rhetorical overlapping and dual identities in which he is trying to be simultaneously father and son, writer and reader, creator and creation. Stephen's performance in the library was a lengthy attempt to posit a syllogism in which Shakespeare is the father and the work is the son, the father is the past and the son is the present, the past is the inheritance and the present is the inheritor, and that, in simultaneous identity they are the same. That would mean that Stephen, as the son, is the same as Shakespeare, the father of all his race, and so Stephen (and not Moore) is the Irishman who will write the Irish national epic. The instructions of the father were: "Remember me." And to do so is to pray for but also to revere. Stephen, suddenly, repositions Shakespeare in the role of father/Father/creator:

> Cease to strive. Peace of the druid priests of Cymbeline, heirophantic: from wide earth an altar.
> *Laud we the gods*
> *And let our crooked smokes climb to their nostrils*
> *From our bless'd altars.*[52]

For the moment, at least, Stephen will be content to serve as worshiper at the altar of Shakespeare and to be the inheritor of genius, rather than to attempt to be the original or to overcome it. William H. Qullian argues that by the time Stephen has left the library with Buck Mulligan, he has exhausted his own ideas and his attempts to contend with Shakespeare: "Stephen has gone as far as he can with his own aesthetic theory and that has not been far enough." Qullian adds that, at the end of "Scylla and Charybdis," "all possibilities seem to be closed."[53] What Qullian does not consider is that Stephen still has open the possibility to write in Shakespeare's shadow, which he had been doing prior to his argument anyway. Stephen has come to the understanding, in his discussion of fathers and sons, that they constitute each other: "A father . . . is a necessary evil" because it is the existence of a son which makes a man a father, and the existence of a father which makes a man a son. They inform and create each other because without each other they cannot exist.

BANISHMENT

Kiberd quotes Joyce as having said that "the Irish, condemned to express themselves in a language not their own, have stamped on it the mark of their own genius and compete for glory with the civilized nations. The result is then called English literature."[54] They were still exiles—Kiberd writes that, in 1904, when Joyce was writing *Ulysses* far away in Trieste and Paris, the Irish people as a whole "were suffering from that most modern of ailments: a homeless mind" because their "traditional patterns of living had been gravely disrupted, but without the material compensations which elsewhere helped to make such losses tolerable."[55]

Perhaps it should come as no surprise that when Irish writers read *Hamlet,* they read the story of themselves. Every reader or viewer of *Hamlet* reads, on some level, the story of him or herself. Everyone seems to want to be Hamlet. It is the watershed role for every actor—the role that every actor wants and fears. From Richard Burbage to David Garrick to Lawrence Olivier to Mel Gibson (not forgetting actress Sarah Bernhardt along the way) actors have used this role of deep complexity and exhausting requirements to demonstrate their skill and prowess as artists. We will probably never know the "ur-Hamlet," Kyd's Hamlet story pre-dating Shakespeare's with the plot he must have reworked. We do know that, whatever was already there in the story, Shakespeare brought to it a remarkable understanding of the sorrow and faith which are part of loss.

Shakespeare creates in Hamlet a figure who is fascinating, sympathetic, and tragically doomed. Hamlet is wronged by Claudius, but Claudius, once he takes the throne, is in control and Hamlet is offered the frustrating choice either to "suffer the slings and arrows" or to "take arms against" his troubles and end both them and himself. By violently including the Irish in the story of pragmatism winning over all, despite its potential ugliness, Shakespeare demonstrates the futility of fighting against the invader. By impressing them so sympathetically as the doomed hero of what Stephen reads to be the ultimate literary paternal figure, Shakespeare is, however, offering the Irish a new inheritance.

Salman Rushdie writes in *Imaginary Homelands* that "a man without strong feeling or powerful affiliations, survives. The self-interested modern man is the sole survivor . . ."[56] Hamlet is not a man consumed entirely by pursuit. The investigation, after all, is his own idea, the act of revenge was his father's. He does not survive physically, but, with the exception of Horatio, an outsider along for the ride, Hamlet may be the only inhabitant of Elsinore whose soul survives intact. Survival of the soul despite the fall of all those around him may be the secret to the mysterious appeal of Hamlet as a character. Prior to his departure to England, he is less bent on revenge than he is on truth, and after his return to Elsinore he does not even mention his filial promise—only through the intrigues of other characters is Hamlet provided with occasion for revenge.

Rushdie writes that "Joyce's wanderer" Bloom and other modernist characters like him "are what we have instead of prophets and suffering saints. But while the novel answers our need for wonderment and understanding, it brings us harsh and unpalatable news as well."[57] He posits the search as the modern experience and the novel as the essentially modern form of literature:

> What appears plain is that it will be a very long time before the peoples of Europe will accept any ideology that claims to have a complete, totalized explanation of the world. Religious faith, profound as it is, must surely remain a private matter. This rejection of totalized explanations is the modern condition. And this is where the novel, the form created to discuss the fragmentation of truth, comes in. The film director Luis Buñuel used to say: 'I would give my life for a man who is looking for the truth. But I would gladly kill a man who thinks he has found the truth.' (This is what we used to call a joke, before killing people for their ideas returned to the agenda.) The elevation of the quest for the Grail over the Grail itself, the acceptance that all that is solid *has* melted into air, that reality and morality are not givens but imperfect human constructs, is the point from which fiction begins.[58]

When Joyce was writing, it was a return to a time when killing people for their ideas had returned with a vengeance. The time being returned to was the very early modern crisis of faith and identity in which Shakespeare was writing *Hamlet*. People were being killed for their ideas then too, and Shakespeare, as Greenblatt so poignantly points out in *Will in the World*, would have seen what was left of those people every time he looked at the piked heads on London Bridge. What is frequently overslooked is the essence of the period now called "early" modern period. The period is called so because it anticipates and contains the emergence of the very issues dealt with by modernists, issues of instability and fractured contemplation of the world.

Texts of the time may not reflect the same kind of wrestling with instability for which modern texts are distinguished, for certainly the early modern period saw some of the most stringently totalizing writing in English history, but that very attempt to grapple with the whole, to create it and reinvest it, is the essence of the literature of early empire and the motive behind cultural impressment. Empire seeks to create a total unit, one with layers and levels of belonging, but a unit nonetheless. The strength with which it attempts to create a whole and the ferocity with which it attempts to hold that whole together is an implicit recognition of the fractures it must overcome.

Chapter Five
Question and Answer

The last night of the 2005 Shakespeare Association of America in Bermuda, I waited for nearly an hour at the bus stop to go into the town of Hamilton for dinner. I was speaking with a friend about the pre-release screening of the Derry Film Initiative *Hamlet,* shown the day before, when the three Irish fellows presenting the film appeared at the bus stop as well.[1] Friendly and in good spirits about the film's reception, they chatted idly with my friend and me about the conference, the film, and the long wait for the bus. Well into the interminable wait, they laughed amongst themselves that they ought to sneak over to the nearby marina, "pirate" one of the boats, paint "Free Ireland" across the side, and sweep jubilantly across to the other side of the island where the pubs awaited them.

I was struck by how drastically their private conversation differed from the public answers they had given to the crowd after the screening of their overtly political film. The Derry *Hamlet* is filmed entirely in black and white and uses a documentary format. The character of Hamlet is the primary documentary camera operator, with frequent voice-overs by Horatio. Characters are in modern dress, including guards in para-military uniform, and are surrounded in their municipal Derry buildings by surveillance cameras from which parts of the "footage" are also supposedly taken. Other editorial and interpretive choices include setting the violent encounter between Hamlet and Ophelia in an empty theatre, using a protest flyer against Claudius as his "portrait" when Hamlet compares him to his father for Gertrude, completely removing of the Fortinbras plotline, and performing Hamlet's "To be or not to be" speech entirely in Irish Gaelic.

Stephen Cavanagh (director/Hamlet), Colin Stewart (Guildenstern), and producer Richard Hughes gave pleasant and yet strangely dismissive answers during the question and answer period after the screening. Asked directly to address the political choices that went into the film, the three answered a seemingly bewildered: "political choices?" Despite follow-up questions regarding the setting, the costumes, the surveillance cameras, and the use of Gaelic for the most crucial speech of the film, the three men flatly insisted that there were "no politics" in the film. Asked why he removed Fortinbras completely, Cavanagh answered "for time" and because he could not afford a large enough cast to fill all the roles. Asked why he did *Hamlet* at all, Cavanagh answered that he had just always wanted to play Hamlet. Asked why they filmed Claudius's post-mousetrap confession through surveillance cameras in a bathroom stall (where he pleads for forgiveness after being sick), the three replied in so many words that they thought it would be interesting. When asked questions which might have required culturally or politically contentious answers, Stewart and Hughes were evasive and brief. Despite the fact that he answered more questions, and at somewhat more length, than the others, Cavanagh was no more forthcoming. The majority of their answers gave the impression of an almost whim-based low-budget production into which they put very little interpretive effort.

However, when asked why they chose a documentary format, they went directly to the text. Explaining that they felt the play functioned through Hamlet's understanding and perception, and that Hamlet himself was an artist of sorts, they felt that in their production it made sense for Hamlet to constantly be filming Elsinore and its inhabitants. Scenes in which Hamlet is not present were filmed through surveillance cameras. The primary "lens" of the play is Hamlet's, both interpretively and literally. Because Hamlet asks Horatio with his dying breaths to tell the story of what happened, they chose to present their film as Horatio's compilation of Hamlet's collected evidence, with voice-overs to narrate. So despite time, budget, and cast limitations, apparently quite a lot of pre-production interpretive choices went into framing the film. The film was, to the audience, overtly political. The effect of the para-military guards and surveillance cameras in a documentary setting was very like newsreel footage of IRA activity in Northern Ireland. The protest flyers were strikingly similar to sectarian propaganda. The effect of the "To be or not to be" speech in the recovered language of Irish Gaelic was stunning in its political implications and post-colonial re-reading. It restricts any real understanding of the performance to a small group of Gaelic speakers and serves as a reminder that the language being spoken was nearly lost through British oppression. Any who do not speak Gaelic are forced to rely on memory for the English words of the speech, serving as a reminder that the speech resonates so thoroughly in Western culture that it can be recalled, at least partially, at will. As part of its sponsorship by the Derry Film Initiative, the film is set in Derry, the place of Orangemen marches ending in bloody results in recent decades, and a place of relentless sectarian violence for centuries. The very fact that they call the city "Derry" instead of "Londonderry" gives away the political perspective of which side they and the film are on.

The removal of the entire Fortinbras plot altered the text by removing the primary foil for Hamlet as a son without a father. Laertes is still there, but his attempted rebellion is quickly dispatched by the clever Gertrude and, without Fortinbras, Hamlet is left with no comparison. The removal, too, of the only glimmer of hope at the end gave the conclusion of the film a desolate absence of any promise for order in Elsinore. Claudius, the only pragmatist with whom Hamlet must contend, is killed and Hamlet, the poet/artist, dies speaking the last words. The rest is silence, indeed. There is no winner in this film, there are only contenders who lose in their bids for power.

SILENCE

Irish readers might well be sensitive to the implications of removing Fortinbras from the end of the play. His entrance signals the end of Hamlet's family on the Danish throne, the end of Danish rule of Denmark. But because he is viewed favorably by Claudius and establishes himself as a quick man of action, like Claudius and like Laertes, he is set up to be the opposite of the intellectual hero. George Bernard Shaw wrote in 1894 of his disappointment in English performances of the play's end:

> When first I saw Hamlet I innocently expected Fortinbras to dash in, as in Sir John Gilbert's picture, with shield and helmet, like a mediaeval Charles XII, and, by right of his sword and his will, take the throne which the fencing foil and the speculative intellect had let slip, thereby pointing the play's most characteristically English moral.[2]

It should come as no surprise that English performances of Shakespeare fail to live up to what Shaw imagines when he reads. He reveals a reliance on more than just text—he is also using the visual aide of Gilbert's illustrations (available still in the Globe Illustrated edition).[3] Reading rather than viewing allows a completely individual relationship to the play, unencumbered by the readings and perceptions of directors, actors, producers, etc. It allows the reader to feel a direct connection to the author, as though the text itself is a communication through which stories are transmitted directly to the reader. It is an individual act. Shaw finds others' readings to be less than his, they conflict with his understanding of the play and seem specious, erroneous, and vain. They are based, in his view, on the vanity and arrogance of actors who enlarge parts for their own glory, who add props and stage business for more time in the limelight, who cut scenes and combine characters in order to promote, through Shakespeare, their own value systems. Perhaps it is this to which Shaw is the most sensitive, as an Anglo-Irishman with a combined and so naturally also fragmented identity. The play performed on the stage is the play interpreted for him by Englishmen, not the play as he experiences it when he reads it alone, absent of any imperial apparatus.

His use of the illustration and the context in which he recalls it reveal much about Shaw's reading of the play and its value systems. Gilbert's illustration is intricate and packed from border to border with dramatic imagery of the end of Act Five. Despite Shaw's reaction, the illustration itself does not focus so entirely on Fortinbras' entrance. That character, in fact, takes up only about one fifth of the total illustration of that scene. Fortinbras is sketched in the center left of the scene, not entirely in the sketch, as his right arm and a bit of hem are cut off by the sketch's border. His armor is impressive, but the only weapon showing is his shield in his left hand. His helmet and its shadow obscure any real expression on his face. He and the soldiers visible behind him are bent at the waist, rushing in as though against a strong wind.

The majority of the illustration is a perfect riot of spectacular death. Directly in Fortinbras' path, Claudius lies sprawled backwards down steps with poisoned chalice rolling away from his dead hand, spilling its contents on the floor. In the background, up the steps, Gertrude is being carried off by what appear to be shirtless servants. In the foreground, Horatio glances up at the entering Fortinbras while holding up a wilting Hamlet whose tragic face looks more pale than the others' in contrast with his black tunic. In front of Hamlet, Laertes lies collapsed on a discarded sword. Fortinbras is not the center of the illustration, is not, in fact, even primary in the illustration. He is one part of the overall scene. The sword Shaw mentions is not actually visible in the drawing.

It is, however, that "characteristically English moral" that perhaps places Shaw most firmly in the camp of those Irish readers who see Fortinbras as the fortunate English invader, prepared for war but finding that those who were not prepared for war had left him an empty throne which he may easily occupy after a few eulogistic words. The "fencing foil," appropriate for courtly duels but not for the battlefield, would have hardly stood up to the sword that Fortinbras surely carries with the impressive armor. The "speculative intellect," the best tool for self-reflection and philosophical inquiry into what dreams may come, feels flimsy compared with "will." The invader need only slow down long enough to step over the bodies and take the place that becomes his by the right of might and of no one else's being left to take it. This, according to Shaw, is an essential English moral—to dash in and acquire whatever has been dropped by those busy thinking instead of than defending.

The removal of Fortinbras from the end then removes from the play a distinctive mark of what pragmatism can accomplish. Removing him from the end of the play does substantially more than just shorten its running time. Removing him removes the character who takes the throne at the end and so also removes any preferential treatment the play may seem to have for men of action over men of intellect. Removing him ends the play with the emphasis still on how the first "invader," Claudius the pragmatic interloper, brought to ruin a good kingdom and the life of a good prince. Removing him gives Hamlet the last words.

A pile of corpses might seem to leave the Derry Film Initiative *Hamlet* with a closed ending, but with no intruder to pick up the pieces of order, the film is instead left as a set of questions quite open and unanswered. It would have been useful and illuminating to hear these choices explained by those who made them. The questions the audience posed to Cavanagh, Stewart, and Hughes were not designed to elicit self-incriminating answers. But when asked anything that might require an answer revealing a position on the "Irish Question," their answers said nothing.

QUESTIONS WITHOUT ANSWERS

The conversation at the bus stop demonstrates that Cavanagh, Stewart, and Hughes are hardly free from political views. Away from the crowd, away from the official setting in which they presented their film to an audience, their political viewpoint made its way into their speech. The reluctance to speak openly about issues they freely spoke of privately and amongst themselves may be best described by another Northern Irish artist, Seamus Heaney, who most clearly records the phenomenon of "Northern Reticence" in "Whatever you say say nothing."[4] His *North* collection, in which the poem appears, is generally open in its declaration of political sympathy for the embattled Northern Irish Catholic, and Heaney frequently writes bitterly towards England. "Whatever you say say nothing," however, is less about sides and more about the suffocating climate that the two sides create. Using occasional allusions to Shakespeare to editorialize on the questions of callous reporters, Heaney writes a paradox of the need to answer and the inability to do so in a poem animated by the conditioned behavior of silence.

The Shakespeare references are small but crucial. The first, mentioned previously in Chapter Four, is part of his description of the crush of reporters "in search of 'views/ on the Irish thing'" in a place where "bad news is no longer news." Frustrated with their "jottings and analyses," he writes that "The times are out of joint." As in *Hamlet*, in which the outsider's administration brings conflict rather than stability for the poetic soul, the present is unsound and unsolvable; violence will lead only to more violence. Heaney uses the second Shakespeare reference to characterize the ever-returning revenge between the two sides. Frustrated by his inability to speak his thoughts openly, Heaney describes himself as "Expertly civil-tongued with civil neighbours."

The reference to *Romeo and Juliet* echoes the opening of the play, in which the Chorus describes irreconcilable conflict:

> Two households, both alike in dignity,
> In fair Verona, where we lay our scene,
> From ancient grudge break to new mutiny,
> Where civil blood makes civil hands unclean. (1.1.1–4)

That "ancient grudge," whose origin no one remembers, ends with the complete destruction of the future of both families when their children attempt to resolve the conflict through alliance. It is a play about learning the far-reaching consequences only after they have been brought to pass, but it is also a play full of street-fighting and the maneuvers of the powerful, in which the sides never resolve their differences, even after they have destroyed each other. In such a context, Heaney's conflict deepens. The poem is the closest he can come to voicing his frustration in a place in which speech can have fatal consequences:

> 'Religion's never mentioned here,' of course.
> 'You know them by their eyes,' and hold your tongue.
> 'One side's as bad as the other,' never worse.
> Christ, it's near time that some small leak was sprung
>
> In the great dykes the Dutchman made
> To dam the dangerous tide that followed Seamus.
> Yet for all this art and sedentary trade
> I am incapable. The famous
>
> Northern reticence, the tight gag of place
> And times: yes, yes. Of the 'wee six' I sing

> Where to be saved you only must save face
> And whatever you say, you say nothing. (III.1–12)

His frustration is the condition of a poet who is conditioned to not reveal anything. Yet while in the open he says nothing when he speaks, in his writing he casts the conflict which gags him in the terms brought to him by the other side: in the English language of the other side and in contextualizing references to the dominant writer of the other side's language. The severe fighting between the Catholic Home Rulers and Protestant Unionists has created a situation in which it is so dangerous to reveal one's feelings that the inhabitants of the "wee six" Ulster counties have learned to speak without really speaking.[5] Heaney may joke that "Smoke signals are loud-mouthed compared with us," but in his poetry he can speak with a slight degree of safety by encoding his frustration in poetry. Even there, however, he cannot freely speak of his views; he is "incapable." He can speak only in codes so tightly formulated that nothing is revealed. Even his "art and "sedentary trade" do not allow him a place to speak openly. Despite the passion with which he vents, the poem only reinforces his point—it voices only the frustrations of silence, and never the view of his side. The Northern Reticence, of which not only Heaney but the Derry Film Initiative *Hamlet* team are victims, does not allow for open political discussion, but does allow for encoding politics into art. The politics that this poem reveals are less about sides and more about suffocating under a political obfuscation of difference in origins.

That is not the case with other poems in the *North* collection. Several poems demonstrate the confusion of being separated from origins by an occupying culture which has become one's own. In "Bone Dreams," Seamus Heaney seeks an ontology prior to colonial existence, phrasing his search in terms of English cultural exports. Attempting to understand and connect with what is potentially a relic of life before English oppression, Heaney can find no way out of English frameworks in a disturbingly violent romance with the life which the bone represents to him. To Heaney, the bone represents a primordial Irish woman, and he is a man unable to court her in any way that does not include English conventions. Finding the bone in the grass, the speaker's first reaction after touching it is a desire to "wind it in/ the sling of mind/ to pitch it at England/ and follow its drop/ to strange fields" (I.12–16).[6] Seeking to connect with the bone, the speaker tries to "push back/ through dictions,/ Elizabethan canopies" (II.5–7). He does not push past the language, the canopies of diction, but is pushing at something through them, or, by using them. The phrases, and their paradigms of belonging, are a barrier blocking meaning and yet the means of reaching it.

He is trying to reach a previous language, and that language is violent—it has "the iron/ flash of consonants/ cleaving the line" (II14–16). That previous language has much to offer as well. It has "the coffered/ riches of grammar/ and declensions" (III. 1–3) and he calls it to "Come back past/ philology and kennings," where it can "re-enter memory/ where the bone's lair/ is a love-nest/ in the grass" (IV.1–6).

He courts his "lady," the bone, in the terms of the marking of and encroachment upon land that characterize invasion and oppression: "I am screes/ on her enscarpments,/ a chalk giant/ carved upon her downs./ Soon my hands, on the sunken/ fosse of her spine/ move towards the passes" (IV.10–16). So the violence of time and cultural re-mapping that divides him from her is the very means through which he courts her. Part V works as a mini-blazon in which he re-reads her skeletal structure though English cultural terms: "the long wicket/ of collar-bone" shapes her through the English games of croquet or cricket, "the Hadrian's Wall/ of her shoulder" re-creates in her the Roman barrier built to keep out the barbaric Celts of Scotland. He does not separate or distinguish between references to language and visual images, nor does he treat differently military images such as "earthworks" and more benign cultural images like the one referring to cricket. Heaney cannot romance his own ontology except in the terms he has been forced to inherit. Like the Derry *Hamlet*'s reinvesting of Shakespeare's play with deeply Irish conflicts and issues, Heaney works in "Bone Dreams" to use, for his own dissident purposes, the culture into which he was impressed. The Derry *Hamlet* reaches for something uniquely Irish, but does so through a play which casts Ireland as the victim. Attempting to reach a pre-English existence, these artists can search only through the master's language and culture, and so Englishize the pre-English existence they are trying to reach and re-enlist the culture they are trying to free through description.

Re-inscription of the oppressor's culture is a post-colonial construct which theorists and critics have dealt with extensively.[7] Once an imperial power has separated a culture from its independent past through generations of oppression, the occupied culture can free itself from the governance, but not the culture of the oppressor. The link with the past has been interrupted and cannot be reclaimed without acknowledging the interruption. Heaney must push through the language he gained in his impressment in order to describe his experience and reach something like his origins, but even when his linguistic archeology is completed he is left with the bones of his past and the efforts he used to reach them. The experience is not a uniquely Irish one, it belongs as well to other Englishized cultures. In *Midnight's Children,* Salman Rushdie encodes the eternally re-capitulating relationship of oppressor and oppressed in the conditions upon which the protagonist's family buys their house from the Englishman who is leaving with the retreating British government—they may purchase the house only if they agree to carry on the English custom of pre-dinner drinks in the courtyard. The family concedes, thrilled to be purchasing such a lovely home, and the required happy hour leads the father to become an alcoholic over the next few years—described by the narrator as possessed by the "djinn bottle"—a configuration of images in which the father is simultaneously haunted by demons of his own culture and the most famous corrupting drink of the imperial culture.[8] The consequences of attempting to take up authoritative residence in one's own country are, culturally, similar to the consequences of continuing to wilt under the yoke of oppression. India and Ireland, however, have different histories with the empire. England set a date with India and walked out. In Ireland, even the part of it that has thrown off the empire sees itself fragmented and separated from the six Ulster counties. The Republic must attempt to recreate itself within its independence, but it is haunted by the part of itself which is still under English hegemony.

Both parts of Ireland, however, experience themselves through the lens of Englishness, even in, or perhaps even more so in, attempts to identify themselves without it. They have their own djinn bottles, the British paradigms they had to swallow as part of reclaiming Irishness. The paradox of finding their Irishness within the constructs through which they were impressed has a long history in the confusing and contradictory means through which England claimed authority over the island.

THE NAME CONQUEST BEING ABSURD

Previous chapters of this study discuss briefly Queen Elizabeth's fluctuation in perception of the Irish Question and methods in approaching it.[9] Her removal and later reinstatement of Lord Grey, her varying degrees of intensity towards subjugation of the island, and her refusal to turn entirely to violent means of oppression frustrated Edmund Spenser and others. A royal proclamation from 1599 deals with her reluctance and reveals the combined anger and sympathy with those fighting English dominance. The proclamation's available summary explains:

> Recites the trouble taken by the Queen to bring Ireland to obedience by peaceable means. The present rebellion is caused by three sorts, some who have been hardly treated by her ministers, some fearing the

power of adverse factions and having no defense against other rebels, and some incited by seminary priests. The Queen does not wish any conquest or extermination of rebels. The name Conquest being absurd. To show her good will, a just and merciful minister has been appointed to Ireland. [Earl of Essex]

—The Queene Maiesties Proclamation declaiming her princely resolution in sending ouer of her Army into the Realme of Ireland. Richmond: 31 March 1599.[10]

Perhaps the first impression is the complete exoneration of the average Irish person of blame in the ongoing insurrection. The proclamation sorts rebels into three kinds: those who have been mistreated by her own officers, those who are essentially peer-pressured into rebellion, and those (much like the accusations identified in Barnaby Riche) who have been led astray by Catholic priests who oppose the Protestant "heretic queen." The repeated use of words which would issue from a benevolent ruler indicate both generosity of spirit towards the Irish people and a sense of them as her own people towards whom she wishes no ill will: "peaceable means," "her good will," "a just and merciful minister." The Irish people seem helpless and in need of her assistance because they have been "hardly treated" by previous officers in charge of Ireland. They are fearful of locals who might hurt them for complicity with the English, and they are misled by Catholic priests who owe allegiance to a Pope who has promised forgiveness to any willing to kill her.[11] The reference to "seminary priests" might, in fact, be an understatement, since Pope Gregory XIII had actually sent soldiers to Ireland to rebel against the Queen, gaining ground and keeping it for over a year. At any rate, the Queen apparently held the Irish unaccountable for the actions to which they were incited by Catholic leaders.

She does not want the rebels "exterminated," because she feels, apparently, that their rebelling is not their fault. Her feelings on the "extermination" of rebels could change—the "just and merciful minister" whom she appoints to address these ills will turn out to be a complete disaster. When he failed utterly to quell much of anything in Ireland and returned to stage *Richard II* as a prologue to his own rebellion against her, he found himself exterminated in short order.

Yet while "extermination" seems appropriate enough to warrant no further comment, "conquest" is absurd. The additional phrase reflects the Queen's insistence upon the Irish as her own subjects, and one does not conquer one's own subjects. The phrase, within the context of the proclamation regarding unrest, depicts the Irish in a way typical of the period, as unruly children in need of a good parent. The queen was, of course, that good parent, willing to use only peaceable means and working to find just the right minister to keep the Irish in hand. The proclamation's phrasing contains the same paradox which makes cultural impressment an act ripe for re-reading. It depicts the Irish as British subjects who need quieting. The queen perceived the Irish to be subjects who needed discipline, rather than as a nation that needed conquering, and it was this perception that guided her reluctance towards the more generally violent measures espoused by Spenser and Sidney (see Chapter One). According to official royal doctrine, the Irish were already members of the empire, but they were members who clung to separateness. It was, however, that very separateness, that inferiority which made them like children, on which the English had to insist while bringing them to heel.

Cultural impressment, the enlisting of another culture in a process of imperial self-identification, seeks to create a unified whole. Yet it fails to do so, because part of the process is to both acknowledge a separate ontology for that other culture and to confuse that ontology by declaring the culture a rightful belonging of the empire. The empire forces upon the enlisted culture the language and literature which are the impressing culture's evidence for presumed superiority and presents them as models of cultural material, but it must insist upon separateness in order to do so. The imaginative models for the impressed culture are those in which it appears as a separate part of the whole, and the permanent fragmentation which results creates ambiguity through which the impressed culture can self-identify. Referring to her "Irish subjects" as such, as people already belonging to her and deserving of kind treatment, may seem less violent than overt oppression, but it is merely a more subtle and underhanded violence. The impressed culture finds itself claimed as a belonging, used for imperialist purposes and against itself. Despite its totalizing goals, however, cultural impressment remains an inconclusive act. The dominant culture can never entirely consume through the force it uses to impress the thing which it must acknowledge as separate. The impressed culture can never reclaim the authority from which it has been separated, nor can it entirely dominate a language and literature it has inherited. Once a culture has been impressed, both the empire and the impressed culture can only contend with each other through the fragmented remains of their identities.

Salman Rushdie writes in the title essay of *Imaginary Homelands* that "It may be argued that the past is a country from which we have all emigrated, that its loss is part of our common humanity," but he suggests that "the writer who is out-of-country and even out-of-language may experience this loss in an intensified form."¹² Rushdie, certainly a better expert than most on the terms of exile from home, culture, and even security, argues that the writer who is separated from his homeland must necessarily be aware of discontinuity with the past. He is more aware of the loss than most because he is unable to immediately access the reminders of the past through anything but fragmented memory. Rushdie feels that all human memory is fragmented to some extent, but the exile who is forced to acknowledge the distance between fragments is perhaps best suited to describe the fragmentation that is part of all modern experience. Rushdie states clearly that "all description is itself a political act" and wonders if description from the perspective of separation might not be useful. He decides that because all people perceive incompletely, the writer who has been separated from the tangible evidence of his ontology can describe his experience and "speak properly and concretely on a subject of universal significance and appeal." He writes that "human beings do not perceive things whole; we are not gods but wounded creatures, cracked lenses, capable only of fractured perceptions." He adds, "those of us who have been forced by cultural displacement to accept the provisional nature of all truths, all certainties, have perhaps had modernism forced upon us."¹³ The provisional nature of all truths, but, most particularly, the provisional nature of identity, could be a wounding experience, but Rushdie encourages writers from the margins to use it to investigate the givens, the "truths," which are used in imperialism. As such, the investigation can permanently call into question those truths and so create an autonomy within the question—a dominance within ambiguity. Such an investigation operates freely within the absence of closure and resists resolution, even at the cost of its own victory, since it is also at the cost of imperial victory.

In *Radical Tragedy,* Dollimore refutes previous criticism which seeks a coherent political unity in the structure of early modern drama. He argues that "the very appeal of this notion of structural coherence has in practice neutralised the destabilizing effect of contradictory dramatic *process,* subordinating it to notions of totality, effacing it in the closure of formalist (and often, by implication, universalist) truth." In other words, a search for a coherent structure dismisses or ignores the subversive representation of the marginalized with which Dollimore's work is concerned. To focus too much on whole-ness at the end of a play turns reading into a process which ignores whatever is closed out in the play, and so fails to recognize the radical implications of its pre-closure presence. In *Henry V, Richard II,* and *Hamlet,* for example, to focus one's reading on order reinforced or suggested at the ends of these plays would be to ignore the subversive presences of Macmorris,

King Richard, and Hamlet in favor of the closure provided by King Henry V, King Henry IV, and Fortinbras.

Dollimore continues that drama of this period "does often effect some kind of closure, but it is usually a perfunctory rather than a profound reassertion of order (providential and political)." That "perfunctory" reassertion of order does not sufficiently close out the subversive elements—or, rather, it does so unconvincingly. A critical focus on order then overlooks the superficial nature of the closure in a search for a totalizing meaning of the play.[14] Fragmentation, an inevitable effect of presenting subversive elements within the whole, is then never adequately resolved.

Focus on subversive elements must be informed by the context of attempted closure. Because the other is given space and presence on stage to justify the closure of the dominant force, the fragmented identity which that other inhabits on stage—the one the dominant seeks to close—becomes its final identity: In the existence of the play, it continues to be a fragment which must be unified with the rest. Fragmentation becomes, in the play, the essence of the marginal identity, and when a post-colonial writer attempts to counterattack, to re-conquer the terms, he or she finds that fragmentation is the continued existence. Seamus Deane describes this phenomenon in the introduction to *Nationalism, Colonialism, and Literature* when he writes that nationalism, as an effect of being colonized, becomes a copy of its oppressor. Deane writes that

> It was only when the Celt was seen by the English as a necessary supplement to their national character that the Irish were able to extend the idea of supplementarity to that of radical difference. This is a classic case of how nationalism can be produced by the forces that suppress it and can, at that juncture, mobilize itself into a form of liberation.[15]

His examination of nationalism in Ireland results in the conclusion that "The major communities in the North, Protestant and Catholic, unionist and nationalist, are compelled by the force of circumstances . . . to rehearse positions from which there is no exit."[16] As Dollimore points out, the marginal existence becomes one of repeated inclusion, but the very repetition prevents a total closure, since the experience continues as long as the play has a beginning as well as an end. Deane's finds this in his observations of Northern Ireland:

> The bulk of the Irish people are ignorant of and alien to the Irish language and its ancient literature; northern Protestants are alien to both

that and to their own complex earlier history in Ireland. To remove ourselves from that condition into one in which all these lesions and occlusions are forgotten, in which the postmodernist simulacrum of pluralism supplants the search for a legitimating mode of nomination and origin, is surely to pass from one kind of colonizing experience into another. For such pluralism refuses the idea of naming . . ."[17]

Deane's point that pluralism, or fragmentation, is the means through which origins are sought, is typical of the paradoxical search for ontology and refusal of available past which characterizes Irish reappropriations of Shakespeare. In O'Casey's work, where characters operate without a knowledge of the past, or in Beckett's, where characters are in desperate need of a past they are unable to remember, it is the ambiguity which provides them with some autonomy in their search for themselves. For Yeats, the past is a place for poets, and so he wants to remove from it those who privileged realists and recreate it through his own vision. For Shaw, the past does not exist. All that exists are present malefactors who misinterpret a language over which he himself claims mastery. For Joyce, all are fragmented, the past is a nightmare from which he is trying to awake, and it is in dreaming that he finds the truth of the provisional nature of things.

Rushdie writes that "we can find in that linguistic struggle a reflection of other struggles taking place in the real world, struggles between the cultures within ourselves and the influences at work upon our societies. To conquer English may be to complete the process of making ourselves free."[18] But Rushdie gets ahead of himself. English cannot be conquered because it is not a landscape or a tangible thing that will sit still for him. English, for one thing, is a language created from disparate languages absorbing one another—Norman French and Anglo-Saxon combined and recombined to create English. The impressed can never entirely conquer English, because it will always be the language of the force that impressed them. They can, however, excel in using it—Yeats, Shaw, Beckett, and Heaney are all Nobel Laureates in Literature and Joyce's *Ulysses* was named the "greatest novel of the twentieth century.[19] Joyce's novel *A Portrait of the Artist as a Young Man* shows an earlier Stephen grappling with the language he inherited. Stephen replies to the blind nationalism of another fellow: "My ancestors threw off their language and took another, Stephen said. They allowed a handful of foreigners to subject them. Do you fancy I am going to pay in my own life and person debts they made? What for?"[20]

Despite the acclaim that the writing of the colonized might receive, writing in English means writing in a language which requires that post-colonial writers understand themselves through other eyes, and therefore their work may contend with the empire and seek to conquer, but total conquest is impossible. Seamus Deane describes colonialism as "a process of radical dispossession" and explains that colonized people lack "a specific history and even, as in Ireland and other cases," lack "a specific language." He characterizes Irish authors writing in English as taking "a vengeful virtuosity in the English language, an attempt to make Irish English a language in its own right rather than an adjunct to English itself."[21] This complicates the idea Rushdie suggests when he considers the language issue with which he and his fellow Indian writers have grappled: "I hope all of us share the view that we can't simply use the language in the way the British did; that it needs remaking for our own purposes. Those of us who do use English do so in spite of our ambiguity towards it . . ."[22]

Perhaps here, as in the Queen's proclamation, the word conquest is "absurd." A dominant language is not something with which a former colony can abscond nor is it a territory a former colony can inhabit to the exclusion of others. In the idea of "remaking it," perhaps ambiguity is more than a necessary evil—perhaps it is the point. Even were an othered culture to dominate English discourse or writing or use in the present, that culture would necessarily be participating in the terms of English's previous victory over them, and so reinforcing that victory by their attempt to erase it with conquest. By making conquest their goal, however, they refuse to submit to those who used English to impress them. As long as there is ambiguity, in their feeling towards it and in who has mastery of it, the writers from the empire's margins can confute the empire and its dominance. They can continually fight to define themselves, they can use the terms of English for their own purposes, and so pervert the power structure which impressed them. By forcing The Question to remain a question, they prevent resolution. They can use the question which remains a question to investigate themselves and to contend with the writer who culturally impressed them, who cast them as victims for better or worse.

WE PUPPETS SHALL REPLAY OUR SCENE

George Bernard Shaw, who wrote extensively on Shakespeare throughout his career, frequently cast his writing in terms which both lauded and envied Shakespeare's place in the canon. While much of Shaw's writing expresses a frustration with others' interpretations of Shakespeare's plays, encoded within those writings are shades of a writer contending with another, far more prominent, writer. Shaw's own bold statements which assert a "correct" understanding of Shakespeare reveal a writer who attempts to assert a certain control over the more prominent writer, but that tone of contention in his other writings becomes an overtly figured battle in one of Shaw's last written pieces, written for a small group of friends at a house party. Shaw knew that his life and his writing career were waning—the introduction to "Shakes Versus Shav," the last piece included in *Shaw on Shakespeare,* includes the note that Shaw wrote in his preface to the short piece: "this in all actuarial possibility is my last play and the climax of my eminence, such as it is."[23] Shaw is typically writing an ironic slight of himself and his career in a way that humbles his reputation—the piece to which he refers is a puppet show. The content of the puppet show, in a paradoxical move of content combined with genre, is a fight between himself and the writer he loved, defended, criticized, and emulated throughout his career. Shaw's "Shakes" is a writer deeply flawed when it comes to realism, but greatly superior in imagination, and certainly superior in reputation. The battle between Shakes and "Shav," the Shaw puppet, is a battle over craft and recognition. Shakes appears on the puppet stage to identify himself as "William Shakes," the writer of "renown not for an age/ But for all time." He states his purpose:

> Hither I raging come
> An infamous imposter to chastize,
> Who in an ecstasy of self-conceit
> Shortens my name to Shav, and dares pretend
> Here to reincarnate my very self . . .[24]

Shaw, according to his own "reincarnation" of Shakespeare, has dared to emulate Shakespeare and to "shorten" Shakespeare's name to "Shav." Shaw places himself in a Shakespearean trajectory and creates a Shakespeare who is aware of it and is displeased. Shav may have caused the rift, but it is Shakes who picks the fight: "Tell me, ye citizens of Malvern,/ Where I may find this caitiff. Face to face/ Set but this fiend of Ireland and myself;/ And leave the rest to me."

Shaw creates for his self-puppet a world renown "almost rivalling" Shakespeare's and Shav appears, saying: "who art thou, that knowest not these features/ Pictured throughout the globe? Who should I be/ But G. B. S.?"[25] Shakes challenges him, not to a duel, but to a brawl: "For one or both of us the hour is come./ Put up your hands." The text then includes stage directions for a very funny fight: "*They spar. Shakes knocks Shav down with a straight left and begins counting him out, stooping over him and beating the seconds with his finger.*" Shav recovers: "*At the count of nine Shav springs up and knocks Shakes down with a right to the chin.*"

This is not to be a merely physical fight. The puppet show moves from fisticuffs to verbal sparring which turns on a contest of literary greatness. Throughout the remainder of the play, Shakes will present his own characters to speak for his imaginative greatness, and Shav will trot out characters written after Shakespeare to battle Shakes for supremacy in genius. Shav fights Shakes's imagination with examples of dramatic realism, poetic skill, and the truthful representation of relationships, all the while trying to convince an arrogant Shakes, who will not concede his place in the canon, that others have written as well or better in recent centuries. Shakes's question "Couldst write Macbeth?" inspires Shav to call for Sir Walter Scott's Rob Roy with the answer, "No need. He has been bettered/ By Walter Scott's Rob Roy. Behold, and blush."[26] The Macbeth and Rob Roy puppets then challenge each other to a fight, but in startlingly different accents. Macbeth's is the poetic perfect English of Shakespeare, and Rob Roy's is a humorously overdone Scottish accent:

> MACBETH. Thus far into the bowels of the land
>   Have we marched on without impediment.
>   Shall I still call you Campbell?
> ROB [*in a strong Scotch accent*] Caumill me no Caumills.
>   Ma fet is on ma native heath: ma name's Macgregor.
> MACBETH. I have no words. My voice is in my sword. Lay on, Rob Roy;
>   And damned be he that proves the smaller boy.
>
> *He draws and stands on guard. Rob draws; spins round several times like a man throwing a hammer; and finally cuts off Macbeth's head at one stroke.*
>
> ROB. Whaur's your Willie Shaxper the noo?
>
> *Bagpipe and drum music, to which Rob dances off.*
>
> MACBETH [*headless*] I will return to Stratford: the hotels
>   Are cheaper there. [*He picks up his head, and goes off with it under his arm to the tune of British Grenadiers*].[27]

Shaw boldly attacks Macbeth with Rob Roy in a fight of realism. Rob Roy is shown immersed in colloquial language which, overdone here for the sake of getting laughs, goes past an accurate representation of Scottish speech to show though exaggeration the distance between a realistically portrayed Celt and the too-Anglicized Macbeth with his King's English. The language is not all: the Rob Roy puppet appears to win the fight with Macbeth (Shaw is, perhaps, fighting a representation war on behalf of Scott?) and exits to the sound of bagpipes, while Macbeth exits to the music of the British military.

Even their background music serves to underline their associations: Rob Roy with accurate music for his home, Macbeth with the music of British invasion. It serves as a reminder that after writing plays to please the English Elizabeth, Shakespeare had written Macbeth to please the Scottish James, but James was a Scot who had become king of another country. By ascending the throne of England, James drew Scotland into the British Empire peacefully, and so succeeded in doing what the English had never completely accomplished through warfare: make Scotland a holding of England.

According to the realism-driven Shaw, Macbeth, while a stunning character, misses the mark of correct portrayal and so presents an English idea of Scotland. The battle lines drawn here are ones of difference not only of place, but of time, in which Shaw presents Scott as improving upon Shakespeare though advances in literary representation. It is important to note that, although Rob Roy decapitates Macbeth, separating his body from the organs for thought and speech, he does not silence the Shakespearean character, who continues to speak as he exits.

The inability to silence Shakespeare despite an apparent victory over him will continue through the puppet show, when Shav presents himself as a contender with Shakespeare. Asked "Where is thy Hamlet? Couldst thou write King Lear?" Shav presents his own *Heartbreak House:* "Aye, with his daughters all complete. Couldst thou have written Heartbreak House? Behold my Lear." The debt to Shakespeare's Lear is clear in Shotover's lines:

> I builded a house for my daughters and opened the doors thereof
> That men might come for the their choosing, and their betters spring
>   from their love;
> But one of them married a numskull: the other a liar wed;
> And now she must lie beside him even as she made her bed.[28]

The "young woman of virginal beauty" replies: "Yes: this silly house, this strangely happy house, this agonizing house, this house without foundations. I shall call it Heartbreak House." *Heartbreak House* does have a foundation—it has King Lear, and Shakes recognizes his own play in the structure of Shav's. He recognizes one of the central ideas of another play as well: to Shotover's ending line "Enough. Enough. Let the heart break in silence," Shakes responds "You stole that word from me: did I not write/ 'The heartache and the thousand natural woes/ That flesh is heir to?'" Shav is aware that Shakes did not invent the inevitability of grief, he only wrote it brilliantly: "You were not the first to sing of broken hearts. I was the first that taught your faithless Timons how to mend them." In other words, Shakes did not begin it, but Shav ended it. Shakes, ever the wiser, replies: "Taught what you could not know." Regardless of attempts to better Shakes, Shav can instead provide only a proposed improvement.

His attempts to displace Shakes as master of the field now fully take the form of conflicts between immortality and inheritance. Shav concedes his inability to master the poetic master. Shakes points out the limited existence of all writers, saying that the "great globe itself,/ Yea, all which it inherit, shall dissolve. . . ." Yet Shav returns that writers will continue to contend with the great Shakespeare, both in person and in the continuing existence of their words: "Tomorrow and tomorrow and tomorrow/ We puppets shall replay our scene. ."

Shav, unable to speak without quoting Shakes, unable to argue without reinforcing Shakes's position, may find a temporary victory by pointing out flaws, but in doing so re-situates himself as a follower and successor and so succeeds only in reinscribing Shakes's stranglehold on supremacy. Succumbing finally to rhyming couplets of iambic pentameter, Shav separates Shakes's immortality as writer from mortality as human in a recasting of Hamlet's description of the vulnerable human body:

> Immortal William dead and turned to clay
> May stop a hold to keep the wind away.
> Oh that the earth which kept the world in awe
> Should patch a wall t' expel the winter's flaw!

It is not the "earth," however, of Shakes's body which keeps "the world in awe;" that, truly, is gone. It is his words that live, something Shakes recognizes and immediately points out: "These words are mine, not thine." Giving up on victory, Shav will content himself with co-existing. Whether or not Shakes is willing to do the same would depend entirely on performance choice and interpretation. Shav concedes:

> Peace, jealous Bard:
> We both are mortal. For a moment suffer
> My glimmering light to shine.
> *A light appears between them.*
> SHAKES. Out, out, brief candle! [*he puffs it out*].
> *Darkness. The play ends.*[29]

If Shakes suffers Shav's "glimmering light to shine," it is only for a moment. Shakes puts out Shav's light, and accompanies his action with one of his most famous quotes from the play the two first fought over. Shaw has presented himself, not only as a puppet contending with Shakespeare for literary recognition, but also as a light Shakespeare can blow out with his poetry. By presenting himself as Shakes's candle, Shaw inserts himself into Shakespeare's work, tucking himself into an image Shakespeare created and can blow out. By blowing it out, Shakes is forced to acknowledge the threat that Shav poses and so bring him recognition as a contender. Shaw's puppet show, written in fun, nevertheless digs up serious issues for the writer. He openly acknowledges what he sees as Shakespeare's ineptitude with realism (an anachronistic, presentist frustration), but continually reinforces him as the greater writer.

Yet all the while, he sets himself up in mock arrogance as a contender for greatness and creates a battle which he will lose, not only to Shakes's better abilities, but to a "jealous" refusal to admit a rival. The cycle of attacking, and so reinforcing, the creator of one's own situation is the classic postcolonial case, in which the oppressed reinforces the structure created by the oppressor. Shaw does not merely attempt to deconstruct Shakespeare's mastery of literature—he acknowledges that mastery but yet continues futile attempts to chip away at it. He inserts himself into Shakes's words, but as the fragile thing Shakes can easily eliminate.

ENDINGS AND OTHER QUESTIONS

Insertion of one's self into the text allows some control of the interpretation, but the re-reading by the impressed both critiques and reinscribes the impressment. Writing about the impressing work allows for an exterior critical control of the text. Creating and participating in a performance of the text, however, is a means of critically controlling the text from the inside. Written critique can comment on the text and the interpretive choices of others, but performance is the acting of interpretive choices. It has the danger of more fully reinscribing the master by putting the work, literally, back in the spotlight without much narrative control. Staging the text re-enacts the impressment, but it does so with the potential to subvert the glorification of the impressing force, the imperial press gang. Demonstrating interpretation through performance does not allow for explanations or lengthy analysis, as is possible in written interpretation.

As Dollimore points out in *Radical Tragedy*, any text which attempts to close out a subversive force must first represent it, and so can never completely erase the threat because while the text continually closes out the threat, it also therefore continually first gives it a voice.[30] Conversely, however, focusing on the subversion by identifying one's self as that threat is the very thing which allows the Irish to both reappropriate and write against the means of their impressment—an interpretation of the text by an impressed other which focuses on the subversive elements in the text must, therefore, also continually reinscribe the impressing force which closes them out in the end. Inserting themselves into the text interpretively continually re-enacts their impressment and their re-reading may expand and explore the subversion, but at the inevitable cost of finding themselves subjugated again and again. Just as, in Dollimore's words, the oppressor "cannot control what it permits," and the oppressed may subvert, but cannot control, the oppressing force when it re-stages its fall. In attempted conquest, it bequeaths to the impressed culture the guidelines for unification which acknowledge difference and so confute the attempted unity. The impressed culture can then use the means of its subjection as the same means through which it resists.

Irish performances of Shakespeare are as abundant as any other culture's, but the strange politics that come into an Irish performance are oddly current in the context of Orangemen's parades, cease fires, and weapons turnovers. England's first colony, Ireland may yet be its last colony as long as there are Ulster Protestants who cling with all their might to English control. The post-revolution Republic of Ireland does not seem to have the preoccupation with a play like *Hamlet* that Northern Ireland does. Residents of the weary and embattled cities of the six Ulster counties produce complicated re-readings of Shakespeare, and some of those have been mentioned in this study already—Seamus Heaney (from Derry) and his frequent mentions of Shakespeare in *North* and *Field Work* and Ciaran Carson's "Hamlet" along with other references in *Belfast Confetti*. Northern Irish men performing Hamlet take on deeper connotations, such as the full-length *Hamlet* by Belfast-born Kenneth Branagh in 1996. But Irish writers in both the North and the Republic find themselves grappling with a cultural identity often defined through their colonial experiences, and through those who culturally colonized them, because rejecting that experience means rejecting the means through which they have been separated from a continuity of Irishness. They must see themselves, then, either as a part of an empire or as a part reclaimed from an empire, and so it is through fragments that they can read themselves.

The inclusion of Macmorris, the dethroning of Richard, and the death of Hamlet all function to violently include characters with Irish characteristics in stories which glorify English pragmatism and expansion. The absence of closure for the lauded pragmatism, however, exists on a larger level than just in the model Dollimore explores of eternally recapitulating opposites that reappear every time the story starts over. The absence of closure occurs in cultural impressment because the impressment cannot consume something it enlists as an included other—the practice itself attempts to simultaneously identify the enlisted culture as the contradictory ideas of same and different. The resulting paradox gives the enlisted culture a fragmented means of self-identification. The work of the post-colonial writer is to negotiate between the fragments to discover the "provisional truths" of culture and nationalism. Shakespeare's Irish characters found themselves recycled by the Irish in ways which reveal the Irish relationship to the empire. Captain Macmorris knows that he serves King Henry and the empire, but in asking "What ish my nation?" he cannot articulate his own ontological differences. Macmorris's combined and conflicting nationalities develop into the Irish stereotypes of soldier and servant. Reappropriated by Sean O'Casey and Samuel Beckett, both characters are alienated from the servitude in which they find themselves, but one is more complicit and one is more rebellious. As Joxer and Boyle, and Didi and Gogo, the divided Macmorrises become marks of permanent servants of absent masters—servants in collusion and in conflict with each other, and in desperate need of a past through which to understand themselves.

Richard's dethronement at the hands of his cousin Henry of Bolingbroke pits idealism in a sympathetic but losing battle with pragmatism. His agility with words is admirable but incapable of securing his place on the throne or the stability of his kingdom, and the poetry with which he articulates his experience serves to underscore the fragile fiction of the authority he lost. While Macmorris is recycled as a stereotype with the complication of a dual cultural identification, Richard becomes a more sympathetic figure to Irish writers like Yeats and Shaw because of the depth with which Shakespeare draws Richard's character and the tragedy of his fall from power. So when Yeats and Shaw rail against an English misunderstanding of Richard as a character, they rail against what they see as the callous depiction of Richard as being an inept ruler because of his poetic nature rather than despite it. Their defenses of Richard take the form of lashings against English pride in pragmatism and their own identification with the Celtic nature of the king whom Shakespeare showed as tragically helpless against the power of his ambitious relative. Reading for impressment through the plays presents a forceful representation of idealism and poetry caving to pragmatism and security, but also complicates the impressment by fleshing out the representation of Irish character and so creating a greater sympathy with the fall of the idealist and more space for an Irish dissident reading.

After an almost nominal representation of the Irish in Macmorris and a conflicted sympathy for Richard, Shakespeare created in Hamlet strong Irish associations with a character perhaps most tragic in his fall. The multiple re-readings of Hamlet by Irish artists enact an attempt to control and re-create the narrative by insertion of themselves into it, similar to Shaw's insertion of himself into Shakespeare's constructions as the light which the Shakes puppet can blow out at will. Stephen Daedalus's syllogism in which he presents the Irish as inheritors of Shakespeare's tradition, as literary children and artistic creations, most clearly describes the process through which an Irish writer attempts to understand himself according to, and against, the representations in which he finds himself in the dominant cultural literature.

All of these dissident re-readings reveal that Shakespeare's cultural impressment of the Irish creates an unresolvable riddle of self-understanding for the Irish writer. The impressment of the Irish in Shakespeare's presentations of Britain and the superiority of Englishness may have been meant to create an imperial closure of definition. Instead, it creates a continuing conflict for the Irish writer attempting to operate within a dominant language and literature inherited as part of belonging to the empire. That literature, like the king's shilling which press gangs slipped into pockets and pints of ale as the exchange of payment for forced service, became both the property of the impressed and symbolic of the loss of autonomy.

SPENDING THE KING'S SHILLING

The empire sees unification of a whole, the impressed sees the parts being unified. The more emphasis there is on the parts during the process of unification (protesting too much?), the more space there is for the impressed to re-read within the structure set in place by the empire. The greater the effort in pressing into service to the empire, the more acknowledgment there is of a difficult fit and so more acknowledgment of difference. The method of impressment must therefore include instruction of how the impressed must function in the whole—how it must alter itself to fit—so that it can function peacefully in its new state of belonging. Instruction was part of military impressment.[31] In cultural impressment, that instruction comes in the narrative function of the story: demonstrating the glory of serving the empire and the futility of rebellion.

Hamlet's advice to the players who will perform his words is a famous one given to actors (who, frankly, tire of hearing it), that an actor should "hold, as t'were the mirror up to nature." Hamlet's advice is to do more than perform realistically and not chew the scenery. It holds more weight than that, considering the early modern ideas of the mirror and its purposes.[32] In *Will in the World*, Stephen Greenblatt uses Shakespeare's frequent images of mirrors and procreation in his discussion on Sonnet 18. Images of mirrors season Shakespeare's plays as well as his sonnets, and Greenblatt's point about the connections between them brings up Shakespeare's preoccupations with lineage and ancestry, with the functions of reflection and preservation, and with replication. Greenblatt unearths a central Shakespearean issue that can be explored in several ways.

The marriage, if you will, of mirrors and procreation in poetry points to, as Greenblatt points out, Shakespeare's focus on the preserving power of language.[33] A mirror reflects a image, but does not preserve it. The mirror's reflection is temporary, it exists only between the moment of stepping in front of it to look and the moment of stepping away. It expires with the removal of the object being reflected. The mirror acts as a means of instruction, as in the *Mirror for Magistrates* and other behavior manuals of the early modern period. A mirror held up to another, particularly if that other is in need of instruction, is a forced self-exploration, a way of showing how one appears in the empire's mirror. Shakespeare used language as a mirror to show Britons what they were and ought to be.

Language is the means to secure memory to a sustainable tether. It is the poet's labor that brings forth the image, and so the construction of language becomes an act of parentage, a creation of something that will reflect back to the world as the writer sees it. The writer is then a sort of mirror, holding him- or herself up to nature to show it what it is and the product, the language, is the reflection of the audience. The mirror reflects what is in front of it at the moment, but in the twentieth century's modernism and post-colonialism, the mirror is revealed to be cracked, and so the cracked mirror is, like Macmorris's service, like Richard's post-royal life, and like Hamlet's Purgatory, not entirely anything. It is a place of contending images, and yet static existence, held together by, and holding together, provisional truths. Understood only through the temporary certainties that surround it, its meaning comes from the strange space it inhabits between them. The focus would ordinarily be on the certainties, the things that can be seen and understood and pointed to. For Shakespeare, however, and for Irish writers who responded to his impressment of Ireland, certainties were not where the real story lay.

Like the image in a mirror, the instructive quality of showing the culturally impressed the whole they ought to see themselves belonging to is a vulnerable thing. Its instructive function collapses with its use because it is dependant on the person viewing the mirror. While the mirror is a totalizing object in the hands of the dominant imperial force, the acknowledged "part" of the empire which gazes into it sees only the parts being strung together.

Seamus Deane suggests that "The definition of otherness, the degree to which others can be persuasively shown to be discordant with the putative norm, provides a rationale for conquest."[34] Once conquered, the otherness has been named and cannot be consumed, since it was the rationale for subjection in the first place. The "rehearsed positions from which there is no exit" are positions of difference tied together by an imagined unity. The postcolonial story reinhabits the early modern subjugation to tell what Deane calls "the story of the fall of modern humankind from a state of bliss into the peculiarly modern condition of alienation."[35]

Shakespeare's becomes, for modernist post-colonial writers, a broken mirror to the impressed. The symbol of Irish art is the cracked lookinglass of a servant for Joyce's Stephen Daedalus. Salman Rushdie, another writer from a former British state, uses the cracked mirror to describe post-colonial experience as well, in the fragmentation of memory. Rushdie, who also understands the modern experience to be one of alienation, writes that "imaginative truth is simultaneously honourable and suspect" and so his narrator in *Midnight's Children,* who experiences independent India from its and his birth, is suspect in his narration. Rushdie suggests that "when the Indian writer who writes from outside India tries to reflect that world, he is obliged to deal in broken mirrors, some of whose fragments have been irretrievably lost." Used for describing the post-colonial experience, however, "the broken mirror may actually be as valuable as the one which is supposedly unflawed." It is Rushdie's word "supposedly" which animates the statement, because it inserts his idea of "provisional truths" into the idea that there was ever, could ever be, an unflawed totalizing view within the mirror. For Rushdie, the mirror is always suspect, and so a broken mirror at least acknowledges the fragmentation with which the post-colonial writer must grapple. Because of this, the broken mirror is "not merely a mirror of nostalgia. It is also . . . a useful tool with which to work in the present."[36]

When Karl Ragnar Gierow of the Swedish Academy introduced Samuel Beckett at the Nobel Laureate ceremony in 1969, he said: "Mix a powerful imagination with a logic inabsurdum, and the result will be either a paradox or an Irishman. If it is an Irishman, you will get the paradox into the bargain."[37] Beckett's experience was the colonial experience of paradoxical fragments—exile (real or metaphorical), a simultaneously collective and fractured sense of self and nationhood, an ambiguous relationship to language. Described through the cracked mirror, the experience is one of contention without resolution, of questions without answers. But by setting up a permanent fracturing, a permanent state of questioning, the empire creates a situation it cannot win and one in which its target can continually evade and seek to counter the attempted consumption. To be always both other and British is the inevitable result of cultural impressment: to attack the impressing force through its own language of conquest, to live in a city with both an English and a local name, to find oneself in a "superior" text as both drawn into the empire as its belonging and sacrificed to its totalizing goals.

Stephen Daedalus's observation, that there is a permanently servile and devastatingly fragmented existence in the lookinglass of the colonized subject,[38] anticipated the experience of millions of colonized subjects who discovered during the twentieth century the means to independence. Many of the nations that freed themselves from Britain in that century found themselves further fragmented: the British colony of India became India, Pakistan, and Bangladesh; Egypt and Anglo-Egyptian Sudan became Egypt and Sudan; the British mandate of Iraq became Iraq and Kuwait; the protectorate of Palestine became Israel and Palestine, two nations trying to occupy the same space; and the British colony of Ireland became The Republic of Ireland and Northern Ireland.[39] These areas, previously understood through the eyes of the master and so like each other in their non-Englishness, tore themselves into pieces in the search for ontological truths of difference. But through the difference, through the cracked mirrors of imagined homelands and pasts from which they have been separated, they can contend with the materials through which they were impressed. Although there are no winners, as in the Derry *Hamlet* there is no Fortinbras dashing in at the end and no happy ending for the poetic prince, the rest is not silence. The rest is words, through which the enlisted servants in British culture can use the ambiguity of the situation into which they were forced to cash in the king's shilling for a sovereign literature of their fragmented identity.

Notes

NOTES TO THE INTRODUCTION

1. Benedict Anderson, *Imagined Communities* (London: Verso, 1983). The quotation here is from page 6.
2. For a study of seventeenth-century uses of nostalgia in literature for defining order and national identity, see Leah S. Marcus, *The Politics of Mirth: Jonson, Herrick, Milton, Marvell, and the Defense of Old Holiday Pastimes* (Chicago: U of Chicago P, 1986). Marcus's study examines state-prompted historicizing of custom in order to codify order and subversion. According to Marcus, the state upheld its authority by sanctioning traditional celebrations and ceremonies, an endorsement which connected the state to customary national origins. The separation of celebration into an "escape-valve" holiday both allowed for subversion and set it apart from everyday rule and authority of order. Writers encouraged to respond to a state appeal to "public mirth" then created subversion in an atmosphere contained by the state, although they took "considerable liberty" with the "upheaval of hierarchy" which accompanies the atmosphere of festival (8).
3. David J. Baker, *Between Nations: Shakespeare, Spenser, Marvell and the Question of Britain* (Stanford: Stanford U P, 1997).
4. Richard Helgerson, *Forms of Nationhood: the Elizabethan Writing of England* (Chicago: Chicago U P, 1992) The phrase "the kingdom of our own language" acts as Baker's controlling idea for the study, and Baker uses the phrase for the title of the introduction, where he first introduces Spenser's idea.
5. Stephen Greenblatt, *Renaissance Self-Fashioning: From More to Shakespeare* (Chicago: U of Chicago P, 1980). Greenblatt's primary term for the focus of what was beginning to be called "New Historicism" was the "poetics of culture" (5). In later works, such as *Shakespearean Negotiations*, Greenblatt's use of "New Historicism" begins to eclipse the previous term, although the idea behind it, an examination of cultural practices as texts to be analyzed and texts as cultural practices, remains both his pivotal methodology and

the better descriptor for the direction towards which scholars continue to apply his theory.
6. Greenblatt, *Renaissance Self-Fashioning* 9.
7. Stephen Greenblatt, *Shakespearean Negotiations* (Berkeley: U of California P, 1988) 3.
8. Greenblatt, *Shakespearean Negotiations* 5.
9. Greenblatt, *Shakespearean Negotiations* 37.
10. The difference indicates a separation in their understandings of the subversion of dominant discourses by both the authors of plays and their critics—Sinfield's choice of words configures both author and critic as engaged in the construction of ideologies and Dollimore configures author and critic as engaged in thinking about and considering what is already there.
11. Jonathan Dollimore, *Radical Tragedy* (Durham: Duke U P, 1993) xxi.
12. Alan Sinfield, *Faultlines:Cultural Materialism and the Politics of Dissident Reading* (Berkeley: U of California P, 1992).
13. Sinfield 9.
14. Jonathan Dollimore, "Shakespeare, Cultural Materialism and the New Historicism," *Political Shakespeare*, ed. Jonathan Dollimore and Alan Sinfield, 2nd ed. (Ithaca: Cornell U P, 1985, 1994) 12.
15. Declan Kiberd, *Inventing Ireland* (Cambridge: Harvard U P, 1995) and *Irish Classics,* (Cambridge: Harvard U P, 2001).
16. Kiberd, *Inventing Ireland* 3. Kiberd's other major work, *Irish Classics,* is less applicable to my study and will not be used here.
17. Kiberd 6.
18. Kiberd 652.
19. Terry Eagleton, *Heathcliff and the Great Hunger* (London: Verso, 1995).
20. Eagleton 1–4.
21. Eagleton 127.
22. Edward Said, *Culture and Imperialism* (New York: Vintage, 1993).
23. Said, *Culture and Imperialism* 70–71.
24. Said, *Culture and Imperialism* 4.
25. Edward Said, *Reflections on Exile and Other Essays* (Cambridge: Harvard U P, 2000).
26. Said, "Reflections on Exile" 174.
27. Said, "Reflections on Exile" 178.
28. Said, "Reflections on Exile" 175.
29. Salman Rushdie, *Imaginary Homelands: Essays and Criticism 1981–1991* (London: Penguin, 1991). Rushdie does not cite or acknowledge Benedict Anderson's *Imagined Communities,* but the similarity in titles indicates a familiarity with Anderson's concept. Rushdie's title essay, however, is written from an intensely personal perspective which, while concerned with the place his past holds in his imagination, pertains more to the imagined past for an exile who is separated from that past.

30. Rushdie 15.
31. Rushdie,132.
32. Kiberd 271.
33. Kiberd 1.
34. For a short history of military impressment and a study of its representations in eighteenth-century British literature, see Dan Ennis, *Enter the Press Gang* (Newark: U of Delaware P, 2002).
35. Kiberd 37.
36. William Butler Yeats, "At Stratford-On-Avon," *Essays and Introductions* (New York: Collier, 1961) 103.

NOTES TO CHAPTER ONE

1. For more on the Essex Rebellion, see: Philip Edwards, *The Making of the Modern English State, 1460–1660* (New York: Palgrave, 2001) 212–215; or *The Oxford Companion to English History*, ed. John Cannon, Revised Ed. (Oxford: Oxford U P, 2002) 355; for more on the use of Richard II as part of Essex's attempted coup and the controversy surrounding the deposition scene, see David Bevington's introduction to the play in *The Complete Works of Shakespeare,* revised 4th ed., ed. David Bevington (New York: Longman, 1997) 721.
2. Richard Helgerson, *Forms of Nationhood: The Elizabethan Writing of England* (Chicago: Chicago U P, 1992) 1.
3. While upholding Tillyard's point about the Tudor Myth in general, Irving Ribner argues that such a reading is ridiculously simplistic and turns on Tillyard, pointing out that the primary problem with Tillyard's reading is that he reads it from *Richard II* to *Richard III* as a single unit, rather than seeing it as two separate units written with two sets of leads to investigate. Ribner argues of the second tetralogy that the stories of the Lancastrian rise were written under apprehension about the type of man who should succeed Elizabeth, and that the plays reflect this in their portrayal of different types of kings who hold characteristics believed to be essential for effective rule (157–167). See E. M. W. Tillyard, *The Elizabethan World Picture* (London: Chatto & Windus, 1943), and Irving Ribner, *The English History Play in the Age of Shakespeare* (Princeton: Princeton U P, 1957).

    Inside Shakespeare's plays, which may or may not be written with the goal of pleasing the wearer of the crown and supporting the myth of providential placement on the throne, are a number of monarchs who rise and fall through their own constructed myths. Most of these myths fail to completely secure the throne for the claimant. These monarchs and would-be monarchs construct their own myths of having a right to rule, and Shakespeare offers a variety of methods and degrees of success, investigating how kings construct their myths, and how those myths either succeed or fail. While Shakespeare certainly makes constructed mythology an important part of crown-snatching in the first tetralogy—York's creative and incantatory recitation of lineage, Richard III's ideals of might equals right, and Richmond's maritally and martially supported claims and appearance to save the country from the scourge of Richard III—Shakespeare seeks its source in the second tetralogy and the rise of the Lancastrians. Whether or not one subscribes to the Tillyardian idea of Shakespeare as publicist for the Tudor myth, something was started when Richard II was unkinged, something that made it possible for subjects of the king to see themselves as potential rulers.

4. Benedict Anderson, *Imagined Communities* (London: Verso, 1983) 11.
5. Anderson 12.
6. Ania Loomba makes much the same argument about Anderson's positioning of this phenomenon as one belonging to the eighteenth century in *Shakespeare, Race, and Colonialism* (Oxford: Oxford U P, 2002) 11. Loomba points out that "recent writers have traced the emergence of a similar dynamic in Elizabethan England," citing specifically, Liah Greenfeld, *Nationalism: Five Roads to Modernity* (Cambridge: Harvard U P, 1992).
7. Irving Ribner, *The English History Play in the Age of Shakespeare* (Princeton: Princeton U P, 1957) 9–10.
8. Ian Robinson argues that Thomas Cranmer's prose in *The Book of Common Prayer* is noteworthy for its ability to not only translate, but also transform, Latin into a thoroughly English prose which is remarkable for its indebtedness to the English writing tradition; see *The Establishment of Modern English Prose in the Reformation and the Enlightenment* (Cambridge: Cambridge U P, 1998). Robinson argues that, in fact, the thoroughness with which Cranmer did this renders the Prayer Book's "rhythm . . . so reliable that its extraordinary distinction can still be overlooked" (83). Cranmer's English prose in the Prayer Book was shifting English from a vulgar vernacular barely fit for courtly conversation to a language equal to Latin in its reverence. Robinson ends the chapter with the statement that "the well-formed sentence was developed in English not as a result of the activities of the Royal Society, to purify the language and make it fit for science, but to approach God" (103). If God was not an Englishman, the English language was at least fit for his Almighty ears.
9. For a collection of the full 1662 version with documents from the earlier 1549 version, with introduction by Diarmaid MacCulloch, see *The Book of Common Prayer* (London: Everyman, 1999). The preface to the 1549 Prayer Book gives its reasons for existence: the chaos that has resulted from differing "uses" in worship, radical omissions from the order of service chosen by individual priests and congregations, and the lack of spiritual searching that comes from repetition and recitation of a book one does not own (17–19). The preface concludes with advice on the appropriate means of refereeing disagreements and "diversity" in the use of the new Book. But the

Proclamation accompanying the 1548 Order of Communion demonstrates that the disagreements had been ongoing for some time and forced quick and repeated publication as an implementation of order. The new Book sought to halt chaos through edict. The direction of the ongoing reforms of the published liturgies was going to be one which made dissention answer to a divine law feared by those who did not fear the law of England. The Proclamation accompanying the 1548 Order of Communion is rife with language of unity and obedience. The Proclamation employs 551 words. The first 251 concern themselves almost entirely with statements of unity and reverence, the good of the country and the good of the church. In the latter half of the Proclamation words of conciliation overtake words of reverence and holiness: obedience, obedient, conformity, content, stay, quiet, quietness, and quietly all appear in the second 250 words (2). Subjects of the king are advised to "follow authority (according to the bounden duty of subjects)" rather than seeking to "arrogantly" follow "their own private authority."
10. Diarmaid MacCulloch, *The Boy King Edward VI and the Protestant Reformation* (Berkeley: U of California P, 2002) 11.
11. David J. Baker, *Between Nations: Shakespeare, Spenser, Marvell, and the Question of Britain* (Stanford: Stanford U P, 1997) 8.
12. Baker 12.
13. Baker 5–6.
14. Baker 14.
15. Current scholarly attempts to differentiate between "England" and "Britain" are important in order to draw distinctions for the works we read, but overzealous attempts to find such distinctions in the period may be anachronistic. The practice of naming is a tricky one, but the overlapping of name usage points to a fluidity in perception of boundaries, personalities of place, and community. In *The Napoleonic Wars: an Illustrated history, 1792–1815* (New York: Hippocrene, 1979), Michael Glover defends his synonymous use of "England" and "Britain" with the statement: "I must apologize to my Irish readers for using the term 'Britain' for what became in 1801 the United Kingdom, but Scottish and Welsh readers will expect no apology from me because Napoleon habitually referred to the whole of the United Kingdom as 'England.' It may be said in his defense that in his day most educated Scotsmen, Welshmen and Irishmen did the same" (2).
16. Stephen Greenblatt, *Shakespearean Negotiations* (Berkeley: U of California P, 1988) 37.
17. Nicholas Canny, *Making Ireland British, 1580–1650* (Oxford: Oxford U P, 2001) 64.
18. Canny 64–65.
19. Canny 123.
20. Richard Helgerson's *Forms of Nationhood* proves that this trend of national writing extended far beyond "literary" writing and into writing in several

disciplines—including law, cartography, travel and exploration, and theology. While Helgerson is careful in pointing out that this trend of national writing was not in any way an organized effort, he nevertheless demonstrates that a cultural trend was at work, in which writers from many disciplines fed from each other to explore Englishness in their written endeavors.

The history of the representation of Irishness as a foil for Englishness needs more scholarly attention; major explorations of the practice focus their attention on, or beginning shortly before, the early modern period. See *Representing Ireland: Literature and the Origins of Conflict, 1534–1660*, eds. Brendan Bradshaw, Andrew Hadfield, and Willy Maley (Cambridge: Cambridge U P, 1993); David Armitage, *The Ideological Origins of the British Empire* (Cambridge: Cambridge U P, 2000); Philip Edwards, *The Making of the Modern English State, 1460–1660* (New York: Palgrave, 2001); Nicholas Canny, *Making Ireland British, 1580–1650* (Oxford: Oxford U P, 2001); Patricia Palmer, *Language and Conquest in Early Modern Ireland: English Renaissance Literature and Elizabethan Imperial Expansion* (Cambridge: Cambridge U P, 2001); *British Identities and English Renaissance Literature*, eds. David J. Baker and Willy Maley (Cambridge: Cambridge U P, 2002).

21. Philip Sidney, "Discourse on Irish Affairs," *Miscellaneous Prose of Sir Philip Sidney*, eds. Katherine Duncan-Jones and Jan Van Dorsten (Oxford: Clarendon, 1973) 8–12.
22. Sidney 11.
23. Barnaby Riche, *A Short Survey of Ireland* (London, 1569) B2.
24. Riche, *A Short Survey* B2.
25. Riche, *The Irish Hubbub, or, The English Hue and Crie* (London, 1618) 6.
26. Riche, *The Irish Hubbub* Title page.
27. Riche, *The Irish Hubbub* 1–2.
28. Baker 74
29. The enchanted forest, for example, in Book I contains characters who represent both Catholic and pagan faiths. They mix and mingle freely, they work together, and they are always evil. The actions of ill-intent are treated equally in the tale, and those actions are frequently centered around permanently separating Redcrosse from Una, whose name means "truth." The implications of this being written at a time when the Protestant church in England was still vulnerable and when religion colored heavily the depiction and perceived origins of Irish "difference" are hard to miss.
30. Edmund Spenser, *A View of the State of Ireland*, eds. Andrew Hadfield and Willy Maley (Oxford: Blackwell, 1997) 85.
31. Spenser, *View* 21.
32. Spenser, *View* 20.
33. Spenser, *View* 20–21.
34. Spenser, *View* 85.
35. Spenser, *View* 93.

36. Spenser, *View* 93.
37. Spenser, *View* 54.
38. Andrew Murphy, *But the Irish Sea Betwixt Us: Ireland, Colonialism, and Renaissance Literature* (Lexington: U P of Kentucky, 1999) 66–79.
39. Helgerson 4.
40. Stephen Greenblatt, *Renaissance Self-Fashioning* (Chicago: U of Chicago P, 1980) 222.
41. Jonathan Bate, "Deep England," What DID Shakespeare Invent? Session, Shakespeare Association of America Annual Meeting, Fairmont New Orleans Hotel, New Orleans, 9 April 2004.
42. It was pointed out to Bate following the presentation that *The Merry Wives of Windsor* is set in a nearly-London area, but Bate countered that Windsor's being more of a suburb of London reinforces his point. I would like to add here that there are a few scenes in the Shakespeare canon set in London, but several are in Westminster which, like Windsor, is only more recently part of the metropolitan area. The others, specifically the tavern in Eastcheap, are in the City, but Eastcheap was, appropriately for Bate's theory, in an area of the city known for being a cattle market for outer-London farmers, and thus possibly the street with the most pastoral associations. More recently, Stanley Wells has mentioned that, while Shakespeare "draws upon London life in his English history plays, especially in the tavern scenes" of *Henry IV*, parts one and two, they are set in previous centuries, and so do not then have the "contemporary metropolitan associations" one finds in the works of Shakespeare's fellow writers. For more, see Stanley Wells, *Shakespeare & Co.:Christopher Marlowe, Thomas Dekker, Ben Jonson, Thomas Middleton, John Fletcher and the other Players in His Story* (New York: Pantheon, 2006) 106–107.
43. The OED defines "impress" as "To levy or furnish (a force) for military or naval service, to enlist; spec. To compel (men) to serve in the army or navy (in recent use, only the latter); to force authoritatively into service." The definition comes with the note that, before the end of the 16th century, this use of the word "was evidently felt as the same word as 'press'" or "'press into service.'" There are two uses of the word in this sense in Shakespeare. One is from *1 Henry IV:* "under whose blessed Crosse/ We are impressed and ingag'd to fight" (1.1.21). The other is from *Macbeth:* "Who can impresse the forest, bid the Tree Unvixe his earth-bound Root?" (4.1.95). The first demonstrates that, early in his career, Shakespeare was familiar enough with the concept to use it metaphorically as well as literally. The Henriad carries repeated scenes treating the problematic issues of military conscripts, volunteers, and substitutions—for example, Falstaff's description of the rag tag bunch he brings to fight Hotspur and company is that they are "food for powder."
44. William Soper, *The Navy of the Lancastrian Kings: accounts and inventories of William Soper, Keeper of the King's Ships, 1422–1427*, ed. Susan

Rose, Publications of the Navy Records Society, v. 123 (London: Allen & Unwin, 1982).
45. Soper 30.
46. Soper 36.
47. Soper 28.
48. Soper 47.
49. No relation to me. *The Autobiography of Joseph Bates* is available online at earlysda.com/bates/joseph-bates2–4.html.
50. *Autobiography of Joseph Bates,* Chapter III, par. 10.
51. Jonathan Dollimore, *Radical Tragedy: Religion, Ideology, and Power in the Drama of Shakespeare and His Contemporaries* (Durham: Duke U P, 1993) 60–61.
52. Terry Eagleton, *Heathcliff and the Great Hunger* (London: Verso, 1995) 260.
53. Eagleton 261.
54. Eagleton 269.
55. Declan Kiberd, *Inventing Ireland: The Literature of the Modern Nation* (Cambridge: Harvard U P) 29.
56. Kiberd 10.
57. Kiberd 268.
58. Kiberd 271.
59. Sandra Gilbert and Susan Gubar demonstrate that all male poets must write under the shadow of Milton, and it is the absence of a "grandmother" which operates as the driving absence-impetus for female writers. By the same token perhaps, Irish writers find themselves writing simultaneously as British writers and not as British writers, both in the shadow of that marvelous Brit, Shakespeare, and in response to him. See Sandra Gilbert and Susan Gubar, *The Madwoman in the Attic: The Woman Writer and the Nineteenth-Century Imagination,* 2nd ed. (New Haven: Yale U P, 2000).
60. Edward Said, "Between Worlds," *Reflections on Exile* (Cambridge: Harvard U P, 2000) 558.
61. Edward Said, "Between Worlds" 565.
62. English dominance creeping over the landscape of Ireland is startlingly captured in Brian Friel's 1980 play *Translations,* in which an English captain in charge of creating updated maps of the area either Anglicizes or outright renames the locations he is mapping. Brian Friel, *Translations* (London: Faber and Faber, 1995).

NOTES TO CHAPTER TWO

1. Alan Sinfield, Faultlines: *Cultural Materialism and the Politics of Dissident Reading* (Berkeley: U of California P, 1992) 127.
2. This is not to suggest that there were no problems with France during this period, since there have been problems between the English and the French

since 1066. But, at this time, the English soldiers being sent to France were there to assist the Protestant claimant Henry of Navarre in capturing the throne from the Catholic claimant of the house of Bourbon, and so were against only the Catholic French. See Philip Edwards, *The Making of the Modern English State,1460–1660* (London: Palgrave, 2001) 248.
3. Philip Henslowe, *Henslowe's Diary*, 2nd edition, ed. R. A. Foakes (Cambridge: Cambridge U P, 2002) 33–38.
4. Edmund Spenser, *A View of the State of Ireland*, 1598, ed. Andrew Hadfield and Willy Maley, (Oxford: Blackwell, 1997). Hadfield and Maley write that the Nine Years' War "almost succeeded in wresting Ireland from the grasp of the English Monarch and placing it under Spanish control." They are contexualizing the issues in Ireland as those issues relate to Edmund Spenser's writing, suggesting that his *View of the State of Ireland* was one part in a long history of work relating to questions of Britain and Ireland, rather than a textual anomaly which is subservient to his other, poetic, works (xx). But the issue they address of the English fear of Ireland as a potential conduit for Spanish invasion of England is one which Spenser also addresses at length in the text of the *View*, most prominently when Irenius works very hard to disconnect any legendary ethnic connection between Spain and Ireland through a convoluted discussion of ethnic origins (45–48).
5. For discussion of theses rebellions in detail, see Nicholas Canny, *Making Ireland British, 1580–1650* (Oxford: Oxford U P, 2001).
6. Sinfield's statement regarding Ireland, which I will be quoting at length, is from *Faultlines*, page 125.
7. Canny 124.
8. Sinfield 125.
9. It must be pointed out up front that, despite his getting comparatively little stage time, of the nation-captains, Macmorris seems to get most of the column inches in post-colonial criticism. Only a few critics, David J. Baker, notably, devote as much effort to exploring the implications of the other nation-captains (primarily Fluellen). See *Between Nations: Shakespeare, Spenser, Marvell and the Question of Britain* (Stanford: Stanford U P, 1997). But for critics interested in not just Ireland, but also questions of belonging, Macmorris is the natural candidate since, in asking "What ish my nation?" one of his few lines is also one of strongest questions of the play.
10. There is plenty of room to read questions of lineage and origin in terms of race and nation. Ania Loomba explores nuances of early modern use of the term "race" in *Shakespeare, Race, and Colonialism* (Oxford: Oxford U P, 2002) to find that fluidity in use of the word can indicate lineage, faith, and nation as well as class, gender, or any other grouping of people. She concludes that use of the word in colonialism is part of a process of systematizing in colonialism and that "Colonial attitudes and behaviour also traveled

from one context to another; English attitudes in America were shaped by their experiences in Ireland" (41).

11. The idea of "Britain" is a question always, and its construction is played out in different versions throughout early modern English literature. David J. Baker, in an anti-Tillyardian frustration with the concept that *Henry V*, or any other play, can represent a completed and universal ideology, points out that we should read *Henry V* "not as a fait accompli of Britishness but as an episode in its ongoing and (still today) unfinished construction" (*Between Nations*, 23). He focuses his work on *Henry V* in exploring the extent to which the "Britain" suggested in *Henry V* was a reality or a vision in process. Leonard Tennenhouse would seem to agree in "Strategies of State and Political Plays" from *Political Shakespeare*, 2nd ed., eds. Jonathan Dollimore and Alan Sinfield (Ithaca: Cornell U P, 1985) 109–128. Tennenhouse argues that in this play, "history is nothing else but the history of forms of disorder, over which Henry can temporarily triumph" and "make a discontinuous political process appear as a coherent moment" (120). In "Heritage and the Market, Regulation and Desublimation" from the same collection, Alan Sinfield defends Stephen Greenblatt against criticism for failing to see the Tudor Myth at work in Shakespeare's plays, when in fact Cultural Materialism in general works to explode the idea that any ideological system, however prominent or effective, is without detractors and, hence, the need for reinforcement (261–262). I believe that *Henry V*, as well as others of Shakespeare's plays, may operate within the period framework provided by the Tudor Myth, but is more invested in exploring the nature of power than they are in stating its infallibility. The room for dissident reading in *Henry V* may be best put by John E. Alvis in "Spectacle Supplanting Ceremony" when he writes that representing a process of unity does not mean representing a "tranquil England." See *Shakespeare as Political Thinker*, eds. John E. Alvis and Thomas G. West (Wilmington: ISI, 2000), 125.

12. Stephen Greenblatt, *Shakespearean Negotiations* (Berkely: U of California P, 1988) 56.

13. Declan Kiberd, *Inventing Ireland* (Cambridge: Harvard U P, 1995). Kiberd traces Macmorris's name and suggests that "he is a descendant of the Norman settlers of the Fitzmaurice clan, some of whom changed their surnames to the Gaelic prefix 'Mac': they remained politically loyal to the crown, despite their identification with Irish culture." Kiberd suggests also that Macmorris's emphasis on work instead of chat at Harfleur "has its roots in his pained awareness that a figure of such hybrid will forever be suspect in English eyes" (12–13). I would point out that it is Fluellen to whom Macmorris makes a point of demonstrating his own dedication, and that Kiberd, whose argument is eminently useful, nevertheless overestimates the Welsh Fluellen's judgment and conception of usefulness.

14. Kiberd 12.

15. Pistol, who learns to fit in with responsible people, is barely acknowledged by the king and falls out of his close company but nevertheless remains in his service. He is thus an example of Henry's shedding of old companions and at the same time something of an exception. While he has not been eliminated entirely, it is not likely Pistol will find himself sharing a pint with his old pal Hal at the tavern again.
16. Sinfield 124.
17. Ernst H. Kantorowicz, *The King's Two Bodies: A Study in Mediaeval Political Theology* (Princeton: Princeton U P, 1957). Kantorowicz's lengthy study does focus on *Richard II* rather than *Henry V*, but discussion of the Body Politic or the Corporal Body comes up often in criticism of *Henry V*.
18. John E. Alvis, in a discussion of "the bonds of comradeship based on mutual usefulness," contends that in "Loving what the king loves and venturing their lives for that for which the king risks his life, they become one with him in a way that no servile subject can know" (109).Using terms like Kantoriwicz's, Alvis investigates the St. Crispin's Day speech in terms of the ceremony so crucial to the Body Politic. See *Shakespeare as Political Thinker*, eds. John E. Alvis and Thomas G. West (Wilmington: ISI, 2000).While he focuses on Bates, Williams, and Court for examples of servants of the king, much of what he writes could be seen to apply to the nation-captains. I would argue, however, that being "one" with the king does not preclude being "servile."
19. Why allow the voicing of Macmorris's confusion in national identity? Perhaps, as Stephen Greenblatt conjectures, "power is not monolithic" and must record its dissenters in order to continue to justify itself (*Shakespearean Negotiations*, 37).
20. In *Political Shakespeare*, Jonathan Dollimore points out more generally in "Shakespeare, cultural materialism and the new historicism" that "appropriation could also work the other way: subordinate, marginal or dissident elements could appropriate dominant discourses and likewise transform them in the process" (12). Subversion does not have to refuse the terms of the discourse, but can instead reinscribe them as they have been traditionalized in order to point out the problems and bring to light the unjustness of the discourse as it has been used.
21. Kiberd 12–13.
22. This line from critic James Agate's review of *Juno and the Paycock* is quoted by Christopher Murray in his introduction to O'Casey's *Three Dublin Plays* (London: Faber and Faber, 1998) ix. All quotes from *Juno and the Paycock* will be from this edition.
23. Murray x.
24. O'Casey, *Juno and the Paycock* 77.
25. O'Casey 115.
26. Terry Eagleton, *Heathcliff and the Great Hunger* (London: Verso, 1995) 314.
27. Eagleton 314.

28. Jeremy Bentham, 1748–1832, entered into the political fray with *A Fragment on Government* (published in 1776). His work on governmental and economic reform is still studied, and his preserved body can still be viewed (original except for the head, which had to be replaced with wax eventually) at the University of London. "Benthamite" became synonymous with "utilitarian."
29. O'Casey 133.
30. O'Casey 147.
31. O'Casey 148.
32. O'Casey 88.
33. Norman Vance, *Irish Literature Since 1800* (London: Longman, 2002) 158.
34. All quotations from the play will be from Beckett's own translation: *Waiting for Godot: A Tragicomedy in Two Acts* (New York: Grove, 1954).
35. Beckett 11.
36. Beckett 9.
37. Kiberd 538.
38. Kiberd 538.
39. Vance 157.
40. Beckett 91.
41. Beckett 67.
42. Beckett 2.
43. Beckett 62–63.
44. Beckett 14.

NOTES TO CHAPTER THREE

1. Jonathan Dollimore, *Radical Tragedy* 2nd ed. (Durham: Duke U P, 1993) xxi.
2. Dollimore goes on to discuss Franco Moretti and the idea of tragedy as an exception to "literature as a conservative form." Moretti contends that tragedy "'contributed, more radically than any other cultural phenomenon of the same period, to discrediting the values of absolute monarchy, thereby paving the way with wholly destructive means, for the English Revolution'" (xxiii). The text under discussion is not, in fact, a tragedy, it is *Measure for Measure,* and Dollimore goes on to explain a reading which uses Moretti to refute F. R. Leavis's attempt to separate complexity from conflict (xxiii).
3. Terence Hawkes, "Bringing Home the Bard," Presented at MLA 2005, Philadelphia as the opening paper of "Presentism and the End of History on Shakespeare Studies." The session focused on the place which presentism has held and lost in Cultural Materialism—not something this study deals with—but nationalism necessarily came to the forefront many times, and Hawkes's cleverism was so appealing that I had to use it.

4. Edward Said, "Reflections on Exile," *Reflections on Exile and Other Essays* (Cambridge: Harvard U P, 2000) 173–186.
5. Said 171.
6. Said 174.
7. Said 175.
8. Said 176.
9. Absentee landlords were an obvious problem for the Irish, who saw their lands turned over to English landlords who seldom bothered to appear there, but were also a serious problem for the English government, which went to some effort to legislate the problem away and force the English owners to spend at least some time on their Irish estates. See Nicholas Canny, *Making Ireland British, 1580–1650* (Oxford: Oxford U P, 2001), chapter 4.
10. Said 177.
11. John Julius Norwich, *Shakespeare's Kings, The Great Plays and the History of England in the Middle Ages:1337–1485* (New York: Touchstone, 1999) 98.
12. Norwich 82.
13. Norwich 87–91.
14. Norwich 73.
15. Charles R. Forker, ed., Introduction, *Richard II,* William Shakespeare (London: Arden, 2002) 67.
16. Forker 3.
17. Joseph Papp, Forward, *Richard II,* William Shakespeare, ed. David Bevington (New York: Bantam, 1980) xv. All other references to the play are from David Bevington, ed., *Richard II, The Complete Works of William Shakespeare,* Updated 4th ed. (New York: Longman, 1997).
18. The argument between Mowbray and Bolingbroke at the opening of the play comes from Bolingbroke's accusation that Mowbray was involved in some way in the death of Thomas of Woodstock, Henry's and Richard's uncle (the youngest brother of Edward the Black Prince and John of Gaunt). The argument in 4.1 involving Aumerle *et al* with the preposterous throwing down of gages also comes from Bagot's accusing Aumerle of the murder. Historical accounts, such as John Julius Norwich's, point out that Richard was unhappy with his uncles' interference, and that Woodstock's power irritated him; see *Shakespeare's Kings: The Great Plays and the History of England in the Middle Ages, 1337–1485.* Whether or not Richard did, in fact, order the murder of Woodstock is open to question, and goes a long way towards confusing sympathy with Richard.
19. David Bevington, introduction to *Richard II, The Complete Works of Shakespeare,* updated 4th ed. (New York: Longman, 1997) 724. The reference is slightly inaccurate—Yeats is actually comparing Richard II to Henry V, but the description certainly fits in a comparison of Richard with his immediate adversary and Hal's father, Bolingbroke. For the essay

Bevington is quoting, see: W. B. Yeats, "At Stratford-on-Avon," *Essays and Introductions* (New York: Collier, 1961) 108. The full quote from Yeats reads: " . . . having made the vessel of porcelain, Richard II, he had to make the vessel of clay, Henry V. He makes him the reverse of all that Richard was. He has the gross vices, the coarse nerves, of one who is to rule among violent people, and he is so 'too friendly' to his friends that he bundles them out of doors when their time is over." Yeats continues in this vein, effectively dismissing heroism in the character of Henry V, and almost victoriously pointing out that Henry's successes were short-lived. The truncated quote, while a memorable description for the characters, fails to deliver the venom with which Yeats increasingly describes this "reverse of Richard."
20. Declan Kiberd, *Inventing Ireland* (Cambridge: Harvard U P, 1995).
21. Kiberd 268–269.
22. W. B. Yeats, "At Stratford-on-Avon," *Essays and Introductions* (New York: Collier, 1961) 102–3.
23. Yeats 104.
24. Yeats 104.
25. Edward Dowden, *Shakespeare: A Critical Study of His Mind and Art* (London: Routledge & Kegan Paul, 1875).
26. Dowden 74.
27. Dowden 73.
28. Dowden 75.
29. Dowden 194.
30. Dowden 199.
31. Kiberd 269.
32. George Bernard Shaw, *John Bull's Other Island* (London: Constable and Co., 1926) vi.
33. Shaw, *John Bull* v.
34. Shaw, *John Bull* viii.
35. Shaw, *John Bull* vii.
36. Shaw, *John Bull* vii.
37. George Bernard Shaw, "The Dying Tongue of Great Elizabeth," First published in *The Saturday Review*, 11 February 1905, Collected in *Shaw On Shakespeare*, ed. Edwin Wilson (New York: Applause, 1961) 140–149.
38. Shaw, *Shaw On Shakespeare* 141.
39. Shaw, *Shaw On Shakespeare* 143.
40. Shaw's contribution to a memoir collection for Beerbohm Tree, reprinted in Shaw's *Pen Portraits and Reviews*. Collected in *Shaw On Shakespeare*, ed. Edwin Wilson (New York: Applause, 1961) 253–254.
41. Shaw, *Shaw On Shakespeare* 253.
42. Shaw, *Shaw On Shakespeare* 254.
43. Shaw, *Shaw On Shakespeare* 254.

NOTES TO CHAPTER FOUR

1. Declan Kiberd, *Inventing Ireland* (Cambridge MA: Harvard U P, 1995) 122.
2. From lines 2,3, and 7. Seamus Heaney, "Whatever you say say nothing," *North* (London: Faber & Faber, 1975) 51–54.
3. Ciaran Carson, "Hamlet," *Belfast Confetti* (Winston-Salem: Wake Forest U P, 1989) 105–108. (This quote from page 106).
4. Carson 108.
5. Many believe that this "Ur-Hamlet" was by Thomas Kyd, but both the play and its authorship are, of course, lost. The story appears to originate with the *Historia Danica* of Saxo Grammaticus (1180–1208) and reappears in French in François de Belleforest's *Histoires Tragiques* (1576). The play called the Ur-Hamlet is frequently attributed to Kyd because of Thomas Nashe's vicious mention of it in his prefatory epistle "to Gentlemen Students of both universities" in *Menaphon,* in the late 1580's, prior to Shakespeare's *Hamlet.* Kyd, like Shakespeare, was without a university education, and would have fallen under the scorn of a university wit like Nashe, in a rebuke similar to Robert Greene's "Groats Worth of Wit" which so famously mentions Shakespeare. There are scholars who consider the possibility that the Ur-Hamlet was an earlier version by Shakespeare, Harold Bloom is one of them; see *The Invention of the Human* (New York: Riverhead, 1998) 383. This seems unlikely for several reasons, not the least of which is that Shakespeare was not known to have written any plays twice, but was rather much more likely to revamp a play by someone else, and frequently did. Scholarship attributing the Ur-Hamlet to Kyd includes Stephen Greenblatt, *Will in the World* (New York: Norton, 2004) 203, 294–322; and David Bevington, *The Complete Works of Shakespeare,* updated 4th ed. (New York: Longman, 1997) 1064. Records of the Ur-Hamlet are summarized in *Hamlet,* ed. Harold Jenkins (London: Methuen, 1982) 82–85.
6. Stephen Greenblatt, *Hamlet in Purgatory* (Princeton: Princeton U P, 2001) 247–248.
7. Barnaby Riche, "A Short Survey of Ireland," London, 1569. Riche's work, ostensibly on Ireland, is much more about Catholicism in general and devotes entire chapters to no fewer than six "marks whereby to know the Antichrist," his consistent name for the Pope. Riche is certain that there are good people in Ireland, but is clear to him that they are corrupted and preyed upon by Catholic priests and other rebels, who force the people to defy the crown.
8. The term "ghostly father" is used to indicate a priest, usually specifying a confessor, in the Catholic faith, in the traditional use of the word "ghostly" to refer to things spiritual. The OED defines the combined term in part 1c. as "a father confessor" and connects it to the similar terms "ghostly advisor" or "director," as well as "ghostly comfort" or "counsel," and states that the

term is "used esp. with reference to what is rendered by a priest to a penitent or one near death." The term "ghostly father" is dated in the OED back to 1290 to refer to a priest (actually, "ghostly fader") and this usage is again given in 1536. The OED also uses a quote from Shakespeare's *Romeo and Juliet* (3.3.49) for the 1592 reference "A Ghostly Confessor." But use of the term "ghostly" has farther reaching applications not specific to members of the clergy and can be used rather as an adjective to remove earthly implications from the proceeding word. Use of the word to refer to ghosts or "disembodied spirits," a use certainly applicable to *Hamlet*, is included as well in part 5 and dates as far back as 1000 and 1300, but is spelled with an "a" instead of an "o," so that the word is potentially conflated with "ghastly." Parts 1–4, however, define the word as pertaining to spiritual or sacred things and are given specifically religious uses.

9. I am operating on the assumption that Hamlet is not actually insane. He does have the excess of emotion that would have qualified to some extent as a symptom of madness, but he deliberately states that he will "put an antic disposition on," and he is very much in control of the situation whenever he is acting the most insane. What is more, Shakespeare gives us a representation of true madness in Ophelia, a state far more obviously insane than any Hamlet pretends to. Perhaps Shakespeare gave us Ophelia's madness in part to demonstrate that Hamlet really is acting the part of madness—he decides to pretend to madness, and he comes out of it, whereas Ophelia's madness ends in death. Hamlet may consider suicide as a possibility, but Ophelia completes it, whether or not intentionally.

10. Greenblatt, *Hamlet in Purgatory* 229.

11. Marjorie Garber argues that this instruction is less clear than it might initially appear to be. Examining the ghost as a *momento mori* which conflates the interchangeable "thresholds" of the "visionary and the visual," Garber sees the ghost as serving the purpose of a reminder of death. For Hamlet to follow this instruction to "Remember me" is to be guided by the father but also to be recalled to the knowledge of death's inevitablity. The instruction provides "a conundrum for Hamlet, a text he must interpret and unpack" and the dramatic action of the play is Hamlet's interpretation of the ghost's direction. See Marjorie Garber, "'Remember Me': *Momento Mori* Figures in Shakespeare's Plays," *Renaissance Drama* 12 (1981) 3–25. The discussion of Hamlet's response to the ghost, and the quotations used here, are from pages 3 and 4.

12. The original Latin text of the *Purgatorio* is available from an edition by Robert Easting, *St. Patrick's Purgatory: Two Versions of Owayne Miles and The Vision of William of Stranton together with the Long Text of the Tractatus De Purgatorio Sancti Patricii*, Early English Text Society (Oxford: Oxford U P, 1991). For a very readable translation, see *Saint Patrick's Purgatory: A Twelfth Century Tale of a Journey to the Other World*, trans. Jean-Michel

Picard (Dublin: Four Courts, 1985). Much of the history of the pilgrimage site included in this chapter comes from Yolande de Pontfarcy's informative introduction to the translated edition.

The highly condensed version of information offered here, combined from Stephen Greenblatt's lengthy history of Purgatory (pages 47–101) in *Hamlet in Purgatory* and from the introduction to the Jean-Michel Picard translation of *Saint Patrick's Purgatory,* is truncated to highlight the Irish associations with Purgatory. Greenblatt's chapter is, necessarily, much broader and serves to reveal deep and passionate theological debates between Protestants and Catholics over the existence of Purgatory, the selling of indulgences and prayers, and the church corruption which fed on a medieval belief that living actions could shorten the Purgatorial tenure of a soul. While Greenblatt provides early texts which reveal the Medieval doctrine of Purgatory, his focus is necessarily on the rift in late sixteenth and early seventeenth religious ideologies created by the Protestant rejection of Purgatory and an application of that rift to a reading of *Hamlet*. Readers interested in an examination of Purgatory's appearance in earlier literature should consult Carol G. Zaleski's "St. Patrick's Purgatory: Pilgrimage Motifs in a Medieval Otherworld Vision," *Journal of the History of Ideas,* 46 (Oct.-Dec. 1985) 467–485.

13. Greenblatt, *Hamlet in Purgatory*. Greenblatt lists Holinshed on 75–76. Shakespeare was certainly very familiar with Holinshed's history of England, and whether or not he was familiar with the work on Ireland, stories of the Irish entrance to Purgatory were widespread enough to be generally known. Greenblatt also lists on page 84 other, continental, versions of the tale by Marie de France, Pérez de Montalbán, Lope de Vega, and Calderón de la Barca which were written after Shakespeare's *Hamlet,* demonstrating that the medieval legend was still in place in the early and mid-seventeenth century.

14. Greenblatt, *Hamlet in Purgatory* 95, 99.

15. Mourning clothes, in black, as well as specially made mourning jewelry, were customary in England from the Middle Ages. The period of mourning varied depending on the relationship to the departed, but mourning for a parent could extend to three or four years. The period of mourning for a widow ended upon remarriage, so Gertrude's mourning is significantly more flexible than Hamlet's. For more on the customs of mourning, see Kathy Lynn Emerson, *Everyday Life in Renaissance England: from 1485–1649* (Cincinnati: F&W, 1996) 70.

16. Greenblatt is quoting Caxton, writing in 1480, in a highly Protestant tract which reported the tales while seriously questioning their validity. *Hamlet in Purgatory* 94.

17. Greenblatt takes these terms from a speech from Brutus in *Julius Caesar:* "Between the acting of a dreadful thing/ And the first motion, all the interim is/ Like a phantasma or a hideous dream" (2.1.63–69). Greenblatt argues

that, as Shakespeare's career continued, he developed the technical skill to widen the structural space between that "first motion" and the "acting of the dreadful thing" in order to represent inwardness, and inward insurrection. Stephen Greenblatt, *Will in the World* (New York: Norton, 2004) 302–303.
18. Greenblatt avoids wading in too definitively to scholarly debate on Shakespeare's personal faith, but rather suggests him as caught in the middle of a time we mistakenly read in extremes. Chapter 3 of *Will in the World*, called "The Great Fear," places Shakespeare in infamously-recusant Lancashire during both a formative time in his own life and a crucial time of recusant subversion in Elizabeth's reign. Greenblatt presents extensive evidence that Shakespeare served as a tutor in recusant households before returning to Stratford, and that Will's father, while ostensibly Protestant for the sake of his office, was nevertheless a recusant who signed a "spiritual last will and testament" that had been secretly circulated by Jesuits. Greenblatt suggests that Shakespeare evidenced no concrete ties to either Protestantism or Catholicism in his later life; he argues rather that, while for reasons of security John Shakespeare "was both Catholic and Protestant," Will, traumatized by the danger of the conflict and fascinated by the charisma of men on both sides, "was on his way to being neither." 113.
19. Greenblatt, *Hamlet in Purgatory* 13–14.
20. Greenblatt, *Hamlet in Purgatory* 16–17.
21. Greenblatt writes that while Purgatory could be ridiculed in an attempt to dispel it as a theory, it could not be "represented as a frightening reality. Hamlet comes closer to doing so than any other play of this period. But Shakespeare, with his remarkable gift for knowing exactly how far he could go without getting into serious trouble, still only uses a network of allusions: 'for a certain term,' 'burned and purged away,' 'Yes, by Saint Patrick,' '*hic et ubique.*'" *Hamlet in Purgatory* 236–237
22. Hamlet describes Elsinore as a prison, but removes any association with a physical prison and instead gives it a spiritual and metaphorical dimension when he tells Rosencrantz and Guildenstern: "I could be bounded in a nutshell and count myself a king of infinite space, were it not that I have bad dreams." The prison is a place like dreams—the space between sleeping and waking—and is then itself a kind of Purgatory. (2.2.254–258)
23. Greenblatt, *Hamlet in Purgatory* 229.
24. Kiberd 32.
25. Eagleton 256.
26. Eagleton 256–257.
27. Eagleton 127.
28. James Joyce, 18. All references to this work come from *Ulysses: The Complete and Unabridged Text, as Corrected and Reset in 1961* (1934), (New York: Vintage International, 1990).
29. Joyce 201.

Notes to Chapter Four

30. Joyce 212.
31. Joyce 208.
32. Vincent John Cheng, *Shakespeare and Joyce: A Study of Finnegan's Wake* (University Park: Pennsylvania U P, 1984) 73–74.
33. Hugh Kenner, *Ulysses,* Revised ed. (Baltimore: Johns Hopkins U P, 1987) 111.
34. Joyce 200.
35. Joyce 192.
36. Joyce 193.
37. Kenner 112.
38. Joyce 185.
39. Joyce 198.
40. Joyce 198.
41. Joyce 190.
42. Joyce 188.
43. Joyce 189.
44. Joyce 208.
45. Joyce 197.
46. Joyce 197–198.
47. Joyce 212. It must be added here that Joyce himself is read as both Stephen (beginning with Stephen Hero and *A Portrait of the Artist as a Young Man*) and as Leopold Bloom. The journey in *Ulysses* is Bloom's journey through a day in Dublin, but Stephen holds a large place in the work as well. Many of Stephen's concerns as an artist are Joyce's, but Bloom's family life, and the positioning of Joyce's wife Nora as Bloom's wife Molly, create a new overlapping sense of father and son in the novel. For more on this see Sydney Bolt, *A Preface to Joyce,* 2nd ed. (Edinburgh: Pearson, 1992) 97–98. Bolt, too, reads Joyce as contending with the greatness of Shakespeare and presenting Stephen as needing the same identification as well. Bolt reports that Joyce admired Shakespeare above all other writers because of his "richness," which Joyce understood as a "complex density" (102). A "complex density" certainly describes Joyce's work as well.
48. Kenner 113.
49. Joyce 194.
50. Joyce 213–214.
51. Joyce 218.
52. Joyce 218.
53. William H. Quillian, *Hamlet and the New Poetic: James Joyce and T. S. Eliot* (Ann Arbor: UMI Research P, 1983) 36.
54. Kiberd 39.
55. Kiberd 329.
56. Salman Rushdie, "Is Nothing Sacred?" *Imaginary Homelands: Essays and Criticism 1981–1991* (London: Penguin, 1991) 423.

57. Rushdie 423.
58. Rushdie 422.

NOTES TO CHAPTER FIVE

1. Stephen Cavanagh, dir., *Hamlet*, perf. Stephen Cavanagh and Colin Stewart, Derry Film Initiative, 2005.
2. George Bernard Shaw, "The Religion of the Pianoforte," First published in *The Fortnightly Review*, February 1894, Collected in *Shaw On Shakespeare*, ed. Edwin Wilson (New York: Applause, 1961) 246.
3. Sir John Gilbert's illustrations of Shakespeare's works are available in *The Globe Illustrated Shakespeare: The Complete Works Annotated*, ed. Howard Staunton (New York: Gramercy Books, 1979). The opening illustration for *Hamlet*, the only one containing the figure of Fortinbras, is on page 1850.
4. Seamus Heaney, "Whatever you say say nothing," *North* (London: Faber & Faber, 1975) 51–54.
5. Ulster remains the location of the most intense sectarian violence, particularly in the cities of Portadown, Belfast, and Derry/Londonderry. Ulster's history is even darker than that of the area now in the Republic: the failure of Tyrone's rebellion in 1607 led many to flee and leave massive areas of land in Ulster open for James I to confiscate. Redistribution of lands to those loyal to the crown and a carefully managed program of colonization continued, despite some resistance. Religious conflict grew, but William of Orange's decisive victory at the Battle of the Boyne in 1690 left little question as to who would remain in control of the area. The Ulster Orangemen still march on 12 July to celebrate the victory. The marches are routed through the Catholic areas of the cities, and the march almost routinely sparks off violence. What is known as the Orange Order, more formally called the Loyal Orange Institution, was founded in 1795 and held its first parade commemorating William III's victory at the Battle of the Boyne the following year. This organization claims that the parade routes are "traditional" and the violence is instigated by the IRA for political gain, whereas Catholic residents claim that the parade routes are deliberately chosen to cause conflict. In 1999, British troops constructed barricades, trenches, and moats to reroute the march in Portadown (the founding city of the Orange Order). In March of 2005, the Orange Order broke off its historic association with the Ulster Unionist Party, with the Party's assent, over concessions given to Sinn Fein in the Good Friday accord. General histories on Ireland and religious conflict include *The Oxford History of Ireland*, ed. R. F. Forster (Oxford: Oxford U P, 2001), Forster's earlier history *Modern Ireland:1600–1972* (London: Penguin, 1990), and Nicholas Canny's *Making Ireland British:1580–1650*

(Oxford: Oxford U P, 2001). Histories of more recent events include Tim Pat Coogan's *The Troubles:Ireland's Ordeal 1666–1996 and the Search for Peace* (New York: Palgrave, 2002), and Brian Feeney's *Sinn Fein:A Hundred Turbulent Years* (Madison: U of Wisconsin P, 2003)
6. Seamus Heaney, "Bone Dreams," *North* (London: Faber & Faber, 1975) 19–23.
7. Investigation of the paradigm of the colonial participation in systems brought in by the oppressor has developed through Benedict Anderson's *Imagined Communities* (London: Verso, 1983), which examines patterns in the collective work of nationalist movements and applied more specifically to literature and imperial control in Edward Said's *Culture and Imperialism* (New York: Vintage, 1994). Perhaps the most useful application of it for this study is Seamus Deane's introduction to the combined work of Terry Eagleton, Frederic Jameson, and Edward Said in Irish Literature: *Nationalism, Colonialism, and Literature* (Minneapolis: U of Minnesota P, 1990).
8. Salman Rushdie, *Midnight's Children* (London: Penguin, 1980).
9. This is discussed at more length in Chapters One and Three, primarily in the placement, removal, and replacement of Sir Philip Sidney's father, Henry Sidney, Lord Grey as Lord Chamberlain of Ireland. Queen Elizabeth frustrated her councillors repeatedly with her reluctance to resort to violent measures to quell Ireland.
10. The original full text proclamation uses similar words; the summary can be found in *Tudor and Stuart Proclamations—A Bibliography of Royal Proclamations of the Tudor and Stuart Sovereigns 1485–1714*, ed. Robert Steele (Clarendon: Oxford 1910).
11. In 1570, Pope Pius V excommunicated Elizabeth and declared her subjects free from obedience to her (on pain of excommunication themselves). Pope Gregory XIII found excommunication too light and declared that any who wished to kill the queen would be absolved from the sin of murder in that case. For more on the relationship between Queen Elizabeth and theVatican, see Carolly Erickson, *The First Elizabeth* (New York: Summit, 1983).
12. Salman Rushdie, "Imaginary Homelands," *Imaginary Homelands: Essays and Criticism 1981–1991* (London: Penguin, 1991) 9–21. Quotation from page 12.
13. Rushdie, "Imaginary Homelands" 12.
14. Jonathan Dollimore, *Radical Tragedy* (Durham: Duke U P, 1984) 60.
15. Seamus Deane, Introduction, *Nationalism, Colonialism, and Literature* (Minneapolis: U of Minnesota P, 1990) 13.
16. Deane 15.
17. Deane 19.
18. Rushdie, "Imaginary Homelands" 17.

19. Perhaps, however, Rushdie is on to something with the idea of mastery in English. Irish recipients of the Nobel Prize in Literature are William Butler Yeats (1923) George Bernard Shaw (1925), Samuel Beckett (1969), and Seamus Heaney (1995). Writers from other former British holdings have been awarded for their writing in English, including Derek Walcott from Saint Lucia (1992) and V. S. Naipaul who was born of Indian immigrants in Trinidad (2001). The list of Nobel Laureates in Literature, along with biographies and transcripts of introductions and speeches, is available at nobelprize.org/literature/laureates/index.html.
20. James Joyce, *A Portrait of the Artist as a Young Man* (London: Penguin, 1964) 203.
21. Deane 10.
22. Rushdie 17.
23. George Bernard Shaw, "Shakes Versus Shav," *Shaw on Shakespeare,* ed. Edwin Wilson (New York: Applause, 1961) 265–269.
24. Shaw 265.
25. Shaw 266.
26. Shaw 266–267.
27. Shaw 267–268.
28. Shaw 268.
29. Shaw 269.
30. Dollimore 60–61.
31. See Chapter One and the *Autobiography of Joseph Bates.* Bates recounts having been given access to shared copies of *The Book of Common Prayer* and the *Life of Nelson* soon after being impressed on a British ship. The books were distributed to calm the impressed sailors and to instruct them as to their duties and obligations.
32. The cracked mirror appears occasionally as an identifying post-colonial mark and works as a means of describing the fragmentation of the colonial self and the fractured identity of the exile. An investigation of mirror imagery in Shakespeare and its relationship to the cracked post-colonial mirror could lead to a whole study in itself. Some general resources on mirrors include Herbert Grabes's *The Mutable Glass: Mirror-imagery in Titles and Texts of the Middle Ages and the English Renaissance* (Cambridge: Cambridge U P, 1982) and Philippa Kelley's "Surpassing Glass: Shakespeare's Mirrors" *Early Modern Literary Studies* 8.1 (2002): 21–32. The most encompassing study of the function of the mirror is Sabine Melchior-Bonnet's *The Mirror: A History,* trans. Katharine H. Jewett (New York: Routledge, 1994, 2002).
33. Stephen Greenblatt, *Will in the World* (New York: Norton, 2004) 238.
34. Deane 12.
35. Deane 9.
36. Rushdie, "Imaginary Homelands" 11, 12.

Notes to Chapter Five

37. nobelprize.org/literature/laureates/1969/press.html.
38. Stephen makes the statement while shaving in a mirror. Buck teases Stephen with Oscar Wilde's quote from the preface to *The Picture of Dorian Grey:* "The rage of Caliban at not seeing his face in a mirror." Stephen counters with: "It is a symbol of Irish art. The cracked lookingglass of a servant." James Joyce, *Ulysses* (New York: Vintage, 1990) 6. Stephen modifies Buck's more traditional observation of Caliban, who cursed Prospero in the language he was taught to speak—instead offering an image, not of one who fails to find himself in the mirror the master gives him, but of one who finds only fragments of his image in reflection.
39. The English East India Company established trade in India in around 1610, and was augmented by the Portugese trade interests which came to England as part of Catherine of Braganza's dowry when she married Charles II in 1662. The crown gained sovereign control in 1857, openly acknowledged when Queen Victoria added "Empress of India" to her list of titles. India gained independence in 1947, agreeing to the partitioning of Pakistan, and Bangladesh split from India the following year. India, which is primarily Hindu, and Pakistan, which has Islamic ties with the Middle East, are still battling over the territory of Kashmir.

    Egypt's primary attraction for the British was the Suez Canal, which allowed trade access to India. The British occupied Egypt to take control of the canal in 1882. The country was declared a British protectorate in 1914, but Egypt gained control of all but the canal in 1922 and finally gained independence in 1952. The Sudan, which had previously been an Egyptian dependancy, was re-conquered by the British for Egypt in 1898. Sudan gained its own independence in 1956.

    Iraq became a British mandate under the League of Nations after WWI. The mandate was relinquished in 1932 and Iraq once again became independent. It did so, however, without the territory of Kuwait, which became a separate country that gained its independence from Britain in 1961. Considering Kuwait to be rightfully a part of Iraq, and a part rich in the oil that drives what there is of Iraq's economy, the Iraqi government invaded Kuwait in 1990, setting off the First Gulf War.

    Palestine became a British mandate in 1922 and was beset by difficulties from the beginning. Supporting Jewish immigration, the British were assisted by the United Nations in an attempted partitioning of Palestine into separate Jewish and Palestinian states in 1948. But the British were hardly gone before civil war broke out and Israel declared itself a sovereign nation the same year. The fighting has yet to cease.

    Ireland's first English military invasion came under the reign of Henry II in 1171. Ireland's many rebellions through the following eight centuries culminated in desperate fighting at the beginning of the twentieth century and finally the Anglo-Irish Treaty of 1921, which granted free republic status to all of Ireland but the six Ulster counties. The result, with the Republic of Ireland in the south and Northern Ireland in the still British-controlled north, has been one of violence and anger that continues still.

This information, necessarily simplified, can be found in a more complete form in the entries and maps of *The Oxford Companion to British History*, ed. John Cannon, revised ed. (Oxford: Oxford U P, 2002), and *The Oxford Illustrated History of Britain,* ed. Kenneth O. Morgan (Oxford: Oxford U P, 1984).

Bibliography

Alvis, John E. "Spectacle Supplanting Ceremony." *Shakespeare As Political Thinker.* Ed. John E. Alvis and Thomas G. West. Wilmington, DE: ISI, 2000.
Alvis, John E. and Thomas G. West. *Shakespeare as Political Thinker.* Wilmington, DE: ISI, 2000.
Anderson, Benedict. *Imagined Communities.* London: Verso, 1983.
Baker, David J. *Between Nations: Shakespeare, Spenser, Marvell and the Question of Britain.* Stanford: Stanford U P, 1997.
Baker, David J. and Willy Maley, eds. *British Identities and English Renaissance Literature.* Cambridge: Cambridge U P, 2002.
Bate, Jonathan. "Deep England." What DID Shakespeare Invent? Session, Shakespeare Association of America Annual Meeting. Fairmont New Orleans Hotel, New Orleans. 9 April 2004.
Bates, Joseph. *The Autobiography of Joseph Bates, 1792–1872.* 8 July 2003. <http://www.earlysda.com/bates/joseph-bates2-4.html>.
Beckett, Samuel. *Waiting for Godot: A Tragicomedy in Two Acts.* New York: Grove, 1954.
The Book of Common Prayer. London: Everyman, 1999.
Bradshaw, Brendan, Andrew Hadfield, and Willy Maley, eds. *Representing Ireland: Literature and the Origins of Conflict.* Cambridge: Cambridge U P, 1993.
Canny, Nicholas. *Making Ireland British, 1580–1650.* Oxford: Oxford U P, 2001.
Carson, Ciaran. "Hamlet." *Belfast Confetti.* Winston-Salem: Wake Forest U P, 1989. 105–108.
Cavanah, Stephen, dir., *Hamlet,* perf. Stephen Cavanagh and Colin Stewart. Derry Film Initiative, 2005.
Cheng, Vincent John. *Shakespeare and Joyce: A Study of Finnegan's Wake.* University Park: Pennsylvania U P, 1984.
de Grazia, Margreta and Stanley Wells, eds. *The Cambridge Companion to Shakespeare.* Cambridge: Cambridge U P, 2001.
de Pontfarcy, Yolande. Introduction. *Saint Patrick's Purgatory: A Twelfth Century Tale of a Journey to the Other World.* By H. of Saltrey. Trans. Jean-Michel Picard. Dublin: Four Courts, 1985. 9–33.

Deane, Seamus. Introduction. *Nationalism, Colonialism, and Literature.* By Terry Eagleton, Frederick Jameson, and Edward W. Said. Minneapolis: U of Minnesota P, 1990. 13.

Dollimore, Jonathan and Alan Sinfield, eds. *Political Shakespeare.* 2nd ed. Ithaca: Cornell U P, 1994.

Dollimore, Jonathan. *Radical Tragedy: Religion, Ideology, and Power in the Drama of Shakespeare and His Contemporaries.* Durham: Duke U P, 1993.

———. "Shakespeare, Cultural Materialism and the New Historicism." *Political Shakespeare.* Ed. Jonathan Dollimore and Alan Sinfield, 2nd ed. Ithaca: Cornell U P, 1994. 2–17.

Dowden, Edward. *Shakespere: A Critical Study of His Mind and Art.* London: Routledge & Kegan Paul, 1875.

Eagleton, Terry. *Heathcliff and the Great Hunger.* London: Verso, 1995.

Eagleton, Terry, Frederic Jameson, and Edward W. Said. *Nationalism, Colonialism, and Literature.* Minneapolis: U of Minnesota P, 1990.

Edwards, Philip. *The Making of the Modern English State, 1460–1660.* New York: Palgrave, 2001.

Emerson, Kathy Lynn. *Everyday Life in Renaissance England: from 1485–1649.* Cincinnati: F&W, 1996.

Erickson, Carolly. *The First Elizabeth.* New York: Summit, 1983.

Forker, Charles R., ed. Introduction. *Richard II.* By William Shakespeare. London: Arden, 2002. 1–169.

Garber, Marjorie. "'Remember Me': *Momento Mori* Figures in Shakespeare's Plays." *Renaissance Drama* 12 (1981): 3–25.

Gierow, Karl Ragnar. "The Nobel Prize in Literature 1969." NobelPrize.org. 2005. The Nobel Foundation. 28 April 2005. <http://nobelprize.org/literature/laureates/1969/press.html>.

Glover, Michael. *The Napoleonic Wars: An Illustrated History, 1792–1815.* New York: Hippocrene, 1979.

Greenblatt, Stephen. *Hamlet in Purgatory.* Princeton: Princeton U P, 2001.

———. *Renaissance Self-Fashioning: From More to Shakespeare.* Chicago: U of Chicago P, 1980.

———. *Will in the World.* New York: Norton, 2004.

———. *Shakespearean Negotiations.* Berkeley: U of California P, 1988.

Hawkes, Terence. "Bringing Home the Bard," Presented for "Presentism and the End of History on Shakespeare Studies" Session. MLA 2005, Philadelphia.

Heaney, Seamus. "Bone Dreams." *North.* London: Faber & Faber, 1975. 19–23.

———. "Whatever you say say nothing." *North.* London: Faber & Faber, 1975. 51–54.

Helgerson, Richard. *Forms of Nationhood: the Elizabethan writing of England.* Chicago: Chicago U P, 1992.

Henslowe, Philip. *Henslowe's Diary.* 2nd edition. Ed. R. A. Foakes. Cambridge: Cambridge U P, 2002.

Bibliography

Joyce, James. *A Portrait of the Artist as a Young Man*. London: Penguin, 1964.

———. *Ulysses: The Complete and Unabridged Text, as Corrected and Reset in 1961* (1934). New York: Vintage International, 1990.

Kantorowicz, Ernst H. *The King's Two Bodies: A Study in Mediaeval Political Theology*. Princeton: Princeton U P, 1957.

Kenner, Hugh. *Ulysses*. Revised ed. Baltimore: Johns Hopkins U P, 1987.

Kiberd, Declan. *Inventing Ireland: The Literature of the Modern Nation*. Cambridge: Harvard U P, 1995.

Loomba, Ania. "Outsiders in Shakespeare's England." *The Cambridge Companion to Shakespeare*. Ed. Margreta de Grazia and Stanley Wells. Cambridge: Cambridge U P, 2001. 147–166.

———. *Shakespeare, Race, and Colonialism*. Oxford: Oxford U P, 2002.

MacCulloch, Diarmaid. *The Boy King Edward VI and the Protestant Reformation*. Berkeley: U of California P, 2002.

Morgan, Kenneth O., ed. *The Oxford Illustrated History of Britain*. Oxford: Oxford U P, 1984.

Murphy, Andrew. *But the Irish Sea Betwixt Us: Ireland, Colonialism, and Renaissance Literature*. Lexington: U P of Kentucky, 1999.

Murray, Christopher. Introduction. *Three Dublin Plays*. By Sean O'Casey. London: Faber and Faber, 1998. vii-xiii

"The Nobel Prize in Literature—Laureates." NobelPrize.org. 2005. The Nobel Foundation. 28 April 2005. <http://nobelprize.org/literature/laureates/index.html>.

Norwich, John Julius. *Shakespeare Kings: The Great Plays and the History of England in the Middle Ages:1337–1485*. New York: Touchstone, 1999.

O'Casey, Sean. *Juno and the Paycock*. *Three Dublin Plays*. London: Faber and Faber, 1998.

The Oxford Companion to British History. Revised Ed. Ed. John Cannon. Oxford: Oxford U P, 2002.

The Oxford History of Ireland. Ed. R. F. Forster. Oxford: Oxford U P, 2001.

The Oxford Illustrated History of Britain. Ed. Kenneth O. Morgan. Oxford: Oxford U P, 1984.

Papp, Joseph. Forward. *Richard II*. By William Shakespeare. Ed. David Bevington. New York: Bantam, 1980. xv.

Quillian, William H. *Hamlet and the New Poetic: James Joyce and T. S. Eliot*. Ann Arbor: UMI Research P, 1983.

Ribner, Irving. *The English History Play in the Age of Shakespeare*. Princeton: Princeton U P, 1957.

Riche, Barnaby. *A Short Survey of Ireland*. London, 1569.

———. *The Irish Hubbub, or, The English Hue and Crie*. London, 1618.

Robinson, Ian. *The Establishment of Modern English Prose in the Reformation and the Enlightenment*. Cambridge: Cambridge U P, 1998.

Rushdie, Salman. *Imaginary Homelands. Essays and Criticism 1981–1991*. London. Penguin, 1991.

Said, Edward. *Culture and Imperialism*. New York: Vintage, 1993.

———. *Reflections on Exile and Other Essays*. Cambridge: Harvard U P, 2000.

Saint Patrick's Purgatory: A Twelfth Century Tale of a Journey to the Other World. trans. Jean-Michel Picard. Dublin: Four Courts, 1985.

Shakespeare, William. *Hamlet. The Complete Works of Shakespeare*. Updated 4th Ed. Ed. David Bevington. New York: Longman, 1997. 1060–1116.

———. *Henry V. The Complete Works of Shakespeare*. Updated 4th Ed. Ed. David Bevington. New York: Longman, 1997. 849–892.

———. *Richard II. The Complete Works of Shakespeare*. Updated 4th Ed. Ed. David Bevington. New York: Longman, 1997. 721–762.

———. *Romeo and Juliet. The Complete Works of Shakespeare*. Updated 4th. Ed. David Bevington. New York: Longman, 1996. 977–1020.

Shaw, George Bernard. *John Bull's Other Island*. London: Constable and Co., 1926.

———. "The Dying Tongue of Great Elizabeth." *The Saturday Review*, 11 February 1905. Reprinted *Shaw On Shakespeare*. Ed. Edwin Wilson. New York: Applause, 1961.

———. "The Religion of the Pianoforte." *The Fortnightly Review*, February 1894. Reprinted *Shaw On Shakespeare*. Ed. Edwin Wilson. New York: Applause, 1961.

———. "Shakes Versus Shav." *Shaw on Shakespeare*. Ed. Edwin Wilson. New York: Applause, 1961. 265–269.

Sidney, Philip. "Discourse on Irish Affairs." *Miscellaneous Prose of Sir Philip Sidney*. Ed. Katherine Duncan-Jones and Jan Van Dorsten. Oxford: Clarendon, 1973.

Sinfield, Alan. *Faultlines: Cultural Materialism and the Politics of Dissident Reading*. Berkeley: U of California P, 1992.

———. "Heritage and the Market, Regulation and Desublimation." *Political Shakespeare*. 2nd ed. Ed. Jonathan Dollimore and Alan Sinfield. Ithaca: Cornell U P, 1985. 255–279.

Soper, William. *The Navy of the Lancastrian Kings: accounts and inventories of William Soper, Keeper of the King's Ships, 1422–1427*. Ed. Susan Rose. Publications of the Navy Records Society, v. 123. London: Allen & Unwin, 1982.

Spenser, Edmund. *A View of the State of Ireland*. Ed. Andrew Hadfield and Willy Maley. Oxford: Blackwell, 1997.

Tennenhouse, Leonard. "Strategies of State and Political Plays: *A Midsummer Night's Dream, Henry IV, Henry V, Henry VIII*." *Political Shakespeare*. 2nd ed. Ed. Jonathan Dollimore and Alan Sinfield. Ithaca: Cornell U P, 1985. 109–128.

Tudor and Stuart Proclamations—A Bibliography of Royal Proclamations of the Tudor and Stuart Sovereigns 1485–1714. Ed. Robert Steele. Clarendon: Oxford 1910.

Vance, Norman. *Irish Literature Since 1800*. London: Longman, 2002.

Wells, Stanley. *Shakespeare & Co.: Christopher Marlowe, Thomas Dekker, Ben Jonson, Thomas Middleton, John Fletcher and the Other Players in His Story.* New York: Pantheon, 2006.
Wilson, Edwin, ed. *Shaw on Shakespeare.* New York: Applause, 1961.
Yeats, William Butler. "At Stratford-On-Avon." *Essays and Introductions.* New York: Collier, 1961.

Index

A
Absentee landlords, 63, 64, 147 n. 9
Alvis, John E., 144 n. 11, 145 n. 18
Anglicization, 39, 63, 125, 142 n. 62
Anderson, Benedict, 2–3, 14, 136 n. 29, 138 n. 6, 155 n. 7
"At Stratford-upon-Avon," *see* Yeats, William Butler

B
Baker, David J., 3, 15–16, 21, 143 n. 9, 144 n. 11
Banishment, *see* Exile
Bate, Jonathan, 26–27
Bates, Joseph, 28–29, 156 n. 31
Beckett, Samuel, 2, 6, 49–50, 54–59, 156 n. 19
  and history, 56–57, 122
  and Ireland, 54, 59
  and paradox, 133
  and servitude, 10, 50, 54, 59, 130
  Waiting For Godot, 54–59
Bevington, David, 66, 72, 137 n. 1, 149 n. 5
Body Natural/Body Politic, 46–47
Bolingbroke, *see also* Richard II; Henry IV, part One
  as exile, 30
  as pragmatist, 37–38, 64–71, 87
  Yeats on, 72, 75, 94
  Shaw on, 77–78, 130
"Bone Dreams," *see* Heaney, Seamus
Book of Common Prayer, The, 15, 29, 33, 138–139 n. 9, 156 n. 31

British expansion
  cultural, 7, 14, 129
  military, 1, 14–15, 40, 129
British Navy, 27–29, 33

C
Caliban, *see* Shakespeare, William: *Tempest, The*
Cambridge Plot, The, *see* Henry V
Canny, Nicholas, 17–18, 147 n. 9, 154 n. 5
Captain Boyle, *see* O'Casey, Sean
Carson, Ciaran, 82, 129
Carson, Murray, 78
Catholicism, *see also* Recusancy
  as corruptive, 19, 22, 84, 118
  as enemy, 24, 140 n. 29, 142–143 n. 2, 149 n. 7
  and *Hamlet*, 84, 87, 91–92, 95–96
  and language, 15
  practices, 91, 95–96, 150–151 n. 12
  and rebellion, 19, 38–39, 84
  and sectarian conflict, 113, 115, 121, 154 n. 5
  Shakespeare and adherence to, 152 n. 18
Cheng, Vincent John, 99
Claudius, *see Hamlet*
Colonialism, *see also* Nationalism; Postcolonialism
  the colonial subject, 9, 34, 93
  and fragmentation, 9, 32, 121–123, 133, 156 n. 32
  and language, 32–33, 46, 123, 155 n. 7
  and the past, 33–34, 115, 123
  and race, 143–144 n. 10

165

Shakespeare and, 13, 83
Spenser and, 22–24
Coriolanus, see Shakespeare, William
Cranmer, Thomas, 138 n. 8
Cultural violence, 13, 27, 31
Culture and Imperialism, see Said, Edward
Cymbeline, see Shakespeare, William

D

Deane, Seamus, 5, 121–123, 133, 155 n. 7
Deposition Scene, the, *see Richard II:* deposition scene
Desmond, Earl of, *see* Irish rebels
Derry Film Initiative, 109–111, 113, 115
Didi, *see* Beckett, Samuel: *Waiting for Godot*
Displacement, *see* Exile
Dollimore, Jonathan
    on closure, 120–121, 128–129, 145 n. 20
    on dissident reading, 4–5, 9, 31, 60–61, 72
Dowden, Edward, 73–75, 79
Dublin
    Joyce's relationship to, 97–99
    as The Pale, 8, 17, 18, 20
    in *Juno and the Paycock*, 50–51, 54
    in *Ulysses*, 101–104, 153 n. 47
"The Dying Tongue of Great Elizabeth," *see* Shaw, George Bernard

E

Eagleton, Terry, 31
    on ideology of the oppressed, 6–7, 32, 51–52, 98
    on O'Casey, 51–52
    on Joyce, 97–98
Easter Uprising, *see* Irish rebels
Edward III, 28
Edward VI, 15
Edwards, Philip, 39, 137 n. 1, 142–143 n. 2
Elizabeth I, 126, 137 n. 3
    and Catholicism, 39, 118–119, 152 n. 18, 155 n. 11
    and Ireland, 17–18, 38–40, 117–119, 155 n. 9
    and Spenser, 21

Essex, Robert Devereux, 2nd Earl of and Essex Rebellion, 13, 38, 118–119, 137 n. 1
Estragon, *see* Beckett, Samuel: *Waiting for Godot*
Exile
    Beckett and, 59, 133
    and identity, 33, 97–98, 106–108, 156 n. 32
    in *Richard II*, 37, 61–64, 67–71
    Rushdie on, 107, 119–120, 136 n. 29
    Said on, 7–8, 61–63
    in *Ulysses*, 98–99

F

Faerie Queene, The, see Spenser, Edmund
Faultlines, see Sinfield, Alan
Falstaff, *see Henry IV, part One*
Finnegan's Wake, see Joyce, James
Fluellen, *see Henry V*
Forker, Charles, 66
Fortinbras, *see Hamlet*
fragmentation, 34, 107, 119–122, 133, 156 n. 32
Friel, Brian, *Translations* 142 n. 62

G

Gaelic language, 8–9, 32, 54, 102, 109–110
Gaelic League, The, 54, 75, 101
Garber, Marjorie, 150 n. 11
Ghosts, 82, 86, 96
    ghostly fathers (priests), 19, 84, 87, 88, 149–150 n. 8
    Hamlet's father, 84, 86–93, 95, 103, 150 n. 11
    Stephen's theorem, 98–99, 102–104
Gierow, Karl Ragnar, 133
Gogo, *see* Beckett, Samuel: *Waiting for Godot*
Gower, *see Henry V*
Greenblatt, Stephen, 3, 4, 135 n. 5, 144 n. 11
    Hamlet in Purgatory, on inwardness, 84, 151–152 n. 17
    Hamlet in Purgatory, on purgatory, 86, 96, 150–151 n. 12, 151 n. 13,
    Hamlet in Purgatory, on Shakespeare's faith, 91, 152 n. 21
    Renaissance Self-Fashioning, 3, 25–26

Index

Shakespearean Negotiations, 4, 16, 40, 43, 145 n. 19
Will in the World, 91, 107, 131–132, 149 n. 5, 152 n. 18
Grey, Henry Sidney, Lord, *see* Ireland, Lord Deputy of
Guildenstern and Rosencrantz, 90, 109, 152 n. 22

H

Hamlet, 41, 84–90, 107, 150 n. 9, 151 n. 15
   actors of, 106, 109
   as idealist, 11, 81–83
   as Irish, 83–84, 130–131
   and lineage, 82–87, 90–91
   and questioning, 25, 81, 92–96
Hamlet, 5, 10, 26, 120–121, 129, *see also* Ghosts: Hamlet's father
   Claudius in, 85, 87, 106, 112
   in film, 109, 129
   Fortinbras in, 85, 111–112, 134
   in Irish poetry, 81, 82, 114, 129
   and language, 81, 93, 96
   Shaw on, 111–112, 126, 127
   sources for, 83, 106, 149 n. 5
   Stephen's theorem, 98–99, 102–104
   in *Ulysses,* 82–84, 97
   uncertainty in, 91–96, 131–134, 150 n. 11, 150–151 n. 12, 152 n. 22
   Yeats on, 11, 72, 82
Hawkes, Terence, 61, 146 n. 3
Heaney, Seamus, 2, 122, 129, 156 n. 19
   "Bone Dreams," 115–116
   "Whatever you say say nothing," 82, 113–115
Heathcliff and the Great Hunger, see Eagleton, Terry
Helgerson, Richard, 3, 13, 22, 24–25, 139–140 n. 20
Henslowe's Diary, 38
Henry II, 27–28, 157 n. 19
Henry IV, 37, 38, 41, 64, 121
Henry IV, part One, 37, 38, 41, 141 n. 42, 141 n. 43, *see also* Bolingbroke
   Falstaff, 26, 42–44, 141 n. 43
   Hotspur, 141 n. 43

Henry V
   as England, 40, 42, 44–46, 48, 144 n. 11
   historical, 28, 38, 39
   as pragmatist, 38, 88, 121, 147–148 n. 19
Henry V, 3, 5, 10, 29, 36–37, 40, 62, 120; *see also* Henry V; Macmorris
   and the Body Politic, 41–46, 145 n. 17
   Cambridge Plot, The, 41–44, 48
   Dowden on, 73–74
   Fluellen, 10, 40–41, 45–46, 48, 144 n. 13
   Gower, 40–41, 48
   Jamy, 10, 40–41, 45
   Shaw on, 76
   Yeats on, 73, 147–148 n. 19
Henry VI, 28, 30, 64
Holinshed, 60, 88, 151 n. 13

I

Imaginary Homelands, see Rushdie, Salman
Impressment
   cultural, defined, 27, 119
   defined, 141 n. 43
   and doomed rebellion, 83–84, 97, 106, 127–128
   and fragmentation, 11–12, 93, 108, 119, 128–134
   history of, 9, 27–29, 33
   and idealism, 11, 30–31, 61, 64
   and servitude, 10, 37, 41, 47–54, 55–59
   and violent inclusion, 17, 27–30, 39–41, 47–48, 87–88
India, 34, 116–117, 133–134, 156 n. 19, 157 n. 39
Ireland, *see also* Irish Literary Revival; Irish rebels; Irish stereotypes
   as a British belonging, 9, 16–18, 37–40, 119, 134
   The Irish Question, 32, 81, 114, 117
   landscape, 63, 142 n. 62
   New English, 24
   Northern Ireland, 82, 109–111, 113–116, 129, 134, 157–158 n. 39
   Old English, 24
   as a dark England, 7, 32
   sectarianism in, 54, 110–111, 154 n. 5
Ireland, Lord Deputy of, 18, 20, 117–118, 155 n. 9

defended by Sir Philip Sidney, 18
  in *Ulysses*, 99
Irish Hubbub, or the English Hue and Crie, The, see Riche, Barnaby
Irish Literary Revival, The, 8, 97, 100–101,
  see also Gaelic League, The
Irish National Library, 11, 98, 100–105
Irish rebels
  Desmond, Earl of, 38–39
  Easter Uprising, 52
  Irish Republican Army, 110, 154 n. 5
  O'Connell, Daniel, 51
  O'Neill, Hugh, 38
  Pearse, Patrick, 51
  Tyrone's Rebellion, 144 n. 5
Irish stereotypes
  as disruptive, 20–21, 24, 32, 84–85, 118–119
  as drunkards, 20–21, 50–55
  as servants, 10, 41, 49–55, 130
  as imaginative, 6, 74, 76, 79
  as childlike, 16, 19–21, 119

J

James I, 126, 154 n. 5
Jamy, *see Henry V*
John Bull's Other Island, see Shaw, George Bernard
John of Gaunt, *see Richard II*
Joxer Day, *see* O'Casey, Sean
Joyce, James, 2, 6, 93, 97–98, 153 n. 47
  Finnegan's Wake, 97, 99
  Ulysses, 11, 82–83, 97–106, 153 n. 47, 157 n. 38
Julius Caesar, see Shakespeare, William
Juno and the Paycock, see O'Casey, Sean

K

Kantorowicz, Ernst H., 47
Kenner, Hugh, 100–104
Kiberd, Declan, 5–7
  Inventing Ireland, on English writers, 9–10, 32–33, 49–50, 82, 144 n. 13
  Inventing Ireland, on Irish writers, 49–50, 72, 74–75, 97, 106
  Irish Classics, 6
King Lear, see Shakespeare, William

King's shilling, the, 27, 29, 131–134; *see also* Impressment
Kyd, Thomas, 106, 149 n. 5

L

Lancaster, 37, 68
Leopold Bloom, *see* Joyce, James: *Ulysses*
London, 26–27, 78, 99, 103, 141 n. 42
Loomba, Ania, 138 n. 6, 143–144 n. 10

M

Macbeth, see Shakespeare, William
MacCulloch, Diarmid, 15, 138–139 n. 9
Macmorris, *see also Henry V*
  and inclusion, 16, 40–41, 129, 132, 145 n. 19
  as Irish, 25, 30, 86, 93, 143 n. 9
  as servant archetype, 41, 49–50, 55–56, 59, 144 n. 13
Maley, Willy, 38, 139–140 n. 20, 143 n. 4
Mirrors, 98, 103, 131–134, 156 n. 32, 157 n. 38
Modernism, 120, 132
Munster Plantation, *see* Spenser, Edmund
Murphy, Andrew, 24
Murray, Christopher, 50, 145 n. 22

N

National identity, 15, 135 n., 145 n. 19, *see also* Irish stereotypes
  of Britishness, 15–19, 30–34, 40–45, 47–49, 144 n. 11
  of Englishness, 18, 36, 61, 74–76, 131–134
  of Irishness, 12, 30–31, 117, 139–140 n. 20
  self-definition, 13–14, 17, 29–31
Nationalism, *see also* Colonialism; Post-colonisalism
  and exile, 8, 62
  in literature, 49, 130
  rejection of, 51, 122
  and reinscription, 121, 155 n. 7
Nelson, Horatio, Admiral, 27, 29, 33, 156 n. 31
Nobel Prize in Literature, 122, 133, 156 n. 19

Index

Norman law, 22–23
Northern Ireland, *see* Ireland
Norwich, John Julius, 64–66, 147 n. 18

O

O'Connell, Daniel, *see* Irish rebels
Odyssey, The, 82–83
O'Neill, Hugh, *see* Irish rebels
Orangemen (Orange Order), 75, 110–111, 129, 154 n. 5
O'Casey, Sean, 6, 10, 49–55, 122, 145 n. 22

P

Pale, The, *see* Dublin
Papp, Joseph, 66–67
Pearse, Patrick, *see* Irish rebels
Pope Alexander VI, 88–89
Pope Gregory XIII, 118, 155 n. 11
Pope Pius V, 19, 84, 149 n. 7, 155 n. 11
Post-colonialism, *see also* Colonialism; Nationalism
   and identity, 7–8, 130, 132–133, 156 n. 32
   and language, 32, 110, 122–123
   and literature, 2, 32
   Post-Colonial theory, 2, 5–6, 30, 143 n. 9
   and reinscription, 7, 116, 121, 128, 133
Purgatory, *see also* St. Patrick's Purgatory
   as Catholic signifier, 87–89, 91, 150–151 n. 12
   and fragmentation, 90–97, 132
   in *Hamlet*, 84, 87–89, 92–93, 152 n. 21, 152 n. 22
   as Irish signifier, 88–89, 151 n. 13
   and melancholy, 89–90
   in *Ulysses*, 102

Q

Quillian, William H., 105

R

Radical Tragedy, see Dollimore, Jonathan
Recusancy, 15, 91, 152 n. 18
Reappropriation, 1, 32–33, 62–63, 97, 122
Reflections on Exile, see Said, Edward
"The Religion of the Pianoforte," *see* Shaw, George Bernard

Ribner, Irving, 14, 137 n. 3
Richard II, 25, 41
   and inheritance, 30, 37–38, 85–86, 97
   as Ireland, 61–66, 93
   as poet king, 60, 64–71, 84, 96, 147–148 n. 19
   as tragic protagonist, 11, 61, 64, 120–121, 129–130
Richard II, 10–11, 88, 120, 137–138 n. 3, 145 n. 17, *see also* Bolingbroke; Richard II
   deposition scene, 67–71, 132
   Dowden on, 73–74
   and Essex Rebellion, 13, 118, 137 n. 1
   John of Gaunt, 37, 64, 67, 78, 137 n. 18
   Northumberland, 66, 68
   Shaw on, 71–72, 75–80
   and Thomas of Woodstock, 69, 71, 147 n. 18
   Yeats on, 60, 71–75, 79–80
Riche, Barnaby, 22, 31, 39, 84, 118
   The Irish Hubbub, or the English Hue and Crie, 20–21
   A Short Survey of Ireland, 19, 147 n. 7
Robinson, Ian, 138 n. 8
Rosencrantz and Guildenstern, 90, 152 n. 22
Rushdie, Salman, 7, 156 n. 19
   Imaginary Homelands, 8, 106–107, 119–120, 122–123, 136 n. 29
   Midnight's Children, 116–117

S

Said, Edward
   Culture and Imperialism, 7, 155 n. 7
   Reflections on Exile, 7–8, 33–34, 61–63,
Saint Patrick, 88–90, 102, 152 n. 21
Saint Patrick's Purgatory, 88–90, 150–151 n. 12, 151 n. 16
Sectarianism, *see* Ireland
Scotland, 15–16, 37, 40, 116, 125–126
Scott, Sir Walter, 125–126
"Shakes Versus Shav," *see* Shaw, George Bernard
Shakespeare, William, *see also Hamlet; Henry IV part One; Henry V; Richard II*
   as Celtic, 31–32, 71, 73

as character in "Shakes Vs. Shav," 124–128, 131
Coriolanus, 4, 72
as cultural icon, 1–2, 6, 112, 153 n. 47
as cultural inheritance, 1–2, 6, 11–12, 13
Cymbeline, 105
and dominant ideology, 4, 5, 11, 60–61
Julius Caesar, 26, 151–152 n. 17
King Lear, 4, 126
and language, 48, 60, 66–71
as literary father, 98–104, 105–106, 142 n. 59
Macbeth, 5, 50, 125–126, 141 n. 43
and mirrors, 131–133, 156 n. 32
and national identity, 9, 14–18, 25–27, 30, 64
and religious belief, 91, 152 n. 18, 152 n. 21
subversive uses of, 9–10, 32–33, 72, 122, 129
Tempest, The, 30, 157 n. 38
Timon of Athens, 72, 126
and the Tudor Myth, 137–138 n. 3, 144 n. 11
Two Gentlemen of Verona, 99
Shaw, George Bernard, 6–7, 71–72, 79–80, 122, 156 n. 19
as Anglo-Irish, 2, 75–76
"The Dying Tongue of Great Elizabeth," 76–79
John Bull's Other Island, 75–76
"The Religion of the Pianoforte," 111–113
"Shakes Versus Shav," 123–128, 131
as theatre reviewer, 11, 130
Short Survey of Ireland, A, see Riche, Barnaby
Sidney, Sir Henry, *see* Ireland, Lord Deputy of
Sinfield, Alan, 4, 9, 136 n. 10
Faultlines, 5, 10, 36, 38–40, 42–43, 49
Political Shakespeare, 5
Somerset, Edward Seymour, Duke of, 15
Soper, William, 27–28
Spain, 39, 143 n. 4
Spenser, Edmund, 15, 26, 32, 84, 117
as courtier, 21–22
The Faerie Queene, 22, 24
and Munster Plantation, 17

View of the State of Ireland, A, 3, 21–25, 29, 31, 143 n. 4
Stephen Daedalus, *see Hamlet:* Stephen's theorem; Joyce, James: *Ulysses*
Swift, Jonathan, 75
Synge, John Millington, 32, 100, 101, 102

T
Tempest, The, see Shakespeare, William
Tennenhouse, Leonard, 144 n. 11
Timon of Athens, see Shakespeare, William
Tree, Beerbohm, 76–79
Two Gentlemen of Verona, see Shakespeare, William
Tyrone's Rebellion, *see* Irish rebels

U
Ulster, *see* Ireland: Northern Ireland
Ulysses, see Joyce, James

V
Vance, Norman, 54, 57
View of the State of Ireland, A, see Spenser, Edmund
Violent inclusion, *see* Impressment
Vladimir, *see* Beckett, Samuel: *Waiting for Godot*

W
Wales, 16, 29, 37, 40, 49
Wanderers, representations of, 56, 62, 71, 82–83, 107
"Whatever you say say nothing," *see* Heaney, Seamus
Wilde, Oscar, 7, 98, 157 n. 38
William of Orange, 114, 154 n. 5
Woodstock, Thomas of, *see Richard II*

Y
Yeats, William Butler, 6, 7, 71–72, 101, 122
"At Stratford-upon-Avon," 11, 72–73
on Dowden, 73–74
and imagination, 74–76, 130
and language, 60, 79, 82, 156 n. 19
and the past, 32, 122
and reappropriation, 32, 79–80, 130

For Product Safety Concerns and Information please contact our EU
representative GPSR@taylorandfrancis.com
Taylor & Francis Verlag GmbH, Kaufingerstraße 24, 80331 München, Germany